COLORADO AMERICAN INDIAN CIVICS

Other books by Roberta Carol Harvey from Sunstone Press

The Earth Is Red: The Imperialism of the Doctrine of Discovery

The Eclipse of the Sun: The Need for American Indian Curriculum in High Schools

The Iron Triangle: Business, Government, and Colonial Settlers' Dispossession of Indian Timberlands and Timber

All That Glitters Is Ours: The Theft of Indian Mineral Resources

Social Contributions of Colorado's American Indian Leaders for the Seven Generations to Come

Warrior Societies A Manifesto

A Brief Colorado Indian History of 1800s, Through a Factual Lens

Stealing the Last Arrow The Department of Interior Indian Probate Proceedings

Colorado American Indian Civics

ROBERTA CAROL HARVEY
A Citizen of The Navajo Nation
EDITED BY MALIN BIRD BEAR

© 2024 by Roberta Carol Harvey
All Rights Reserved
No part of this book may be reproduced in any form or by any electronic or mechanical means including information storage and retrieval systems without permission in writing from the publisher, except by a reviewer who may quote brief passages in a review.

Sunstone books may be purchased for educational, business, or sales promotional use.
For information please write: Special Markets Department, Sunstone Press,
P.O. Box 2321, Santa Fe, New Mexico 87504-2321.
Printed on acid-free paper
∞

eBook: 978-1-61139-757-4

LIBRARY OF CONGRESS CATALOGING IN PUBLICATION DATA
(ON FILE)

WWW.SUNSTONEPRESS.COM
SUNSTONE PRESS / POST OFFICE BOX 2321 / SANTA FE, NM 87504-2321 /USA
(505) 988-4418

Dedication

My faith. Without it, my writing would be impossible.
I am so truly grateful.

Acknowledgment

My Family

Nobody has been more helpful to me in the pursuit of this project than the members of my family for whom I am so very thankful. I could not have the time for research and writing without their active support. They encouraged me and made sure that whatever resources I needed for this project were available: computer, printer, supplies, etc. Thank you to my most beloved husband (who made breakfast, lunch and dinner and took over all daily family responsibilities so I could focus on this project) whose love provides such joy and stability in my life. Thank you to my son, Aaron, for sharing his vast knowledge of historical and contemporary native issues. I included Chapter 13 on the Indian Child Welfare Act as a result of listening with him to Rebecca Nagle's, This Land Podcast.

About the Cover
Breastplates are handcrafted from long bone beads which are strung on strong cord with spacer beads and leather between them. They were originally worn as armor for protection from arrows and spears. After the introduction of the bullet in the late 1600s, the breastplates had no purpose except to give the warrior a sense of personal and spiritual strength. They are used in dances and ceremonies. This breast plate was made for Sander Bird Bear, Mandan-Hidatsa Tribes, Fort Berthold Reservation, North Dakota, by his Shimá Sání (maternal grandmother), Roberta Carol Harvey (Diné). It was prayed over while being made and blessed with traditional prayer and the smoke of sage burnt over palo santo wood in an abalone shell. The four elements are present: water (the shell as a water vessel), earth (the plant material and wood being burnt, gifts from Mother Earth), fire (lighting the sage) and air (represented by the smoke produced). The smoke is fanned with an eagle feather, with the quill wrapped in red felt and secured with deer sinew. The smoke carries prayers upwards to our deities. The author has come to realize how important it is to support our American Indian artists. American Indians are about 1% of the U.S. population, with artists being a small subset of the population, so we are creating unique art. I have a carved sign at my front door with our Diné sense of how we are to live: "Walk in Beauty." Also, in my study, I have a sign to remind myself of where I am: "Lo Here, the Holy Place." In purchasing American Indian art, you are getting a piece, many times, prayed over and blessed by the artist.

Symbolism of the Eagle
By Geoffrey M. Standing Bear, Principal Chief of the Osage Nation
Using eagle parts in ceremonies is a long held tradition among Native American people. Not only are the feathers worn during ceremonies, but they're also used on a daily basis to bless oneself or others. "My elders once told me to look at [an eagle's wing] like the Catholics do a crucifix," he says. "I bless myself every morning and say a prayer with it." According to Standing Bear, Native Americans believe that the eagle is closer to God than humans are. "The eagle flies above us and has been here longer than we have and knows God better than we do," he says. "It has holy powers that we can draw from by respectful use of its feathers [and other body parts]. We show our respect and distill blessings to another person by taking the feathers and touching them on the head and on the heart and on the hands to bless their minds, their emotions and their experiences in life." Tink Tinker, also a member of the Osage Nation in Oklahoma, agrees. Tinker is a professor of American Indian cultures and religious traditions at the Iliff School of Theology in Denver. "The eagle is one of our closest relatives," he says. "We believe that all of our relatives have distinct energy or power attached to them, and we use the eagle for its powers to help with healing and to give people strength, courage, wisdom and generosity. We use [the feathers] ceremonially to bring the intrinsic energy of the eagle into the ceremony. They're not just symbols, they have actual power that relates closely to the Indian people." By federal law, it's illegal to possess, use or sell eagle feathers—a policy that is meant to deter hunters from poaching wild eagles for their feathers or body parts. However, the law, which is part of the Bald and Golden Eagle Protection Act and the 100-year-old Migratory Bird Treaty Act, stipulates that Native Americans who are members of federally recognized tribes can obtain a permit under the Federally Recognized Tribal List Act of 1994 to gain access to golden eagles and bald eagles. Native Americans may give feathers or other eagle items as gifts to other Native Americans and may hand them down within their families. They may not, however, give them to non-Native Americans. In the 1970s, the U.S. Fish and Wildlife Service established the repository "in recognition of the significance of these feathers to Native Americans." It is located within the Rocky Mountain Arsenal National Wildlife Refuge in Commerce City, a suburb of Denver.

Contents

Preface ≈ 31

   Primary Source Reliance

   American Indians; Indians; Native Americans; Indigenous Peoples Nomenclature

   Names; Spelling

   Disclaimer

   Settler Colonialism

1: Background ≈ 35

   574 Tribes

   Key Definitions

   Federally Recognized Tribes in Colorado

   Denver's Urban American Indian Population

   Hub of American Indian Country

   Denver City Council Land Acknowledgement

   Denver Indian Center

March Denver Powwow Co-Founders

American Indian Employment Preference within BIA Won in Littleton, Colorado

Attorney Harris Sherman: Reflection on Littleton, Colorado, Victory

Political Classification Status of Federally Recognized American Indian Tribes and Their Members

Ending Use of Mascots in Colorado Public Schools

In-State College Tuition Rates for Certain Native Students

2: Federal Historical Context ⇜ 49

U.S. Federal American Indian Policy

U.S. Predicates Authority over American Indians Based on Broad Interplay of U.S. Constitution's Treaty Power, Commerce and War Powers Clauses

U.S.-American Indian Treaties

Law of Nations regarding Treaties

American Indian Nations Considered Sovereigns of Soil

1780: President Thomas Jefferson: Empire of Liberty—Future of Commerce and Expansion

Marshall Trilogy

1830: Indian Removal Act

President Jackson's Justification for Indian Removal Act

Tenor of Times - They May Begin to Dig Their Graves and Prepare to Die

Secretary of War Threatens Cherokees. They Will Be Left to Whims of

Georgia

Impact of U.S. Supreme Court Cases on Indian Removal Act

Indian Removal Act Passed

Removal of Indian Nations Became Mandatory

1845: Manifest Destiny of U.S. to Possess Whole Continent

1873: President Grant's American Indian Peace Policy Debacle

President Grant Breaches His Own American Indian Peace Policy

December 7, 1875: President Grant's Message - Gold in Black Hills; Sioux (aka Lakota) Unwilling to Cede Them; End Sioux Rations

December 20, 1875: Deadline Notice for Sioux to Be on Their Reservation by January 31, 1876, Received by Cheyenne River Agency

December 22, 1875: Deadline Notice Received by Standing Rock Agency, Agent Requests Extension of Time due to Difficult Winter Weather Conditions; Impossible for Sioux to Comply with Deadline

January 31, 1876: Deadline for Sioux to Be on Their Reservation

U.S. Military Prepares for Winter Campaign

January 21, 25, 1876: Department of Interior Will Share Sioux Intelligence with War Department

February 1, 1876: Sioux Indians Turned Over to War Department for Such Action as Military Deems Proper

February 7, 1876: War Dept. Assumes Authority over Sioux Indians

February 1876: U.S.—Sioux War Commences

The Big Lie: Lakota's "Utter Defeat" Was Due to Their Own "War Lust"

3: SQUATTING ∽ 67

    Land and Preemption Acts

    Encroachment on American Indian Lands

    Squatters' Claims Clubs

    Territorial Legislatures and Courts Legalized Squatting

    Bureaucratic Inefficiency due to Communication within Command Structures Prevents Military Enforcement Against Illegal Squatting

    Reservations Swarm with Squatters

    Squatters and Settlers as Hired Guns

4: BRIEF COLORADO HISTORY ∽ 73

    Indigenous Peoples in Colorado Pre-Contact

    Contact with Spain

    Mexican Land Grants

    U.S. Military Expeditions Conducted Surveillance on American Indian Tribes

    1852: First Colorado Court Decree for Irrigation Rights

    1857: Denver City Promoters

    1858: Discovery of Gold in Colorado

    1859: Miners' Court

    Colorado's Gold Rush's Impact on Farming

    1862: Homestead Act

    1863: First Agricultural Society Established

Agricultural Colonies

Investment in Irrigation

   1861: Colorado Established as Territory

   Gold and Silver Production Priority for Funding Union Army during Civil War

   Southern Confederacy Seeks to Win Western Part of U.S. to Exploit Precious Metals

   October 1863: Commissioner of Indian Affairs Dole Confirms Mineral Wealth of Colorado Territory

   1864: Four Colorado Forts

5: SAND CREEK MASSACRE ∽ 83

   June 3, 11, 13, 1864: Governor Evans Demands Federal Troops Be Sent to Denver

   June 15, 1864: Major McKenny Warns General Curtis that Colorado's Volunteer Cavalry May Start Plains Indian War

   June 27, 1864: Governor Evans' First Proclamation - Orders Indians to Move to Forts

   August 11, 1864: Governor Evans' Second Proclamation - Citizens of Colorado Authorized to Kill Hostile Indians

   Analysis of Governor Evans' Second Proclamation of August 11, 1864 - University of Denver's John Evans Study Committee

   August 1864 - November 1864: Cheyenne and Arapaho Indians Repeatedly Seek Peace

   August 29, 1864: Cheyenne and Arapahos Call for Peace Talks

   September 4, 1864: Governor Evans Informed by Indian Agent Colley that Cheyenne and Arapaho Desire Peace

September 14, 1864: Governor Evans Forwards Agent Colley's Letter that Cheyenne and Arapaho Desire Peace to Colonel Chivington

September 18, 1864: Major Wynkoop Reports Meeting with Cheyenne and Arapaho regarding Peace to Acting Assistant Adjutant-General, District of Upper Arkansas

September 28, 1864: Governor Evans Meets with Cheyenne and Arapaho Peace Party; Rejects Peace Offer Alleging State of War with Military in Control

September 29, 1864: Governor Evans Sends Letter to Agent Colley regarding Meeting with Cheyenne and Arapaho Peace Party; That, as Governor, He Rejected Peace Offer due to U.S. State of War

September 29, 1864: Major-General Curtis Asserts Indians Don't Want Peace and Are Trying to Avoid Winter Campaign

October 14, 1864: Colonel Chivington Orders Capt. Nichols, Colorado Third Regiment, to Kill All Indians His Command Encounters

October 15, 1864: Commissioner Dole Orders Governor Evans to Negotiate for Peace with Indians when They Offer, Regardless of U.S. State of War

November 4, 1864: Major Wynkoop Relieved of Command

November 15, 1864: Majors Anthony and Wynkoop Meet with Cheyenne and Arapaho Who Continue to Press for Peace

November 15, 1864: Commissioner Dole Reports to Secretary of Interior that Cheyenne and Arapaho Urge Peace - Military Says Further Punishment Needed

November 16, 1864: Major Anthony Reports to Headquarters that Cheyenne and Arapaho Appealing for Peace

November 28, 1864: Major Anthony Reports Arrival of Colorado Third Regiment at Fort Lyon: 1000 Soldiers

November 28, 1864: Major General Curtis Reports to Brigadier General Carleton that Cheyenne and Arapaho Are Begging for Peace

November 29, 1864: Sand Creek Massacre - Colonel Chivington Reports Killing 400-500 Indians and Leaders; Third Regiment Colorado Cavalry Scalped Dead Indians; Mutilated Their Bodies; Removed Private Parts as War Trophies

December 7, 1864: Colonel Chivington's Second Report to Governor Evans: Killed 500 Indians, Still in Pursuit of Cheyenne and Arapaho

Return of Colorado Third Regiment to Denver

Report on Sand Creek Massacre by Indian Agent Leavenworth

Sand Creek Massacre Reported as "Disastrous and Shameful Occurrence"

Governor Evans' Culpability in Sand Creek Massacre - University of Denver's John Evans Study Committee

May 30, 1865: U.S. Condemns Sand Creek Massacre

April 28, 1865: Instructions to Treaty Commission Appointed to Negotiate for Arapaho and Cheyenne Colorado Land - Offer No Money, No Specific Land for New Reservation

October 11-13, 1865: U.S. Treaty Delegation, Arapaho and Cheyenne Still Recovering from Sand Creek Massacre, Not Ready to Agree to Relinquish Land in Colorado

October 13, 1865: Treaty Council with Arapaho and Cheyenne - Unfortunately for You, Gold Discovered in Your Country

1867: Medicine Lodge Treaties - Cheyenne and Arapaho Treaty Establishing Reservation in Indian Territory

6: RETALIATORY AMERICAN INDIAN MILITARY CAMPAIGNS

January 6, 1865: Battle of Fort Rankin: Capt. O'Brien's 60-Man Cavalry Ambushed by 1000 American Indian Warriors; 14 U.S. Soldiers and Four U.S. Civilians Killed

1868: Battle of Beecher Island: Tenth Cavalry Rout Allied Forces of Northern Cheyenne, Arapaho, and Oglala after Their Week-Long Siege of Colonel Forsyth's Command

1869: Battle at Summit Springs; U.S. Army Force of About 300 Attack Cheyenne Encampment

7: 1887: "Colorow's War"–False Nomenclature to Hide Murder of and Forced Removal of Utes Lawfully Hunting on Ceded Land ◦ 113

White Military Forces Arrayed against Colorow's Band Utterly Disproportionate to Utes Fighting Warriors

1887: Brigadier-General George Crook's Report on Ute Troubles Caused by White Aggression against Lopsided Small Force of Indians Who Had No Desire to Fight

1887: Major-General Alfred H. Terry's Report to Adjutant-General on Colorow Conflict

Without General Crook's Military Report, Totally False 'Historical' Versions, Concealing Murder of and Forced Removal of Utes Lawfully Hunting on Ceded Land, Would Prevail

8: Utes–Treaties and Agreements with U.S. ◦ 119

September 15, 1865: Superintendent Taylor, Upper Platte; Obstruction of Mining Prejudicial to U.S.

1866: Gold, Silver and Coal Discovered on Ute Land; Fertile Land, Timber, Water Power, All Requirements for Profitable Occupation

1868: Ute Treaty of 1868 - Utes Cede Central Rockies

1872: Colorado Citizens Demand Utes Cede Mineral-Rich San Juan Mountains

1873: Incalculable Value of San Juan Mountains Ceded by Utes

1877: Stay Friendly with Utes

9: City and Railroad Development Lead to Colorado Statehood ∽ 125

Colorado Water and Railroad Developers

1867: American Express Co., Shoot Indians

1867: Central City—Bounty for "Indian Scalp with Ears"

1871: Denver Pacific Railway Completed to Colorado

City Developers, Durango, Colorado

1876: Colorado Statehood

10: Push to Remove All Utes from Colorado ∽ 129

Commissioner of Indian Affairs Smith: End Indian Fiction of Sovereignty

1877: Commissioner of Indian Affairs Hayt Recommends Removing All Indians in Colorado and Arizona to Indian Territory to Facilitate Mining and Farming by Whites

1878: Colorado Legislators Petition for Removal of All Utes

1879: Colorado Gov. Pitkin's Message to State Legislature: Need to Remove Indians

1879: Nathan Meeker - Wrong Person to Appoint as Indian Agent at White River Agency or Any Other Indian Agency

September 29, 1879: Battle at Milk Creek; Utes Attack White River Agency

Sample News Headlines from Colorado Newspapers (1878–1879)

Governor Pitkin's Order: Bring In, Dead or Alive, All Hostile Indians

1880: After Thornburgh/Meeker Incidents Utes Forced Out of Colorado

1881: Whites Pour onto Land Left by Uncompahgre Utes with No Shred of Common Decency

Ute Commission. Those Engaged in Meeker Murders, Not Now in U.S. Custody, Are Dead or Have Fled Outside U.S.

Utes Blame Otto Mears for Removal to Utah; Co joe, Ute Sub-Chief, Tries to Assassinate Him

1890: Commissioner Morgan - Southern Utes to Stay in Colorado

11: MINING AND CATTLE INDUSTRIES ∽ 143

Mining Geology

Essentials for Mineral Development

Colorado Moguls: Mining and Real Estate

Metal Processing Enterprises

Colorado Metals Production History

Cattle Enterprises

12: FURTHER FEDERAL ACTIONS IMPACTING TRIBAL AUTONOMY ∽ 149

American Indian Wars

1861: Treaty of Fort Wise, Confine Cheyenne and Arapaho on Reservation, 1/13 Size of Fort Laramie Treaty Lands

1863: Commissioner Dole to Governor/Superintendent Evans - Get Cheyenne and Arapaho that Have Not Signed Treaty of Fort Wise to Do So

1871: Indian Appropriations Act Ends Treaty-Making with American Indian Nations

1887: General Allotment Act

Southern Utes' Land Allotted; Weenuche Band Refuses Allotment

Social and Economic Effects of Allotment

Allotment's Effects on Grazing and Forest Land

Plenary Power of Congress over American Indian Affairs

Bureau of Indian Affairs ("BIA") American Indian Citizenship Ceremony

1924: Indian Citizenship Act. Double Edged Sword

1934: Indian Reorganization Act

1946: Indian Claims Commission—Pre-Cursor to Termination of Indian Tribes

1950–1967: Termination of Tribes' Federal Status

1968: Indian Civil Rights Act

13: INDIAN CHILD WELFARE ACT. A CIVICS MODEL IN ROLE OF JUDICIARY AND PUBLIC INTEREST GROUPS ꙮ 165

"Adoption Cliff"

Ultimate Purpose of Adoption by Christians *"Is to Place Them [Children] in a Christian Home That They Might Be Positioned to Receive the Gospel"*

Southern Baptist Convention's Resolution No. 2 on Adoption and Orphan Care

Academy of Adoption and Assisted Reproduction Attorneys; Eager to Support a "Hot Commodity"

Increasing Number of American Indian Children in Adoption and Foster Pool

Litigation Seeking to Declare ICWA Unconstitutional

    Political Machine Seeking to Dismantle ICWA

    Anti-Tribal Sovereignty Movement

    Opposition to Racial Classifications

    Conservative 'Go-to-Judge' - Federal Judge Reed O'Connor, United States District Court for the Northern District of Texas, Fort Worth

    Law Firm in Multi-Billion Dollar Machine Opposing ICWA: Gibson, Dunn & Crutcher LLP, Law Firm

    SCOTUS Decision in Brackeen ICWA Challenge

    President's Pronouncement on ICWA Case Victory for Tribal Nations

    Tribes' Hope Political Attacks on Tribal Sovereignty Cease

    "ICWA Lives to Die Another Day"

    Op-Ed Written by Legal Counsel for Pacific Legal Org., Adi Dynar, Implies American Indian Societies Are Uncivilized

    ICWA Kills—Another Op-Ed Written by Legal Counsel for Pacific Legal Org., Adi Dynar, Proclaims ICWA Is Merely to Protect Tribal Governments' Bruised Egos

    Federal and Colorado Adoption Legislation Enacted Giving Preference to Family and Kin and Restricting Intervention

14: OKLAHOMA CASES REGARDING TRIBAL CRIMINAL LAW JURISDICTION ↜ 183

    2020: *McGirt v. Oklahoma* Case

    2022: *Oklahoma v. Castro-Huerta* Case

    NARF/NCAI Joint Statement on U.S. Supreme Court Ruling in *Oklahoma v. Castro-Huerta*, July 7, 2022

    SUIT's Statement on Sovereignty after Adverse Supreme Court Ruling in *Oklahoma v. Castro-Huerta*

Jurisdictional Quagmire Post-2022 U.S. Supreme Court *Oklahoma v. Castro-Huerta* Decision

15: U.S. Congressional Committees on Indian Affairs ~ 187

U.S. Senate Committee on Indian Affairs

U.S. Senate Committee on Indian Affairs Oversight Hearing on Water as a Trust Resource: Examining Access in Native Communities

U.S. House Natural Resources Subcommittee on Indian and Insular Affairs

Major Congressional Statutes regarding American Indian Affairs

16: New Era of Indian Self-Determination ~ 189

1968: President Lyndon B. Johnson, Indian Self-Determination

1970: President Richard M. Nixon, Indian Self-Determination

1975: Indian Self-Determination and Education Assistance Act

Successive Presidential Administrations Confirm Tribal Sovereignty

President Biden's November 22, 2022, Memorandum regarding Tribal Consultation

Uniform Standards for U.S. and Tribal Government-to-Government Consultation

17: White House Tribal Nations Summit, December 6, 2023 ~ 193

December 6, 2023: President Biden's Historical Contribution of Funding to Tribes for Improvement of Quality of Life

U.S. Government Accountability Office's (GAO) Tribal Advisory Council

Direct Funding to Tribes Critical

18: SOVEREIGNTY OF INDIAN NATIONS ∾ 195

Certain of Indian Nations' Sovereign Powers

Sovereign Immunity from Suit

Collaborating with Other Tribes to Seek Social, Economic, and Educational Opportunities

National Congress of American Indians

NCAI Founding Principles

19: DEVELOPING AND MAINTAINING ACTIVE RELATIONS WITH FEDERAL EXECUTIVE BRANCH, DEPARTMENTS AND AGENCIES ∾ 199

Tribal Communication with Federal Executive Branch

Federal Executive Agencies with Tribal Trust Responsibilities

Department of Interior

Secretary of Interior Deb Haaland

U.S. Military

Procurement Technical Assistance Center ("PTAC")

Environmental Protection Agency ("EPA") Programs

Indian Health Service

Denver Indian Health and Family Services, Inc.

U.S. Department of Health and Human Services' Office of Minority Health Investing in Food Sovereignty, April 2023

20: DEVELOPING AND MAINTAINING ACTIVE RELATIONS WITH STATE AND COUNTIES ∾ 207

Colorado Commission of Indian Affairs

State Office of Liaison for Missing and Murdered Indigenous Relatives

Colorado State Legislation to Protect Colorado Tribal Lands from Annexation without Tribal Consent

Colorado Tribal-State Compacts

Taxation Compacts

Gaming Compacts

No Internet Betting for Colorado Indian Tribes

Southern Ute Indian Tribe Takes Legal Action against Colorado

Tribal Ordinances for Hunting and Fishing

Fishing and Hunting Memorandum of Understanding with State of Colorado

UMUT's Members Gain Access to Brunot Area for Hunting and Fishing

Colorado's General Assembly, 2023, SUIT and UMUT

Colorado's General Assembly, 2024, SUIT and UMUT

SUIT and UMUT Assume State Historic Preservation Officers' (SHPO) Roles

Civil Jurisdiction of State Governments Outside Indian Country

Colorado Counties

21: PUBLIC SERVANTS ⇔ 217

Serving in Federal and State Legislatures

Hon. U.S. Senator Ben Nighthorse Campbell, Northern Cheyenne

Colorado State Legislature: Hon. State Senator Suzanne Williams, Comanche

2010: Colorado State Senator Williams Introduces Indian Mascot Bill

2012: Colorado State Senator Williams Introduces Genocide Resolution, SJR12-0466

2020: Colorado's Official Recognition of Columbus Day Terminated

Federal Judiciary Appointments

Hon. Diane J. Humetewa, Judge, U.S. District Court, District of Arizona, May 2014

Hon. Sara Hill, Judge, U.S. District Court for Northern District of Oklahoma, December 2023

22: SOVEREIGN SOUTHERN UTE INDIAN TRIBE ↩ 223

(1) Power to Establish a Form of Government

SUIT's Constitution

SUIT's Council

SUIT's Boards and Committees

Southern Ute Indian Tribe's Statement on Sovereignty after Adverse U.S. Supreme Court Ruling in *Oklahoma v. Castro-Huerta*

(2) Power to Legislate

(3) Power to Administer Justice

SUIT's Court

SUIT's Legal Department

SUIT's Police Department

(4) Power to Protect Reservation Land

    City of Durango's Unilateral Secret Plan to Annex Southern Ute Indian Reservation Land

    City of Durango's Illegal Unilateral Illegal Secret Plan to Tap into Water at Lake Nighthorse Campbell

(5) Power to Protect Its Children

    Indian Child Welfare Act ("ICWA")

(6) Power to Manage Its Resources

    SUIT's Department of Natural Resources

    SUIT's Environmental Programs Department

    SUIT's Utilities Management

(7) Power to Establish Tribal and Individual Tribal Member Enterprises on Indian Lands, Communities, or Reservations

    SUIT's Businesses

    Sky Ute Casino Resort

    Southern Ute Indian Tribe Growth Fund

    Red Willow Production Company

    Red Cedar Gathering Company

    GF Properties Group

    GF Private Equity Group, LLC

    GF Ventures, LLC

    SUIT's Cultural Museum

(8) Power to Manage Health Care

SUIT's Health Department

(9) Power to Manage Education

Department of Education

Southern Ute Indian Montessori Academy

American Indian Boarding School Trauma Still Present

Bison

SUIT's Bison Herd

23: SOVEREIGN UTE MOUNTAIN UTE INDIAN TRIBE ⌒ 239

(1) Power to Establish a Form of Government

UMUT's Government

Constitution of Ute Mountain Ute Tribe, Preamble

(2) Power to Legislate

1988 UMUT's Law and Order Code

Power to Determine Membership; Power to Exclude Persons from Reservation

(3) Power to Administer Justice

UMUT's Court

UMUT's Legal Department

UMUT's Police Department

(4) Power to Protect Its Children

UMUT Is Indian Child Welfare Act ("ICWA") Advocate

(5) Power to Manage Its Resources

UMUT's Solar Project

2019 Office of Indian Energy Program, Indian Energy Champion Award, Bernadette Cuthair, UMUT

UMUT's Climate Action Plan

(6) Power to Establish Tribal and Individual Tribal Member Enterprises on Indian Lands, Communities, or Reservations

UMUT's Casino

Farming, Ranching and Construction

Weeminuche Construction Authority Received National Minority Enterprise Development Award as Minority Construction Firm of Year

UMUT's Tribal Park

(7) Power to Manage Health Care

Towaoc Health Center

2022: Colorado Health Foundation's Dr. Virgilio Licona Community Health Leadership Award, Bernadette Cuthair, UMUT

(8) Power to Manage Education

Kwiyagat Community Academy

UMUT's Adult Education Family Learning Center

UMUT Actively Engaged in Restoring Language and Culture

24: American Indian Water Rights

"Whiskey Is for Drinking, Water Is for Fighting"

Colorado Ute Indian Water Rights Settlement Act of 1988 (Southern Ute and Ute Mountain Ute Indian Tribes)

New Water Delivery Infrastructure Needed

1922: Colorado River Compact

2019: Colorado River Drought Contingency Plan

2026: Colorado River Basin Managing Guidelines

Ten Tribes Partnership Push for Role in 2026 Colorado River Basin Guidelines Negotiations

Colorado River Basin Tribal Coalition Seeks DOI's Use of Political Influence on Its Behalf

May 3, 2024, Memorandum of Understanding between States and Tribes on Colorado River Management

UMUT's Water Rights

25: PRESERVING AMERICAN INDIANS' RELIGIONS, CULTURES AND LANGUAGES ⇔ 257

1800s BIA Prohibition on American Indian Religious and Cultural Practices

NCAI Policy Issues

2019: United Nations Declares International Decade of Indigenous Languages

Education and American Indian Boarding Schools Legacy

June 2024: U.S. Catholic Bishops Formally Apologize for 'Trauma' Inflicted on Native American Communities

26: WILLFUL VIOLATION OF STATE LAW REQUIRING COLORADO PUBLIC HIGH SCHOOLS TO TEACH CIVICS, INCLUDING SOCIAL CONTRIBUTIONS OF MINORITY GROUPS ⇔ 263

Colorado House Bill 19-1192: Codified as § 22-1-104, C.R.S.

Judicial Review of § 22-1-104

Colorado Attorney General Opinion on § 22-1-104

Colorado Appellate Court Decision on § 22-1-104

Colorado Federal District Court, *Lane v. Owens*, 2003, Cited § 22-1-104 in Dicta as Valid Example of Curriculum Requirement

Colorado Supreme Court Decision regarding Use of Term "Must" by General Assembly (aka State Legislature)

Native American Holocaust in Colorado's Public High Schools

Donna Chrisjohn, Sicangu Lakota/Diné, American Indian Educator

'Our Invisibility and Our Erasure in This Country Is on Purpose'

27: United Nations Permanent Forum on Indigenous Issues ∽ 271

United Nations Declaration on the Rights of Indigenous Peoples ("UNDRIP")

United Nations Summary of Damages to Indigenous Peoples

Appendix 1: U.S. Colorado American Indian Treaties

Appendix 2: Presidential Viewpoints of American Indians

Appendix 3: BIA American Indian Citizenship Ceremony

Appendix 4: American Indian Child Welfare Act—A Civics Model in Role of Judiciary and Public Interest Groups

Appendix 5: Criminal Law Jurisdiction Chart Post *Oklahoma v. Castro-Huerta*

Appendix 6: Major Congressional American Indian Affairs Statutes

Appendix 7: Federal Executive Agencies with Tribal Trust Responsibilities

Preface

Tribes have shaped and are shaping the political, economic and social landscape of Colorado. The state of Colorado realized this as far back as 1998 when Colorado state lawmakers mandated that American Indian history and culture be included in the curriculum of high schools in Colorado, based on the persistent efforts of Comanche State Senator Suzanne Williams. For her, it was a highlight of her 16 years in the House. Senator Williams is a fierce and creative advocate for Native Americans. *She is a hero to me. Her work in civics and her exercise of courageous citizenship is something I hope all Coloradoans get to learn about in their study of Colorado Civics.*

In 2003, the legislature mandated that students must satisfactorily complete a course on the civil government of the United States and the state of Colorado, as a condition of high school graduation, which expressly included the history and culture of certain minorities, effective with the graduating class of 2007 (SB 36, enacted 4/22/2003, § 22-1-104, C.R.S.). The minorities included African-Americans, American Indians and Latinos. Colorado school districts are willfully ignoring § 22-1-104, C.R.S. Students receive diplomas even if they have not been offered or satisfactorily completed the course required under § 22-1-104.

Primary Source Reliance

In the pages that follow the reader will become aware of the author's reliance on numerous direct citations from relevant historical documents. This format derives from the author's perspective that the material under discussion here is best experienced by the contemporaneous voice unfiltered by time or latter-day interpretations and revisions.

American Indians; Indians; Native Americans; Indigenous Peoples Nomenclature

American Indians, also referred to as Native Americans, and Indigenous Americans, are the indigenous peoples of the United States. I primarily refer to them as American Indians as much of the federal legislation, policies and programs refer to them as such. Whenever possible, I use their specific indigenous name. The term 'Indians' used herein refers to American Indians.

Names; Spelling

The names of historical American Indian people and tribes can cause much confusion for historians and readers. People often received several names over the course of their lives. A single person might have a birth name, a clan name, a name related to a good deed or act of bravery, and a French, Spanish, or English name used by Europeans or Americans. A tribal name could be spelled in numerous different ways. Spelling of words differed also. Misspelling and grammatical variances will be noted in the quoted material; please keep this in mind while reading this material.

Disclaimer

The views expressed herein are those of the author and do not reflect any official position of any entity. The laws that affect American Indians' rights and programs are evolving on many fronts - in court decisions, in statutes passed by Congress, and in executive orders and other actions of the President and the executive, legislative and judicial branches. Federal Indian law is in a constant state of flux. The material in this book does not constitute legal advice.

Settler Colonialism

Aaron Bird Bear explained settler colonialism to me as follows:

> Colonialism is suggested to be the policy or practice of acquiring full or partial political control over a nation, occupying it with settlers, and exploiting it economically. Additionally, settler colonialism aims for the dissolution of indigenous societies by establishing a

new colonial society on seized land with the elimination of native societies as an organizing principal. Settler colonialism annihilates to supplant.

This same concept was expressed by General John Pope in 1878:

> *I presume it will not be disputed that all history shows that when a savage and a civilized people are brought together in the same country, the inevitable result has been the dispossession of the savage and the occupation of the lands by civilized man.*
>
> *The first treaty made with an Indian tribe only alienated a small portion of his lands, but as the emigrants pressed forward, increasing daily both their numbers and the routes by which they entered the Indian country, it soon became necessary to make another treaty, and then another, until in time, and a very short time, as it appears, one tribe of Indians after another was dispossessed of its lands until the whole of the vast region east of the Mississippi River fell into possession of the whites.*
>
> *Accepting as inevitable the proposition that in the nature of things, the lands on this continent must in some manner and in large pass from the possession of the Indian into that of the white man ... we bought his lands by driblets, knowing very well that every purchase demanded another purchase in geometrical ratio, and that with every sale the means of livelihood upon which the Indian race had depended for ages, and which was the only mode they knew, were restricted more and more, and that in time every tribe of Indians must, in the nature of the case, be left destitute, except insofar as the government chose to feed and clothe them. The Indian did not know this in the beginning, nor indeed until want was upon him. We knew that he must relinquish in time all of his country. He did not know it, nor in the least comprehended the merciless and resistless progress of white populations. In short, we began the system, knowing perfectly what would be the results; the Indian began and for a long time continued it in ignorance of these ends.* (Emphasis added).[1]

Secretary of the Interior Carl Schurz's (1877 to 1881) exposure to Indians prior to assuming office was limited, and he held a view in keeping with the popular ethnocentrism of the times. He stated:

The underlying support of this proposition [War Department control] was the conviction that the Indian could never be civilized and that the only possible *solution of the problem which he embodied was to confine him*, under strict military supervision, on reservations from which all uplifting contact with white men was barred, *till he should become extinct by virtue of his own incurable barbarism.* (Emphasis added).[2]

Notes:

1. Address by General John Pope before the Social Science Association, at Cincinnati, Ohio, May 24, 1878. Delivered by Request of the Association (Cincinnati: n.p., 1878). Excerpt from: Editor, Cozzens, Peter. "Eyewitnesses to the Indian Wars: 1865-1890: Vol. 5, The Army and the Indian." Apple Books.
2. Carl Schurz, The Reminiscences of Carl Schurz, vol. 3 (New York: The McClure Co., 1908), 385.

1

BACKGROUND

In 1998, Colorado state lawmakers mandated that American Indian history and culture be included in the curriculum of public high schools in Colorado, based on the persistent efforts of Comanche State Senator Suzanne Williams. In 2003, they broadened the law mandating that in order to graduate students must satisfactorily complete a high school civil government course which includes the history, culture and social contributions of American Indians and other groups. Yet tens of thousands of students graduate each year in the state without learning any of the information that is mandated in that single state graduation requirement. This book on Colorado Indian civics is to help fulfill this requirement.

> Ideals, principles, and practices of citizenship have always been part of American Indian societies. The rights and responsibilities of American Indian individuals have been defined by the values, morals, and beliefs common to their cultures. American Indians today may be citizens of their tribal nations, the states they live in, and the United States.[1]

574 Tribes

> *There are 574 ethnically, culturally, and linguistically diverse federally recognized Indian Tribes/Nations in the United States.* These Tribal Nations are distinct political entities whose inherent sovereignty predates the United States and is reflected in their government-to-government relationship with the U.S. government. The United States has undertaken a unique trust responsibility to protect and support Tribal Nations and their citizens through treaties, statutes, and historical relations with Tribal Nations.[2]

The National Museum of the American Indian describes Indian civics as follows:

> American Indian governments and leaders interacted, recognized each other's sovereignty, practiced diplomacy, built strategic alliances, waged wars, and negotiated peace accords. They exist within a vast political and legal landscape.[3]

The Constitution of the United States, treaties, executive orders, statutes, and court decisions have consistently recognized a unique political relationship between Indian nations and the United States. As sovereigns, Indian nations must continually assess the interplay between the executive, congressional and judicial branches of government, public entities and the political climate to protect their sovereignty, right to self-governance, right to self-determination and ability to flourish.

The U.S. Forest Service's National Resource Guide to American Indian and Alaska Native Relations provides "Forest Service leadership with critical information to develop or improve government-to-government relations with all Federally Recognized American Indian and Alaska Native Tribes."

> Indian tribal governments possess inherent powers of self-government.
> No two tribal governments are exactly alike.
> There are no single or standard answers for any given issue that can be equally applied to all tribes.
> Indian peoples are diverse, as well.

Dozens of other tribes are recognized by various state governments, whose authorities and responsibilities differ according to the laws of the states.

Key Definitions

> The following definitions, unless otherwise noted, are from the Forest Service National Resource Book on American Indian and Alaska Native Relations, 1997.
>
> Federal Power. The Indian Commerce Clause, Article I, Section 8, Clause 3 of the U.S. Constitution provides Congress with broad powers. "The Congress shall have Power...to regulate Commerce

with foreign Nations, and among the several States, and with the Indian Tribes."

Indian Tribe. Historically, the Federal Government has determined that it will recognize particular groups or Indian tribes under the Indian Commerce Clause of the U.S. Constitution. The Secretary of the Interior has the authority to determine which groups are Federally Recognized. Tribes which are "Federally Recognized" are considered Indian tribes or tribal governments for legal purposes.

Indian. An Indian is a person recognized as an Indian by that person's tribe or community. It is important to understand that the protections and services the United States provides tribal members do not flow from an individual's status as an American Indian in an ethnological sense, but because that person is a member of a Federally Recognized Tribe with which the United States has a trust relationship. This trust relationship entails certain legally enforceable obligations, duties, and responsibilities. "Just as there is great diversity among tribal nations, there is great diversity among individual American Indians. There is no generic American Indian."

Indian Country. The term Indian country is defined in 18 U.S.C. § 1151 and 40 C.F.R. § 171.3 as:

> ...all land within the limits of any Indian reservation under the jurisdiction of the United States Government, notwithstanding the issuance of any patent, and, including rights-of-way running through the reservation;
> all dependent Indian communities within the borders of the United States whether within the original or subsequently acquired territory thereof, and whether within or without the limits of a state; and
> all Indian allotments, the Indian titles to which have not been extinguished, including rights-of-way running through the same.
> Consistent with the statutory definition of Indian country, as well as federal case law interpreting this statutory language, lands held by the federal government in trust for Indian tribes that exist outside of formal reservations are informal reservations and, thus, are Indian country.

Indian Reservation. The Bureau of Indian Affairs defines a reservation as "an area of land reserved for a tribe or tribes under treaty or other agreement with the United States, executive order, or federal statute or administrative action as permanent tribal homelands, and *where the federal government holds title to the land in trust on behalf of the tribe.*" (Emphasis added).[4]

Historian Richard White describes them as follows: "American officials, in attempting to halt conflict between Indians and whites, prevent expensive wars, and open up lands to white settlement, created reservations the way survivors of a shipwreck might fashion a raft from the debris of the sunken vessel. Reservations evolved on an ad hoc basis as a way to prevent conflict and enforce a separation of the races."[5]

Executive Order Reservations. Not all reservations were established by treaty. Some reservations were identified or created by executive order. Between 1871, when Congress discontinued formal treaty making, and 1910, tribes not previously recognized were established by executive order.

Allotted Land. The term "allotted land" refers to land owned by individual Indians that is either held in trust by the United States or is subject to a statutory restriction on sale or other forms of alienation (conveyance or transference of property to another). Most allotted lands are the result of allotment laws that the U.S. government passed in the late 1800s and early 1900s.

Federal Indian Law involves a distinct body of law that relates to the legal relationships between the federal government and Indian tribes. It is dynamic, evolving and encompasses several hundred years of federal policies and interaction with tribes. The sources of federal Indian law include principles of international law, the United States Constitution, treaties with Indian tribes, federal statutes and regulations, executive orders, and judicial opinions.

Code of Federal Regulations. Title 25 ("Indians") of the U.S. Code addresses a myriad of subjects important to the tribal-federal relationship.

Trust Responsibility

The trust responsibility is the U.S. Government's permanent legal obligation to protect tribal lands, assets, resources, and treaty rights, as well as a duty to carry out the mandates of Federal law with respect to American Indians. Federal Indian Policy and "trust responsibilities" have developed from treaties, congressional laws, executive orders and court decisions. Several federal agencies provide direct services or funding to federally recognized tribes and their citizens.[6]

Federally Recognized Tribes in Colorado

There are two federally recognized tribes in Colorado, the Southern Ute Indian Tribe and the Ute Mountain Ute Indian Tribe. The Utes name for themselves is "Nuu-ciu" meaning "The People." It is important to understand that these two tribes are sovereign nations. It is as if you are interacting with another nation entirely, such as France or Belgium or Japan or China. The laws and protocols of these two nations must be adhered to and respected at all times.

The Southern Ute Indian Tribe (hereinafter "SUIT") lies to the south and east of Durango, Colorado. The reservation has tribal member allotments, as well as tribally owned land, dating back into the early 19th century. Land ownership is like a checkerboard with Utes, non-Utes, and state and federal governments having ownership of parcels. Their ownership may be severed with ownership of only the surface estate or mineral estate. There are 307,838 tribally owned acres and 1,408 enrolled members who reside both on and off the reservation.

The Ute Mountain Ute Tribe (hereinafter "UMUT") Reservation spreads across approximately 900 unallotted square miles in the southwest corner of Colorado, as well as parts of New Mexico and Utah. The UMUT has about 2,100 registered members, most of whom reside in Colorado.

The National Congress of American Indians describes tribal governance as follows:

Tribal governance ensures protecting each tribe's territorial integrity and sovereignty over its lands, resources, and population. The tribes determine their own governance structures, pass laws, and enforce laws through police departments and tribal courts that apply within their own territory. They provide multiple programs and services, including, but not limited to, health and human services, education, and energy and land management. They also build and maintain a variety of infrastructure, such as public buildings, housing, and roads.[7]

Denver's Urban American Indian Population

The 2020 Census Data reports that 74,129 American Indian and Alaskan Natives live in the State of Colorado, comprising 1.0 percent of the total population. The cities with the largest populations are Denver and Colorado Springs. During World War II and the years immediately after the war, American Indians from rural areas, particularly from reservations, moved to cities in search of better opportunities. Selected as one of the initial destination cities for the relocation and employment assistance program of the Bureau of Indian Affairs ("BIA"), Denver became a hub for American Indian migrants. Although the federal government hoped to assimilate American Indian relocatees by distancing them from reservation communities, the Denver American Indians created an urban American Indian community to support themselves and showed little interest in losing their tribal or American Indian identities. Despite their diversity, they share the same strong commitment to family and cultural survival.[8]

Hub of American Indian Country

In the far-flung expanse of American Indian country, Denver emerged as the informal capital. Denver has the nation's largest concentration of national American Indian groups, about 15 associations ranging from the leading non-profit American Indian law firm to the leading scholarship fund. Propelling Denver to center stage has been the city's neutrality in tribal affairs and its centrality in transportation. "In the urban American Indian political world, Denver is the primary city," Kevin Gover, past assistant secretary for American Indian Affairs, said. Gover, observed, "If we need a location where we are not favoring one group over another, Denver is neutral ground."

Denver City Council Land Acknowledgement

Land Acknowledgements honor a place's Indigenous people—past and present—and recognize the history that brought us to where we are today.

The Denver City Council Land Acknowledgement reflects the importance of Indian history, culture and social contributions to the state and the past and present "exclusions and erasures of Indigenous Peoples:"

The Denver City Council honors and acknowledges that the land on which we reside is the traditional territory of the Ute, Cheyenne, and Arapaho Peoples. We also recognize the 48 contemporary tribal nations that are historically tied to the lands that make up the state of Colorado.

We honor Elders past, present, and future, and those who have stewarded this land throughout generations. We also recognize that government, academic and cultural institutions were founded upon and continue to enact exclusions and erasures of Indigenous Peoples.

May this acknowledgement demonstrate a commitment to working to dismantle ongoing legacies of oppression and inequities and recognize the current and future contributions of Indigenous communities in Denver.[9]

Denver Indian Center

The Denver Indian Center Inc. (DICI) is an urban cultural gathering center for the American Indian and Alaskan Native community of the Denver Metro area. Incorporated in 1983 to meet the unique needs and challenges facing the Native community, the DICI's mission is "To empower our American Indian youth, elders, families and community by promoting self-determination and economic, mental and physical health through education, advocacy and cultural enrichment."[10]

The Denver Indian Center is the community's lifeline for assistance. The following Client's Comment about the Denver Indian Center captures this essence:

I came to the Indian Center with nothing. I was new to Denver. I didn't know where to go... Now, I am enrolled in programs at the Indian Center and have felt so much support from their staff. I am about to finish training on my new job that I got after participating in the workforce program and I am about halfway through with the Fatherhood program's classes. I see the day that I came to the Indian Center as a big turning point in my life in Denver. I am so grateful for everything...[11]

March Denver Powwow Co-Founders

Watching the March Denver Powwow, which John Emhoolah and Keith Fox, an Arikara, started, Mr. Emhoolah explained that "Every tribe has its own explanation of the meaning of the powwow.... But in the old days it was often a religious ceremony. Powwows historically included more activities considered sacred. That's how the songs were made—to the Creator."[12]

He realized that young American Indians growing up in the cities were not learning about their heritage and gaining the self-esteem which can come from tribal identity and this was his dream for them in founding the Powwow. Then, too, Mr. Emhoolah pointed out, "Denver has a lot of Indians, but we'd never had a big gathering of all the tribes." So, the Denver event helped create and sustain community spirit. Mr. Emhoolah served in many capacities—including head singer, head dancer, judge, arena director or master-of-ceremonies—in powwows all over the country.

American Indian Employment Preference within BIA Won in Littleton, Colorado

On March 14, 1970, local American Indians occupied the BIA Plant Management Engineering Center ("PMEC") in Littleton, Colorado, protesting anti-Indian employment practices by the BIA.

Despite the BIA's mandate to give preference to American Indian employees, non-Indians occupied the better-paying jobs and higher positions at the PMEC. According to the formal complaint filed on March 12, 1970, only 17 of 119 employees at the PMEC were American Indians, despite the provision of American Indian preference in hiring. Fourteen of those 17 American Indian employees earned between $4,300 and $7,100 annually

(GS 4 and below), and only one American Indian employee made over $10,000 per year. Jobs at the federal employment rating, GS 4 and below, were mainly clerical, while supervisory positions were at a level of GS 10 or above. Non-Indian employees occupied all the higher positions (GS 12 and above), and none of the non-Indian employees earned less than $6,800. The American Indian employees further asserted that the PMEC officials' unwillingness to offer training opportunities to American Indian employees halted their career advancement.

The PMEC employees who signed the complaint filed with Edward E. Shelton, Director of the Interior Department's Office of Equal Employment Opportunity, and BIA Commissioner Louis R. Bruce, came to be known as the "Littleton Twelve."

Nine members of the group that occupied the BIA PMEC office in Littleton, Colorado, were arrested and charged with trespassing and interference based on a complaint filed by Charles McCrea, suspended Chief Official of the PMEC office. All of them were tried in Arapahoe County Court, represented by attorney Harris Sherman, on June 23, 1970, and acquitted.

Attorney Harris Sherman: Reflection on Littleton, Colorado, Victory

> The criminal trial of the demonstrators was my very first case and it was in front of an all-white jury. The trial took three days and the jury came back with complete acquittals for all of the defendants. While an exhilarating victory for the group, the reality was that the agency was back to its systematic placement and advancement of white employees at the expense of Native American employees. The Littleton 12 group, along with other organizations, decided to push matters further through the courts. With the assistance of one of America's great law firms, Arnold & Porter, I filed a challenge of the BIA employment practices with the United States District Court in Washington, DC. The plaintiff in that case was Enola Freeman, one of the Littleton complainants. The primary claim in the case was the agency's refusal to follow the Indian Preference Statutes. On December 21, 1972, Judge Corcoran issued his ruling that the BIA had violated the Indian Preference Statutes and ordered the agency to revise its employment practices so that Native Americans would have a preference in hiring, advancement, transfers, and training within the

Agency. This landmark ruling was the beginning of a real transformation within the Agency. The ruling was appealed by the government but that appeal was defeated as well. Thereafter, the BIA started to amend its employment practices across the board to provide the preference.

Unfortunately, the *Freeman* victory was quickly challenged by certain non-Indian employees in the Albuquerque office of the BIA claiming that it violated the civil rights of non-Indian employees. A federal court in New Mexico sided with the non-Indians and thus put in jeopardy the gains of the *Freeman* decision. So we appealed the New Mexico decision, *Mancari v. Morton*, to the U.S. Supreme Court. Gaining review by the Supreme Court is extremely hard to achieve (less than 2%) but because of the importance of this case, the Court granted certiorari and scheduled the case for oral argument. As a young lawyer it was a great privilege to stand before the Supreme Court on behalf of Indian employees and argue the merits of the Indian Preference Statutes. We had a spirited argument and the Court rendered a 9-0 decision on behalf of Indian employees validating the Indian Preference Statutes.

Since then, over time, the BIA and Indian Health Service have become agencies largely run by Native Americans and are a testament to self-determination. It all began in Littleton, Colorado, with the Littleton 12.

Political Classification Status of Federally Recognized American Indian Tribes and Their Members

Tribes are governmental and political entities, not racial groups. This is a principle embedded in U.S. law from the very beginning and explicitly recognized by the Supreme Court in *Morton v. Mancari* in 1974. It was established as a result of the Littleton 12. *Mancari* held that federally recognized Indian tribes and their tribal members represent a "political classification," not a racial class. As such, Congress may enact legislation, and executive branch agencies may implement policy, that is unique to Indian peoples without violating the requirement of equal protection of the law, when such legislation or policies are reasonable and rationally designed to further tribal self-government.

Literally every piece of legislation dealing with Indian tribes and reservations, and certainly all legislation dealing with the BIA, single out for special treatment a constituency of tribal Indians living on or near reservations. If these laws, derived from historical relationships and explicitly designed to help only Indians, were deemed invidious racial discrimination, an entire Title of the United States Code (25 U.S.C.) would be effectively erased and the solemn commitment of the Government toward the Indians would be jeopardized. ... As long as the special treatment can be tied rationally to the fulfillment of Congress' unique obligation toward the Indians, such legislative judgments will not be disturbed. Here, where the preference is reasonable and rationally designed to further Indian self-government, we cannot say that Congress' classification violates due process.[13]

Ending Use of Mascots in Colorado Public Schools

Colorado started its own assessment amid national discussions about the use of derogatory Native American mascots, and in 2016, a state commission, which included tribal representation, recommended schools should eliminate all Native American mascots because of the misrepresentation and stereotypes they perpetuate, unless a school came to an agreement with a federally recognized tribe.[14]

UMUT Chairman Heart praised the Legislature's passage of Senate Bill 21-116 ending the use of American Indian mascots in Colorado public schools. Chairman Heart played a strong role in the Colorado Commission of Indian Affairs' ("CCIA") compliance efforts. The CCIA meetings on this subject are available online. Opposition to the law is discussed in the press.[15]

In-State College Tuition Rates for Certain Native Students

Under Colorado Senate Bill SB21-029, section 23-7-112 IV (b) (effective June 28, 2021), "American Indian students who are registered members of a federally recognized American Indian tribe with historical ties to Colorado" will be eligible for in-state tuition at Colorado public universities and colleges, beginning fall semester 2021-22.[16]

Notes:

1. https://americanindian.si.edu/nk360/about/understandings#eublock10 (accessed online June 21, 2024).

2. Tribal and Native American Issues, U.S. Government Accountability Office. https://www.gao.gov/tribal-and-native-american-issues (accessed online June 21, 2024).

3. https://americanindian.si.edu/nk360/about/understandings#eublock6 (accessed online June 21, 2024).

4. https://www.bia.gov/faqs/what-federal-indian-reservation (accessed online June 17, 2024).

5. Richard White, It's Your Misfortune and None of My Own: A History of the American West (Norman: University of Oklahoma Press, 1991), 91.

6. U.S. Forest Service National Resource Guide to American Indian and Alaska Native Relations. https://www.fs.usda.gov/spf/tribalrelations/pubs_reports/preface.shtml (accessed online July 4, 2024).

7. National Congress of American Indians (2020). Tribal Nations and the United States: An Introduction. Washington, DC, February 2020 (accessed online July 4, 2024).

8. American Indian/Alaska Native Population. https://ccia.colorado.gov/tribes/american-indian/alaska-native-population (accessed online July 4, 2024).

9. htts://www.denvergov.org/Government/Departments/Denver-City-Council/About (accessed online April 8, 2021).

10. https://denverindiancenter.org/ (accessed online April 25, 2023).

11. https://denverindiancenter.org/ (accessed online April 25, 2023).

12. https://www.csmonitor.com/1990/0523/lpow.html (accessed online

April 20, 2023).

13. *Morton v. Mancari*, 417 U.S. at 554-55 (1974).

14. https://www.colorado.gov/pacific/sites/default/files/atoms/files/CSAIRPS-Report-2016.pdf (accessed online April 21, 2023).

15. Ending Use of American Indian Mascots in Colorado Public Schools, Paolo Zialcita, May 19, 2022. https://www.cpr.org/2022/05/19/colorado-schools-native-american-mascots-avoid-fines/#:~:text=State%20lawmakers%20passed%20 SB21%2D116,schools%20to%20meet%20those%20parameters (accessed online April 21, 2023).

> Colorado Politics, PODIUM, Mascot commission makes up its own rules, Mark Hillman, April 20, 2022. https://www.coloradopolitics.com/opinion/podium-mascot-commission-makes-up-its-own-rules/article_f4fbe848-c057-11ec-b754-f7ed694c524c.html (accessed online April 21, 2023).

16. https://www.denverpost.com/2021/06/28/colorado-indigenous-in-state-tuition-law/ (accessed online April 21, 2023).

2
Federal Historical Context

History provides an important understanding of American Indian law and policy. Federal Indian policy has defined the relationship between the federal government and tribes. The major periods are set forth below:

U.S. Federal American Indian Policy

    Colonization/Colonial Period, 1492–1800s
    Treaty-Making and Removal Period, 1778–1871
    Reservation Period—Allotment and Assimilation, 1887–1934
    Reorganization Period, 1934–1953
    Termination, 1953–1967
    Self-Determination, 1967–Present

U.S. Predicates Authority over American Indians Based on Broad Interplay of U.S. Constitution's Treaty Power, Commerce and War Powers Clauses

> For over a century, the Supreme Court has interpreted the Constitution to grant the federal government "plenary" power over "Indian Affairs"—the diplomatic, political, military, and commercial relationships between the United States and Native nations.[1] This authority has been based on an unwieldly interplay between the Constitution's' treaty-making power (Article II, section 2), the war powers clause (Article I, Section 8, Clause 11) and the commerce clause (Art. I, Sec. 8, cl. 3).

Felix Cohen recognized in his seminal Handbook of Federal Indian Law, published in 1942, that the scope of the commerce clause had grown to include more than just commerce:

> The congressional power over commerce with the Indian tribes plus the treatymaking power is much broader than the power over commerce between the states. ... The commerce clause in the field of Indian affairs was for many decades broadly interpreted to include not only transactions by which Indians sought to dispose of land or other property in exchange for money, liquor, munitions, or other goods, but also aspects of intercourse which had little or no relation to commerce, such as travel, crimes by whites against Indians or Indians against whites, survey of land, trespass and settlement by whites in the Indian country, the fixing of boundaries, and the furnishing of articles, services, and money by the Federal Government.[2] It has also been found to apply to Congress's ability to legislate across a wide range of areas, including domestic violence, employment and taxation.

U.S. American Indian Treaties

Treaties are legally binding agreements between two or more sovereign governments. Treaties with Indian nations were negotiated and concluded by a representative of the President and became binding agreements after they were ratified by a two-thirds majority vote of the U.S. Senate. Formal treaty making ended when Congress, with a rider in the Appropriations Act of March 3, 1871, prohibited the federal government from making new treaties with American Indian tribes. The text reads: "No Indian nation or tribe within the territory of the United States shall be acknowledged or recognized as an independent nation, tribe, or power with whom the United States may contract by treaty; but no obligation of any treaty lawfully made and ratified with any such Indian nation or tribe prior to March 3, 1871, shall be hereby invalidated or impaired..."[3]

There are 389 treaties with Indian nations. With the end of treaty making in 1871, the U.S. government continued to enter into similar legal relationships with tribes under statutes, executive orders, and other agreements such as presidential proclamations. A chart of American Indian Treaties and agreements in Colorado is in Appendix 1.

In 1865, Secretary of the Interior Harlan instructed treaty negotiators that "these treaties might be amended by the Senate and such amendments would not require the concurrence of the Indians."[4]

Law of Nations regarding Treaties

The acknowledgement of the sovereign status of Indian Nations is confirmed by the understanding under the Law of Nations regarding the status of the parties to treaties. Emerich de Vattel, a leading international lawyer, states that treaties are made "between sovereigns who acknowledge no superior on earth." He is most famous for his 1758 work The Law of Nations, which profoundly influenced the development of international law. Therein he wrote:

> The Law of Nations: §219. Treaties are sacred between nations. ... Between bodies politic,—between sovereigns who acknowledge no superior on earth,—treaties are the only means of adjusting their various pretensions,—of establishing fixed rules of conduct,—of ascertaining what they are entitled to expect, and what they have to depend on.[5]

> The Law of Nations: §221. ... He who violates his treaties, violates at the same time the law of nations; for he disregards the faith of treaties,—that faith which the law of nations declares sacred; and, so far as depends on him, he renders it vain and ineffectual. Doubly guilty, he does an injury to his ally, he does an injury to all nations, and inflicts a wound on the great society of mankind.[6]

American Indian Nations Considered Sovereigns of Soil

In numerous treaty conferences held between the highest-level of Crown and colonial officials and Indian leaders, Indian nations were considered the sovereign owners of their land. The credibility of the sovereignty of the Indian tribes is recognized by U.S. Supreme Court Justice Story in his *Commentaries on the Constitution of the United States*:

> § 3. There is no doubt, that the Indian tribes, inhabiting this continent at the time of its discovery, maintained a claim to the

exclusive possession and occupancy of the territory within their respective limits, as sovereigns and absolute proprietors of the soil. They acknowledged no obedience, or allegiance, or subordination to any foreign sovereign whatsoever; and as far as they have possessed the means, they have ever since asserted this plenary right of dominion, and yielded it up only when lost by the superior force of conquest, or transferred by a voluntary cession.[7]

1780: President Thomas Jefferson: Empire of Liberty—Future of Commerce and Expansion

Jefferson used the phrase "Empire of Liberty" in 1780, while the American Revolution was still being fought. In his instructions to George Rogers Clark to take Fort Detroit he envisioned a future of commerce and expansion:

> We shall divert through our own Country a branch of commerce which the European States have thought worthy of the most important struggles and sacrifices and ... shall form to the American union a barrier against the dangerous extension of the British Province of Canada and add to the Empire of Liberty an extensive and fertile Country...[8]

This false narrative of spreading liberty across the continent was used to justify removing Indians who were seen as obstacles to progress.

Marshall Trilogy

Three U.S. Supreme Court cases, M'Intosh, Cherokee Nation and Worcester, represent the Marshall Trilogy and fundamentally shaped federal Indian policy and institutionalized major doctrines of federal Indian law: Johnson v. M'Intosh, 21 U.S. 543 (1823); *Cherokee Nation v. Georgia*, 30 U.S. 1 (1831); and *Worcester v. Georgia*, 31 U.S. 515 (1832). The Trilogy, primarily authored by Chief Justice John Marshall, established federal primacy in Indian affairs and excluded state law from Indian country.

M'Intosh incorporated the Doctrine of Discovery into federal law. Under the Doctrine of Discovery whichever European nation first 'discovered' land, then not ruled by a Christian prince or people, could claim ownership of the land as against other European nations, even if it was inhabited. The discovering Christian country acquired the 'fee simple absolute' title to the land, which is a term meaning the unlimited ownership interest in the land. Marshall's ruling changed the nature of Indian ownership of their land—Indians only had the right to occupy the land; they didn't own it. It could be purchased or won by conquest.

Cherokee Nation characterized tribes as 'domestic dependent nations,' not foreign nations. Indian tribes were understood to be wards of the federal government. The federal government was authorized to make decisions for the Indians. The doors to the U.S. Supreme Court to litigate their grievances were slammed.

Worcester held that state law does not apply in Indian Country. This was recently modified by a majority of the U.S. Supreme Court in 2022 in the case, *Oklahoma v. Castro-Huerta*. Under this case, the federal government and the state have concurrent jurisdiction to prosecute crimes committed by non-Indians against Indians in Indian country.

1830: Indian Removal Act

President Jackson's Justification for Indian Removal Act

President Jackson justified the Indian Removal Act based on an understanding that the Indians were savages and had made no improvements to the U.S.:

> What good man would prefer a country covered with forests and ranged by a few thousand savages to our extensive Republic, studded with cities, towns, and prosperous farms, embellished with all the improvements which art can devise or industry execute, occupied by more than 12,000,000 happy people, and filled with all the blessings of liberty, civilization, and religion?[9]

He also refused to recognize them as sovereign nations. Jackson declared, "I have long viewed treaties with the Indians an absurdity not to be reconciled to the principles of our Government." The Indians, said Jackson, were subjects of the United States, pure and simple, "inhabiting its territory and acknowledging its sovereignty." It was a fiction that the tribes were in fact separate and independent entities, and it was absurd to negotiate with them as such.[10]

For additional presidential viewpoints on American Indians see Appendix 2.

Tenor of Times - They May Begin to Dig Their Graves and Prepare to Die

Alfred Balch, Jackson's Commissioner of Indian Treaties, echoed the tenor of the times: "...removal of Indians would be an act of seeming violence — But it will prove in the end an act of enlarged philanthropy. These untutored sons of the Forest, cannot exist in a state of Independence, in the vicinity of the white man. If they will persist in remaining where they are, they may begin to dig their graves and prepare to die."[11]

Hezekiah Niles, editor of the *Niles Weekly Register* newspaper, offered the starkest comment on removal: "The fate of the Indians within the present states and territories—is sealed." The eastern Indian Nations would remove or become extinct.[12]

Just nineteen days into his presidency, Jackson stated his removal policy in a speech to the Creek Indians.

> Where you now are, you and my white children are too near to each other to live in harmony and peace. Your game is destroyed and many of your people will not work and till the Earth. *Beyond the great river Mississippi, where part of your nation has gone, your father has provided a country large enough for all of you, and he advises you to remove to it. There your white brothers will not trouble you; they will have no claim to the land, and you can live upon it, you and your children, as long as the grass grows or the water runs, in peace and plenty. It will be yours forever.* (Emphasis added).[13]

Balch's assurance to Jackson that he would ramrod Indian removal legislation through Congress was underway. On February 24, 1830, Rep. John Bell and the Indian Affairs committee introduced a removal bill—officially, H.R. 287. The Senate version of the bill, submitted at the same time by Bell's counterpart on the Senate's Indian Affairs committee, Hugh Lawson White, was known as S. 102.[14] The House version of the bill was preceded by a report of over 15,000 words that was part opposition to removal, part history of United States Indian policy, especially the peculiarities of the treaty system, and part assertion of the southern Indians' rapid decline and, should they remain, certain extinction.

Secretary of War Threatens Cherokees - They Will Be Left to Whims of Georgia

In 1824, Secretary of War John Calhoun threatened to leave the Cherokees "exposed to the discontent of Georgia and the pressure of her citizens" if they continued to refuse to exchange their land in Georgia for land west of the Mississippi. They responded: "Sir, to these remarks we beg leave to observe, and to remind you, that the Cherokees are not foreigners, but original inhabitants of America; and that they now inhabit and stand on the soil of their own territory; and that the limits of their territory are defined by the treaties which they have made with the Government of the United States."[15]

False arguments that the Indians would be willing to exchange lands were introduced:

> General Carroll, to the secretary of war, describing the difficulties he met with in inducing the Indians to emigrate, says, "The truth is, they rely with great confidence on a favorable report on the petition they have before Congress. If that is rejected, and the laws of the States are enforced, you will have no difficulty of procuring an exchange of lands with them."
>
> General Coffee, upon the same subject says, "They express a confident hope that Congress will interpose its power, and prevent the States from extending their laws over them. Should they be disappointed in this, I hazard little in saying that the government will have little difficulty in removing them west, of the Mississippi."[16]

Reports from Indians that had moved west, however, were dismal and they feared for their survival. General Clark, Superintendent of Indian Affairs, credits the southern Indians fear of moving with the dire stories of the Indians who had moved west. Senator Evans described it as follows:

> The condition of many tribes west of the Mississippi is the most pitiable that can be imagined. During several seasons in every year,

they are distressed by famine, in which many die for want of food, and during which the living child is often buried with the dead mother, because no one can spare it as much food as would sustain it through its helpless infancy.[17]

Impact of U.S. Supreme Court Cases on Indian Removal Act

The U.S. Supreme Court, under *Fletcher v. Peck*, stated in dicta that Georgia held fee title to all land within the state and *Johnson*, determined that Indians had a right to occupy land, but they did not own it.[18]

Since Natives did not own the land, they became prey to an increasingly loud argument within the United States that Indian occupancy of land in close proximity to settlers inevitably led to trouble. To avoid the trouble, Indians should be moved away from the edges of western settlement.[19]

Since under *Fletcher* and *Johnson*, the states held fee title to all land within the state, it led the southern states to enact legislation incorporating Cherokee land into the counties of Georgia and totally abrogating their sovereignty. They would be citizens of Georgia and subject to its laws.

Senator John McKinley (ALA), Thomas F. Foster (GA) and Richard H. Wilde (GA) supported Senator John Forsyth of Georgia's assertion that the Indians possessed no inherent rights to the soil by invoking the well-known Supreme Court case of *Johnson* in which Chief Justice John Marshall had affirmed that the United States held dominion over Indian lands by an established right of 'discovery' and conquest, inherited from the country's European predecessors. The Indians had a right of occupancy, but not a right to title. Furthermore, Congressman Henry Lamar from Alabama argued the Supreme Court case of *Fletcher* supported his position for the Indian Removal Act.

Indian Removal Act Passed

In 1830, Congress passed the act titled: "An Act to provide for an exchange of lands with the Indians residing in any of the states or territories, and for their removal west of the river Mississippi," commonly referred to as the Indian Removal Act of 1830, 4 Stat. 411. The *Fletcher* and *Johnson* decisions bolstered support for the Act in Congress. It passed the Senate by a vote of 28-19. It passed the House by a vote of 102-97. It was signed by President Andrew Jackson on May 28, 1830.

It included funds to pay for removal—$500,000 was appropriated to pay to move Indians west of the Mississippi River. The bill, conspicuously, contained no stipulation which allowed the Indian Nations to refuse relocation or even any indication they might not wish to do so, and nothing further was said of assimilation. It made no mention of the use of force.[20]

Removal of Indian Nations Became Mandatory

Over 60 removal treaties were signed which resulted in the forced westward migration of approximately 80,000 American Indians. Although removal was supposed to be voluntary, the relocation of Indian Nations became mandatory whenever the government decided. Many of the eastern Indian Nations were destroyed or decimated. Millions of acres of lands were opened to settlers moving west.

1845: Manifest Destiny of U.S. to Possess Whole Continent

In an 1839 article in the Democratic Review, John O'Sullivan—a Democrat in the era of Andrew Jackson— articulated American imperialism, outlining the contours of the new nation: "Its floor shall be a hemisphere—its roof the firmament of the star studded heavens, and its congregation an Union of many Republics, comprising hundreds of happy millions, calling, owning no man master, but governed by God's natural and moral law of equality, the law of brotherhood—of 'peace and good will amongst men.'"[21]

In 1845, he gave the 'doctrine of discovery' a uniquely American flavor when he coined the term Manifest Destiny to defend U.S.' expansion and claims to new territory:

> ... the right of our manifest destiny to over spread and to possess the whole of the continent which Providence has given us for the development of the great experiment of liberty... is right such as that of the tree to the space of air and the earth able for the full expansion of its principle and destiny of growth.[22]

The idea of Manifest Destiny, and the desire of Americans to fulfill this destiny, was an extremely powerful force. Thus, the Louisiana Purchase, the annexation of Texas, the War with Mexico and the settlement of the Oregon Territory all opened the continent to the U.S.' domination of Indian nations, bringing them and their lands into the control of the American empire. With the Gadsden purchase in 1853 of what is today southwestern New Mexico and southern Arizona from Mexico, the continental puzzle of the lower 48 states was complete.

1873: President Grant's American Indian Peace Policy Debacle

On March 4, 1873, at his second inaugural address, President Grant's enunciated his American Indian Peace Policy:

> My efforts in the future will be directed to the restoration of good feeling between the different sections of our common country ... by a human course, to bring the aborigines of the country under the benign influences of education and civilization. It is either this or war of extermination. Wars of extermination, engaged in by people pursuing commerce and all industrial pursuits, are expensive even against the weakest people, and are demoralizing and wicked. Our superiority of strength and advantages of civilization should make us lenient toward the Indian. The wrong inflicted upon him should be taken into account and the balance placed to his credit. The moral view of the question should be considered and the question asked, Can not the Indian be made a useful and productive member of society by proper teaching and treatment? If the effort is made in good faith, we will stand better before the civilized nations of the earth and in our own consciences for having made it.[23]

He announced that Christians would be appointed as Indian agents. Many in the military were opposed as they believed Indians would only respond to control by military officers, not preachers.

President Grant Breaches His Own American Indian Peace Policy

The outcry for opening the Black Hills in the Dakotas for gold mining brought President Grant to a crossroads. He had taken office in 1869 on a pledge to keep the West free of war. "Our dealings with the Indians properly lay us open to charges of cruelty and swindling," he had said, and he had staked his administration to a Peace Policy. Now, President Grant was forced to choose between the electorate and the Indians.

The Treaty between the Lakotas and the U.S. had been signed at Fort Laramie in 1868, the year before President Grant took office. "From this day forward," the document began, "all war between the parties to this agreement shall forever cease." All Lakota land was to be inviolate. President Grant would breach this Treaty.[24]

December 7, 1875: President Grant's Message - Gold in Black Hills; Sioux (aka Lakota) Unwilling to Cede Them; End Sioux Rations

Succumbing to the demands of the voting electorate to open the Black Hills for mining, President Grant announced action would be taken to relieve the impasse, starting with denying food rations to the Sioux.

> The discovery of gold in the Black Hills, a portion of the Sioux Reservation, has had the effect to induce a large emigration of miners to that point. Thus far the effort to protect the treaty rights of the Indians to that section has been successful, but the next year will certainly witness a large increase of such emigration. The negotiations for the relinquishment of the gold fields having failed, it will be necessary for Congress to adopt some measures to relieve the embarrassment growing out of the causes named. *The Secretary of the Interior suggests that the supplies now appropriated for the sustenance of that people, being no longer obligatory under the treaty of 1868, but simply a gratuity, may be issued or withheld at his discretion.* (Emphasis added).[25]

President Grant elected to cease the rations.

December 20, 1875: Deadline Notice for Sioux to Be on Their Reservation by January 31, 1876, Received by Cheyenne River Agency

The Lakotas were given until January 30, 1876, to be on their Reservation. The deadline Notice was received by the Cheyenne River Agency on December 20, 1875. Rounding up the Lakota was a near-impossible feat in the dead of winter, yet all who refused would be considered hostile and subject to attack. Many of the Lakotas were snowbound in villages scattered throughout the Unceded Territory.

> Their attitude hadn't changed; they had no truck with the wasichus [whites] so long as they stayed off Lakota land, which their chiefs had no intention of surrendering. Their response to Secretary Chandler's ultimatum was unthreatening and, from an Indian perspective, quite practical: They appreciated the invitation to talk but were settled in for the winter; when spring arrived and their ponies grew strong, they would attend a council to discuss their future.[26]

December 22, 1875: Deadline Notice Received by Standing Rock Agency, Agent Requests Extension of Time due to Difficult Winter Weather Conditions; Impossible for Sioux to Comply with Deadline

The Commissioner's deadline was received at Standing Rock on December 22, 1875. Agent Burke requested that the Indians be given an extension of time because of weather conditions.[27]

January 31, 1876: Deadline for Sioux to Be on Their Reservation

When January 31, 1876, arrived, with no extension granted, not all of the bands of Indians had returned to their reservation. The mechanics for the U.S. to commence war against the Great Sioux Nation were set in motion.[28]

U.S. Military Prepares for Winter Campaign

The military strategic and tactical operations were directed toward an "end state" which included (1) breaking up the Great Sioux Nation; (2) destroying villages; (3) settling tribes on reservations; (4) subjugating the Northern Plains Indians; and (5) ceding the Black Hills to the U.S.[29]

January 21, 25, 1876: Department of Interior Will Share Sioux Intelligence with War Department

The DOI was not a neutral party during the Sioux War; they were active participants providing military logistical support and intelligence. Commissioner Smith informed Interior Secretary Chandler that: "On

January 25, 1876, the Commissioner forwarded to the Secretary of War intelligence relative to the probable movements of Sitting Bull gathered by Agent Burke, Standing Rock Agency."[30]

February 1, 1876: Sioux Indians Turned Over to War Department for Such Action as Military Deems Proper

On February 1, 1876, the Secretary of the Interior notified the Secretary of War: "... Sitting Bull still refuses to comply with the directions of the Commissioner, the said Indians are hereby turned over to the War Department for such action on the part of the Army as you may deem proper under the circumstances."[31]

February 7, 1876: War Dept. Assumes Authority over Sioux Indians

On February 7, 1876, Generals Sheridan, Crook and Terry were notified to carry out the request of the Secretary of the Interior, but specific orders were not issued because of the uncertainty of the location of the Indians. Simultaneous efforts were to be directed against Sitting Bull, Crazy Horse and Dull Knife.[32]

> They [were] to find the enemy in his winter camps, kill or drive him from his lodges, destroy his ponies, food, and shelter, and hound him mercilessly across a frigid landscape until he gave up. If women and children fell victim to such methods, it was regrettable, but justified because it resolved the issue quickly and decisively, and thus more humanely.[33]

February 1876: U.S.—Sioux War Commences

Preparations for the Big Horn Expedition, the official U.S. Army designation of the first campaign of the Great Sioux War of 1876, were undertaken immediately.[34] The 1876 Sioux War was underway.

The Big Lie: Lakota's "Utter Defeat" Was Due to Their Own "War Lust"

Only after the Little Big Horn debacle in 1876, did Congress question the war's origins and the government's objectives. The new secretary of war, J. Donald Cameron, assured Congress, that military operations targeted not the Lakota nation, only "certain hostile parts." The Black Hills, Cameron attested, were a red herring: "The accidental discovery of gold on the western border of the Sioux reservation and the intrusion of our people thereon, have not caused this war..." The Lakota's "utter defeat" was due to their own "war lust."[35]

Notes:

1. Ablavsky, Gregory. "Beyond the Indian commerce clause." Yale LJ 124 (2014): 1012.

2. Cohen, Felix S. Handbook of federal Indian law: With reference tables and index. US Government Printing Office, 1942, Ch. 5, §3.

3. 16 Stat. 544, 25 U.S.C. 71.

4. William. T. Hagan, "United States Indian Policies, 1860-1900," Handbook of North American Indians, vol. 4 (Washington, DC: Government Printing Office, 1988), 53.

5. de Vattel, Emerich, *The Law of Nations or the Principles of Natural Law*, 1797, trans. Charles G. Fenwick (New York: Oceana Publications for the Carnegie Institute, 1964), § 219.

6. Ibid., §221.

7. Story, Joseph. 1 *Commentaries on the Constitution of the United States*. §3 (1st ed. 1833).

8. "From Thomas Jefferson to George Rogers Clark, 25 December 1780," *Founders Online*, National Archives, https://founders.archives.gov/documents/Jefferson/01-04-02-0295. [Original source: *The Papers of Thomas Jefferson*, vol. 4, *1 October 1780–24 February 1781*, ed. Julian P. Boyd. Princeton: Princeton University Press, 1951, pp. 233–238.] (accessed online November 13, 2020).

9. President Andrew Jackson's Message to Congress "On Indian Removal," December 6, 1830; Records of the United States Senate, 1789-

1990; Record Group 46; National Archives.

10. Andrew Jackson to James Monroe, March 4, 1817, Jackson Papers, 4: 93-98.

11. Alfred Balch to Andrew Jackson, January 8, 1830; Andrew Jackson Papers: Series 1, General Correspondence and Related Items, 1775-1885 (15,697).

12. Niles' Weekly Register, December 19, 1829.

13. President Jackson's Message to Congress "On Indian Removal", December 6, 1830; Records of the United States Senate, 1789-1990; Record Group 46; Records of the United States Senate, 1789-1990; National Archives and Records Administration (NARA).

14. Bills and Resolutions, Senate, 21st Cong., 1st Sess., February 22, 1830.

15. Banner, Stuart. How the Indians lost their land: Law and power on the frontier. Harvard University Press, 2005: 199.

16. Letter from General John Coffee to Secretary of War Eaton, October 14, 1829.

17. *Speeches on the Passage of the Bill for the Removal of the Indians, Delivered in the Congress of the United States, April and May, 1830.* Perkins and Marvin, 1830: 172.

18. *Fletcher v. Peck,* 10 U.S. 87 (1810); *Johnson v. M'Intosh,* 21 U.S. 543 (1823).

19. https://www.cmich.edu/research/clarke-historical-library/explore-collection/explore-online/native-american-material/native-american-treaty-rights/land-transfers#:~:text=Since%20Natives%20did%20not%20own,the%20edges%20of%20western%20settlement (accessed online July 4, 2024).

20. Stephens, Kyle Massey, "To the Indian Removal Act, 1814-1830. "

PhD diss., University of Tennessee, 2013. https://trace.tennessee.edu/utk_graddiss/2487 (accessed online July 4, 2024).

21. John L. O'Sullivan, "The Great Nation of Futurity," *The United States Democratic Review*, Volume 6, Issue 23, 1839, pp. 426-430. https://www.mtholyoke.edu/acad/intrel/osulliva.htm (accessed online November 21, 2020).

22. John L. O'Sullivan, "The Great Nation of Futurity," *The United States Democratic Review*, Volume 6, Issue 23, 1839, pp. 426-430. https://www.mtholyoke.edu/acad/intrel/osulliva.htm (accessed online November 21, 2020).

23. Ulysses S. Grant, in Inaugural Addresses of the United States: From George Washington, 1789, to John F. Kennedy, 1961 (Washington, DC: Government Printing Office, 1961), 133-34. Santala, Russel Dale. The Ute campaign of 1879: a study in the use of the military instrument. US Army Command and General Staff College, 1994, pp. 14-15.

24. Id.

25. Ulysses S. Grant, "Seventh Annual Message," December 7, 1875. Gerhard Peters and John T. Woolley, The American Presidency Project. http://www.presidency.ucsb.edu/ws/index.php?pid=29516#axzz-2fUkFG2te (accessed online September 2, 2022).

26. Ulysses S. Grant Launched an Illegal War Against the Plains Indians, Then Lied About It. https://www.smithsonianmag.com/history/ulysses-grant-launched-illegal-war-plains-indians-180960787/ (accessed online July 4, 2024). Doane Robinson, History of the Sioux, op. cit., p. 422.

27. Letter of Indian Commissioner J. Q. Smith to Secretary of Interior Z. Chandler, 144 Cong. 1 sess. V. XIV, (ser 1691), H. EX. DOC. 184, p. 18.

28. U.S., Congress, House, Military Expedition Against the Sioux Indians, 44th Cong., 1st Sess., 1876, House Ex. Doc. 184, p. 10.

29. Blome, Matthew L. The Emergence of Operational Art in the Great Sioux War 1876-1877. ARMY COMMAND AND GENERAL STAFF

COLLEGE FORT LEAVENWORTH KS SCHOOL OF ADVANCED MILITARY STUDIES, 2013.

30. 44 Cong. 1 sess. V. XIV, (ser 1691), H. EX. DOC. 184, pp. 13.

31. Letters Received, Department of the Platte, Letter, Secretary of the Interior to the Secretary of War, 1 February 1876. 44 Cong, 1 sess, V. XIV, (ser 1691), H. Ex. Doc. 184. pp. 16-18.

32. U.S., Congress, House, Report of the Secretary War, 44th Cong., 2d Sess., 1876, House Ex. Doc. 1, Part 2, p. 441.

33. Utley, Robert M. Frontier Regulars: The U.S. Army and the Indian, 1866-1891. Lincoln and London: University of Nebraska Press, 1973, p. 11.

34. U.S., Congress, House, Report of Secretary of War, 44th Cong., 2d Sess., 1876, House Ex. Doc. 1, Part 2, p. 442.

35. Ulysses S. Grant Launched an Illegal War Against the Plains Indians, Then Lied About It. https://www.smithsonianmag.com/history/ulysses-grant-launched-illegal-war-plains-indians-180960787/ (accessed online July 4, 2024). Doane Robinson, History of the Sioux, op. cit., p. 422.

3

SQUATTING

Land and Preemption Acts

Favorable land acts affording settlers the right to purchase the land on which they squatted (preemptive right) at a minimum price were enacted by Congress starting in 1800.[1]

Land subsidies and preemptive rights for squatters were used as tools for compact settlement of lands. Compact settlements made defense against Indians easier which reduced the cost to the government of having to provide military services. It increased the ability to clear lands and reduce game habitat for Indian hunting, making their willingness to move more likely. It made the migration of a group of settlers possible, rather than having them migrate singly. This facilitated the development of settler communities, which in turn encouraged the migration of additional settlers. The resources from these lands would help the federal government reduce its national debt and accumulate capital for its own use and as collateral for credit.

Encroachment on American Indian Lands

As the American white population grew and the demand for land increased, settlers bordering on uncultivated Indian land were often unconvinced of the legitimacy of Indian property rights. The most blatant problem that refused to go away, and would continue to linger, was the prevalence of squatters who simply occupied American Indian land, without any authority whatsoever. It is important to emphasize that this encroachment on Indian land and violation of Indian rights started from the beginning of European peoples contact with Indian nations.

Term 'Squatters' Defined: Squatters were those that simply occupied vacant public domain lands or American Indian lands (even if American Indian title hadn't been extinguished), often making improvements, "and took their chances on confirming legal title at a later date."[2]

The Confederation Congress tried to resolve the issue of squatters in Indian treaties by specifically giving Indians the authority to "punish them as they pleased" as was done under the Treaty of Fort McIntosh in 1785 with the Delaware and Wyandot Indians.[3]

Legitimizing Squatting: *The popular belief on the frontier was that squatters were doing a national service by clearing the land and extending the area of civilization.*

Commenting on the past, Senator Barrett of Wyoming in 1953 confirmed that "The Federal Government recognized squatters' rights."[4]

Squatters' Claims Clubs

> Squatters would form associations to tide the settlers over until Congress should enact a law which would give them proper legal protection, or until they were able to pay for their claims.[5]
>
> While these associations were formed to protect squatters from the law, the associations were almost universally accepted by public opinion. As one newspaper observed, "It is useless to say anything in justification or explanation of combinations of this character, as they have become a part of the established common law of the West, and are based upon that fundamental element of democracy—popular will, and the first law of nature—self-defence [sic]."[6]

When the land they squatted on was put up for bid, they prevented any bidding or competitive pricing.

> At the general land sales at Dubuque, in the Spring of 1840, speculators, although present in force, were awed into silence, subjection and non-interference by the presence, in *large numbers*

of pioneer citizens, with their rifles and revolvers, and had any of the speculators presumed to bid against an actual claim occupant he would have paid the penalty with his life. (Emphasis added).⁷

Territorial Legislatures and Courts Legalized Squatting

As far as practicable, Territorial Legislatures recognized the validity of these "claims" upon the public lands. The Supreme Territorial Court of Iowa held such 'claims' to be valid.⁸

Bureaucratic Inefficiency due to Communication within Command Structures Prevents Military Enforcement Against Illegal Squatting

Tony Randall Mullis provides a clear explanation of the time delays experienced in communicating within and between the Departments of the Interior and War. Add to that a predilection in favor of squatters and settlers, the Indians faced a concrete disadvantage in protecting their lands by the military eviction of intruders.

> The slow communication paths to Washington limited the options available to local agents in their attempts to enforce the applicable laws and treaties. *Before they could ask the local military commanders for military assistance, Indian agents had to forward their request through the Interior Department's chain of command.* Regarding the Delaware situation, for example, their Indian Agent, B.F. Robinson, just had to send a removal request through the Superintendent of Indian Affairs office in St. Louis. From there the Superintendent would send the Agent's application to the Commissioner of Indian Affairs, George Manypenny, in Washington. *If the Commissioner approved the request, he would forward it to the Interior Secretary, Robert McClelland.* Once McClelland made his decision, *it would either end there or he would ask the President for his approval to use troops to evict the intruders. If the President agreed, he would direct the War Department to provide the necessary troops to aid the local agent in removing the illegal settlers. By the time a request reached the Secretary of War, weeks if not months could have passed while more squatters moved onto Indian lands.* Those intruders that were already there continued to improve the land and establish permanent homes for themselves in accordance with what they believed to be their preemption rights under the 1841 law.

> By the time orders from the War Department flowed down its chain of command through the Adjutant General's Office to the Department of the West Headquarters in St. Louis to the respective commanders at either Fort Leavenworth or Fort Riley, even more delays had occurred. Without some sort of local authority to request and use military force as had been given Marshals to enforce federal laws, Indian Agents were at the mercy of the existing communications infrastructure and the government's bureaucracy in their attempts to support and defend their Indian clients. *Perhaps the most contemptible aspect of the intruder removal process was the fact that several of the army officers assigned to Fort Leavenworth and Fort Riley were land speculators themselves...* (Emphasis added).[9]

Reservations Swarm with Squatters

Economic pressures from private settlers and companies in search of valuable resources continued to infringe on the rights of tribes to reside without interference on their reservations.

> *There is scarcely one of the ninety-two reservations at present established on which white men have not effected a lodgement: many swarm with squatters, who hold their place by intimidating the rightful owners; while in more than one case the Indians have been wholly dispossessed, and are wanderers upon the face of the earth.* (Emphasis added).[10]

Squatters and Settlers as Hired Guns

More distressing was the policy to use the squatters as 'hired guns,' a military force against the Indians. They were willing to vigorously protect their alleged land rights.

> *Settlers presented the Indians with a large local militia that made the odds of a victorious attack so low that, realizing their weakness, the tribes sold out cheaply. However, opposed the common law tradition might be to squatters, these settlers played an important role in expropriating Indian lands at minimal cost.* (Emphasis added).[11]

Notes:

1. Terms of Sale under Various U.S. Land Acts 1785-1862, Ohio Lands Book.

2. C. Merton Babcock, The Social Significance of the Language of the American Frontier, 24 AM. SPEECH 256, 257-58 (1949).

3. Griesmer, Daniel R. The evolution of military strategy and Ohio Indian removal in the 1790s. The University of Akron, 2015, p. 55. https://catalog.archives.gov/id/170281455 (accessed online January 13, 2024).

4. https://historytogo.utah.gov/uhg-history-american-indians-ch-4/ (accessed online December 28, 2022).

5. Record: Proceedings and Debates of the 83rd Congress, 1st Session. Volume 99, Part 4. United States. Congress. U.S. Government Printing Office, 1953, p. 1953.

6. M. Stephenson, The Political History of the Public Lands from 1840 to 1862: From Preemption to Homestead (New York: Russell and Russell, 1967), p. 21. HISTORY OF CEDAR COUNTY, IOWA, Western Historical Company, Successors to H. F. Kett & Co., 1878, p. 326. https://iagenweb.org/cedar/1878history/county-bogusclaimants.htm (accessed online December 28, 2022).

7. Bogue, Allan G. "The Iowa Claim Clubs: Symbol and Substance." *The Mississippi Valley Historical Review*, vol. 45, no. 2, 1958, pp. 231–53. *JSTOR*, https://doi.org/10.2307/1902928. (accessed online June 22, 2024).

8. The History of Benton County, Iowa, Containing a History of the County, Its Cities, Towns, &c, Western Historical, 1878, p. 179.

9. Mullis, Tony Randall. "Soldiers were never on more disagreeable service": Peace operations in territorial Kansas and the trans-Missouri West, 1854–1856. University of Kansas, 2002, pp. 41-42.

10. "The Indian Question, Francis A. Walker" (2017). US and Indian Relations, p. 60.

11. Kades, Eric. "The Dark Side of Efficiency: Johnson v. M'Intosh and the Expropriation of American Indian Lands." *University of Pennsylvania Law Review* (2000).

4

BRIEF COLORADO HISTORY

Indigenous Peoples in Colorado Pre-Contact

Prior to the Europeans, the Ute Indians were centered in the mountains and canyonlands, and the Arapaho and Cheyenne on the Great Plains of what would become the state of Colorado. The hunting or wintering sites overlapped along the Front Range of the Rocky Mountains. Comanche and Kiowa Indians also lived and hunted within the present boundaries of the state.

Within the Ute tribe there were subdivisions including Uncompahgre, Weeminuche, Muache, Capote, and others. These subdivisions related primarily to geographic locations and not major cultural differences. The Ute expanded to the point that by the time Europeans came into their land, they ranged from Pike's Peak on the east to the Great Salt Lake on the west, and from Taos in the south, to Wyoming's Green River country on the north.[1]

In 1840, the Kiowa, Comanche, and Lakota joined the Cheyenne and Arapaho in an unprecedented alliance to resolve territorial disputes and counter the growing number of emigrants headed west.

Contact with Spain

> In 1595, the viceroy of New Mexico selected Juan de Oñate y Salazar to lead an expedition of northern New Spain in search of gold. Oñate began the expedition in January 1598 with 400 settlers, soldiers, and livestock. The expedition crossed the Rio Grande at present-day El Paso, Texas, and on April 30, 1598, he claimed all of

New Mexico for King Phillip II of Spain, including what is today southern Colorado. That summer, his party established the colony of New Mexico for Spain and became New Mexico's first governor. Hearing about plentiful game to the north in the San Luis Valley, Oñate sent an expedition there to hunt bison. The party came across a village of about fifty Ute lodges; the Utes greeted them warmly, and some of the Ute men volunteered to help the inexperienced Spaniards hunt bison. Their relations with the Utes remained friendly until the 1630s, when Spaniards attacked a band and took about eighty Utes as slaves. Thereafter, Utes began raiding Spanish parties and communities for livestock and goods.[2]

Mexican Land Grants

After winning independence from Spain in 1821, Mexico issued land grants in present-day New Mexico and Colorado to encourage settlement as a bulwark against rising American influence in the Southwest. In 1833, the Mexican government awarded the Conejos Grant, roughly spanning land between the Rio Grande and Conejos Creek near present-day Alamosa, to fifty families. In 1841, Mexico gave the Canadian trader Charles Beaubien and Mexican official Guadalupe Miranda the contested Maxwell Grant. In 1843-44, the Luis Maria Baca Grant No. 4 and the Sangre de Cristo Grant were granted in south-central Colorado (present-day Costilla County).[3]

U.S. Military Expeditions Conducted Surveillance on American Indian Tribes

Due to the lack of knowledge of the west, President Jefferson conducted exploratory military expeditions during his administration which included: Lewis and Clark to the Northwest Territory and California (1803-1806), Freeman and Custis to the Red River (1806), Hunter and Dunbar to the mouths of the Arkansas and Red Rivers (1804-1805), and Lt. Zebulon Pike to the Rockies (1805-1807). Also, these expeditions conducted military reconnaissance of Indians. It was critical they be *military expeditions* to substantiate discovery claims against other countries (e.g., the Pacific Northwest which was claimed by Great Britain, Spain and Russia).

In 1805, U.S. Army General James Wilkinson ordered Lieutenant Zebulon

Pike to lead 20 soldiers on a reconnaissance of the upper Mississippi River. On a second expedition in 1806-1807, Pike ultimately explored the west and southwest, including today's Kansas, Colorado, New Mexico, Texas and Louisiana. On February 26, 1807, a troop of Spanish soldiers captured Pike and his men, informing Pike that he was in Spanish territory. They were taken to Chihuahua. Neither Pike nor his men were mistreated; the majority were returned to the U.S. on June 30, 1807. The Spanish Governor was reprimanded by his King for releasing Pike before receiving an apology from the U.S. for trespassing.

Major Stephen Long's 1819-1820 expedition mapped the central Plains to the Rocky Mountains. Long was the first Army explorer to include professional scientists on his survey team. He also was the first to use a steamboat for exploration purposes. Setting out from Council Bluffs, he crossed the plains to Colorado, explored the Front Range of Colorado, and then followed the Rocky Mountain Front Range down into New Mexico.

The orders regarding these military expeditions included gathering detailed intelligence, not only on Spain, and thereafter, Mexico, but on the number, strength, allies and military capacity of the Indians.

1852: First Colorado Court Decree for Irrigation Rights

The first Colorado court decree for irrigation rights for a Spanish American user was made covering 13.5 second feet of water from the Culebra River.[4]

1857: Denver City Promoters

Denver already had promoters in 1857. The Denver City Town Company was formed in 1858 with the following members: E. I. Stout, president; General William Larimer, E. E. Whitsitt, James Reed, J. H. Dudley, Charles Blake, Norman Welton, A. J. Williams, General John Clancy, Samuel Curtis, Ned Wynkoop, McGaa and Charles Nichols. Most of their names have been perpetuated in the names of Denver's prominent streets.[5]

1858: Discovery of Gold in Colorado

The first publicized discovery of gold in Colorado was in 1858. Prospectors traveling west to California's Gold Rush panned small amounts of gold at

Cherry Creek, the South Platte River, and Ralston Creek. William Green Russell and a team of prospectors traveled to the South Platte River the next year and discovered gold at the Little Dry Creek, which is credited with launching the Pikes Peak Gold Rush in 1859. The immediate rush to the Denver area resulted in important placer finds near Idaho Springs and Central City. Panning gold from stream and terrace gravels is called placer mining, derived from the Spanish word placer or "pleasure"—the gold is available at one's pleasure.

Gold and other ore deposits were mostly in a northeast-trending belt, known as the Colorado mineral belt. From near Boulder on the northeast this belt extended southwest to the San Juan Mountains and beyond. The Cripple Creek District, the largest gold producer in Colorado, and several minor districts, lay southeast of the mineral belt.

1859: Miners' Court

The first miners' court was created in the Gregory District of Gilpin County, in 1859. Subsequent courts followed the Gregory model. The Gold Hill District was organized by a mass convention on July 23, 1859. Boulder's town company was organized on February 10, 1859.

Colorado's Gold Rush's Impact on Farming

> Colorado's Gold Rush changed farming in northeastern Colorado almost overnight. Miners needed supplies and at first, depended upon foodstuffs imported from the Midwest. Flour cost as much as $50 a barrel here but hungry miners were more than willing to pay these inflated prices. Further, because many of Colorado's Fifty-niners had farming backgrounds they turned to agriculture after they were unable to survive in the mines. These people found the mountain meadows and lands along the foothills fertile and they took up farms in those places. Farmers did not plant crops for survival but rather to sell. Agriculture in northeastern Colorado rapidly changed from subsistence to commercial farming. As fast as Indian title was extinguished by treaties, farmers filed claims.[6]

1862: Homestead Act

The Homestead Act of 1862 (12 Stat. 392) was signed into law by Abraham Lincoln after the southern states seceded. It provided that any adult citizen, or intended citizen, who had never borne arms against the U.S. government could claim 160 acres of surveyed government land. Claimants were required to live on and "improve" their plot by cultivating the land. After five years on the land, the original filer was entitled to the property, free and clear, except for a small registration fee. Title could also be acquired after only a six-month residency and trivial improvements, provided the claimant paid the government $1.25 per acre. After the Civil War, Union soldiers could deduct the time they had served from the residency requirements. Under the Homestead Act, land was ultimately granted in thirty states.

In Colorado, 107,618 claims were filed, granting 22,146,400 acres, amounting to 33% of the state land.

1863: First Agricultural Society Established

The first agricultural society was established in 1863; the plow followed the pick.

> Robert Stubbs: Before ten years Colorado beef will grace the stalls of the butchers in the New York markets, and the spindles of Lawrence will run on Colorado wool. ... It would cost less than one dollar a head to drive one thousand head of cattle from here to the Missouri River ... it is well known that everything can be raised here that can be produced in the Northwestern States, and that in sufficient quantity to abundantly supply home consumption. How to develop these capacities is a subject that should claim the attention of every one who feels an interest in the growth and prosperity of our flourishing young territory.[7]

Agricultural Colonies

Agricultural communities were established, the first being the Union Colony of Colorado, more commonly known as Greeley, Colorado. In 1869 Horace Greeley, editor of the New York *Tribune* and a Western booster, with help from Nathan C. Meeker, a 19th century reformer, organized the "Colony of Colorado", soon renamed the Union Colony. Each member or family paid an initiation fee in exchange for a farm plot, rights to water and a town lot. Greeley and Longmont were started as such colonies. However, by the turn of the century most colonies disappeared as they were swallowed up in a greater wave of the industrialization of agriculture by corporate conglomerates throughout northeast Colorado.[8]

Investment in Irrigation

The period between 1860 and 1869 was particularly active, the investment for irrigation reaching $14,410,037. The largest for any decade, however, was between 1880 and 1889, when $17,150,419 was invested.[9]

1861: Colorado Established as Territory

On February 28, 1861, Colorado was established as a Territory. John Evans was appointed as Territorial Governor and ex oficio Superintendent of Indian Affairs. The Territory was opened to white settlement, even though Indian title had not been fully extinguished. Many tribes continued to view the land as theirs. Territorial officials lost no time in establishing seventeen counties, all of which contained Indian land.

Gold and Silver Production Priority for Funding Union Army during Civil War

Precious metals from the West helped keep Northern banks solvent during the protracted, bloody—and expensive—Civil War and reassured an anxious public that the U.S. would be able to pay its debts. Transporting the gold and silver to banks in the East was difficult.

Southern Confederacy Seeks to Win Western Part of U.S. to Exploit Precious Metals

> The Confederate plan for the West during the Civil War was to raise a force in Texas, march up the Rio Grande, take Santa Fe, turn northeast on the Santa Fe Trail, capture the stores at Fort Union, head up to Colorado to capture the gold fields and then turn west to take California.

In February 1862, a Confederate army invaded New Mexico Territory. The advance into New Mexico Territory (today's New Mexico and Arizona) under Brigadier General Henry Sibley had several ambitious goals, among them claiming the New Mexico Territory and California for the Confederacy, annexing parts of Mexico, and establishing a presence on the Pacific coast to mitigate the Union blockade of Southern ports. Of particular importance was access to the gold and silver mines in the Western states, especially those of California, Colorado, and Nevada.

The New Mexico Campaign was a dismal failure, effectively thwarting Southern ambitions in the West. With the rich gold and silver mines out of reach, the only course left was to try to pirate Union treasure in transit.[10]

October 1863: Commissioner of Indian Affairs Dole Confirms Mineral Wealth of Colorado Territory

On October 31, 1863, Commissioner Dole confirmed the mineral wealth of the Colorado Territory in his Annual Report to the Secretary of the Interior, without referring to the destitution and desperation of the Cheyenne and Arapaho Indians which might lead to war:

> Colorado Territory, resting upon the headwaters of the Platte and Arkansas rivers and the western slope of the Rocky mountains, is rich in mineral wealth, containing gold, silver, copper, iron, coal and salt, alabaster, limestone, and gypsum. None but gold mines have been worked to any extent; these are proving remunerative...[11]

Anticipating treaty negotiations for the cession of Ute lands to the U.S., Lafayette Head, agent at the Conejos Indian Agency in the San Luis Valley, attempted to impress the Utes by bringing a delegation of them to Washington, DC, in February 1863. The delegation included leaders from each of Colorado's Ute bands, including the Tabeguache leaders Shavano and Ouray.

Colorado Territorial Governor John Evans then convened a treaty council at Conejos in October 1863, joining Head and other government officials.

Ultimately, Ouray's Tabeguache, numbering about 1,500, was the only band present in sufficient numbers to legitimize an agreement. They ceded all of the Rocky Mountains east of the Continental Divide, as well as Middle Park, which was targeted for development by influential Front Rangers William N. Byers and Ed Berthoud.

Commissioner Dole reported this to Secretary of Interior John Usher as follows:

> It will be seen that by the treaty negotiated with the Tabequache band of Utahs ... the Indian title is extinguished to one among [sic] the largest and most valuable tracts of land ever ceded to the United States. It includes nearly all the important settlements thus far made in Colorado, and all the valuable mining districts discovered up to this time.[12]

1864: Four Colorado Forts

In the summer of 1864, General Robert B. Mitchell received 1,000 troops to both patrol the Platte River Road and to establish outposts. At the same time, four sites were located and forts built throughout northeastern Colorado.[13]

Notes:

1. Athearn, Frederic J. An Isolated Empire: A History of Northwestern Colorado. 3rd ed. Colorado Bureau of Land Management, Cultural Resource Series No. 2, 1982, p. 53.

2. San Luis Valley. Colorado Encyclopedia. https://coloradoencyclopedia.org/article/san-luis-valley (accessed online April 21, 2023).

3. San Luis Valley. Colorado Encyclopedia. https://coloradoencyclopedia.org/article/san-luis-valley (accessed online April 21, 2023).

4. Decree No. 1 in District No. 54, known as the San Luis People's Ditch, dated April 10, 1852.

5. ALICE POLK HILL, COLORADO PIONEERS IN PICTURE AND STORY, 1915. https://archive.org/details/coloradopioneers00hill_0 (accessed online December 23, 2021).

6. Mehls, Steven F. The new empire of the Rockies: A history of northeast Colorado. No. 16. Bureau of Land Management, 1984. Athearn, Robert G. The Coloradans (Albuquerque: University of New Mexico Press, 1976), pp. 107-109.

7. Steinel, Alvin Theodore. History of Agriculture in Colorado: A Chronological Record of Progress in the Development of General Farming, Livestock Production and Agricultural Education and Investigation, on the Western Border of the Great Plains and in the Mountains of Colorado, 1858 to 1926. State agricultural college, 1926, p. 55.

8. Mehls, Steven F. The new empire of the Rockies: A history of northeast Colorado. No. 16. Bureau of Land Management, 1984.

9. Steinel, Alvin Theodore. History of Agriculture in Colorado: A Chronological Record of Progress in the Development of General Farming, Livestock Production and Agricultural Education and Investigation, on the Western Border of the Great Plains and in the Mountains of Colorado, 1858 to 1926. State agricultural college, 1926, p. 235.

10. GOING FOR GOLD: HOW THE CONFEDERACY HATCHED AN AUDACIOUS PLAN TO FINANCE THEIR WAR, DANIEL SELIGMAN, 7/28/2022. https://www.historynet.com/confederate-plan-to-finance-war/ (accessed online June 21, 2024).

11. Report of the Commissioner of Indian Affairs to the Secretary of the Interior, United States. Office of Indian Affairs. 1863, p. 28.

12. Ibid., p. 139.

13. Mehls, Steven F. The new empire of the Rockies: A history of northeast Colorado. No. 16. Bureau of Land Management, 1984.

5

SAND CREEK MASSACRE

Euro-American contact resulted in a devastating loss of life, disruption of tradition, and enormous loss of lands for American Indians. The Sand Creek Massacre is included in this civics text because it exemplifies the impact of this contact and the role the U.S. federal, Colorado Territory, local military and citizens groups played in destroying the governments of the Cheyenne and Arapaho Indian Nations and ousting them from Colorado.

June 3, 11, 13, 1864: Governor Evans Demands Federal Troops Be Sent to Denver

Governor Evans contacted Colonel Chivington, Major-General Curtis, General Carleton (NM) and General Mitchell to dispatch troops to Denver. Due to the ongoing Civil War and their commitment to other locales, they could not commit their troops. This meant that Colorado would have to use undertrained and undisciplined volunteer soldiers to *"whip these red-skin rebels into submission at once"* as directed by Governor Evans. (Emphasis added).

June 15, 1864: Major McKenny Warns General Curtis that Colorado's Volunteer Cavalry May Start Plains Indian War

Major T.I. McKenny who was sent to Fort Larned by General Curtis to assess the growing Indian hostilities in western Kansas reported:

> In regard to these Indian difficulties, I think if great caution is not exercised on our part there will be a bloody war. It should be our policy to try and conciliate them, guard our mails and trains well to prevent theft, and stop these (military) scouting *parties that are*

roaming over the country who do not know one tribe from the other, and who will kill anything in the shape of an Indian. It will require but few murders on the part of our troops to unite all these warlike tribes of the plains who have been at peace for years and intermarried amongst one another. (Emphasis added).[1]

A day later, Governor Evans wrote to Major-General Curtis to whip the "infernal barbarians:"

June 27, 1864: Governor Evans' First Proclamation - Orders Indians to Move to Forts

TO THE FRIENDLY INDIANS OF THE PLAINS:

Agents, interpreters, and traders will inform the friendly Indians of the plains that some members of their tribes have gone to war with the white people. They steal stock and run it off, hoping to escape detection and punishment. In some instances they have attacked and killed soldiers and murdered peaceable citizens. For this the Great Father is angry, and will certainly hunt them out and punish them, but he does not want to injure those who remain friendly to the whites. He desires to protect and take care of them. For this purpose I direct that all friendly Indians keep away from those who are at war, and go to places of safety. Friendly Arapahoes and Cheyennes belonging on the Arkansas River will go to Major Colley, U.S. Indian agent at Fort Lyon, who will give them provisions, and show them a place of safety. Friendly Kiowas and Comanches will go to Fort Larned, where they will be cared for in the same way. Friendly Sioux will go to their agent at Fort Laramie for directions. Friendly Arapahoes and Cheyennes of the Upper Platte will go to Camp Collins on the Cache la Poudre, where they will be assigned a place of safety and provisions will be given them.

The object of this is to prevent friendly Indians from being killed through mistake. None but those who intend to be friendly with the whites must come to these places. The families of those who have gone to war with the whites must be kept away from among the friendly Indians. The war on hostile Indians will be continued until they are all effectually subdued.[2]

August 11, 1864: Governor Evans' Second Proclamation - Citizens of Colorado Authorized to Kill Hostile Indians

Governor Evans issued a Proclamation to the citizenry of Colorado that the Indians had refused to come into the forts he designated for their safety. He explicitly authorized settlers to organize killing parties targeting Indians perceived as a threat; to take captives; and to hold "for their private use and benefit" any property they capture. Evans further offered to furnish arms and ammunition and to pay any parties that would organize under the militia law of the territory to seek out and kill Indians, recruiting citizens to join the hundred-day volunteers for which Evans had been lobbying Secretary of War Stanton. He had no authority at this time to basically declare war.

PROCLAMATION.

Having sent special messengers to the Indians of the plains, directing the friendly to rendezvous at Fort Lyon, Fort Larned, Fort Laramie, and Camp Collins for safety and protection, warning them that all hostile Indians would be pursued and destroyed, and the last of said messengers having now returned, and the evidence being conclusive that most of the Indian tribes of the plains are at war and hostile to the whites, and having to the utmost of my ability endeavored to induce all of the Indians of the plains to come to said places of rendezvous, promising them subsistence and protection, which, with a few exceptions, they have refused to do:

Now, therefore, I, John Evans, governor of Colorado Territory, do issue this my proclamation, authorizing all citizens of Colorado, either individually or in such parties as they may organize, to go in pursuit of all hostile Indians on the plains, scrupulously avoiding those who have responded to my said call to rendezvous at the points indicated; also, to kill and destroy, as enemies of the country, wherever they may be found, all such hostile Indians. And further, as the only reward I am authorized to offer for such services, I hereby empower such citizens, or parties of citizens, to take captive, and hold to their own private use and benefit, all the property of said hostile Indians that they may capture, and to receive for all stolen property recovered from said Indians such reward as may be deemed proper and just therefor.

I further offer to all such parties as will organize under the militia law of the Territory for the purpose to furnish them arms and ammunition, and to present their accounts for pay as regular soldiers for themselves, their horses, their subsistence, and transportation, to Congress, under the assurance of the department commander that they will be paid.

The conflict is upon us, and all good citizens are called upon to do their duty for the defense of their homes and families.

In testimony whereof, I have hereunto set my hand and caused the great seal of the Territory of Colorado to be affixed this 11th day of August, A. D. 1864. John Evans.[3]

Analysis of Governor Evans' Second Proclamation of August 11, 1864—University of Denver's John Evans Study Committee

The Report of the University of Denver's John Evans Study Committee, of November 2014, castigated Governor Evans.

> Evans's Proclamation of August 11 essentially created an unregulated vigilante force. ... No criteria are offered for violence-hungry settlers, who have been bombarded with anti-Indian sentiment from the state, the military, and local newspapers, and who would be outfitted and paid by the state, to differentiate hostile from friendly Indians. The proclamation does not merely carry a "vigilante tone,"... it is a blanket endorsement of citizen violence against Native people in partnership with territorial civil leadership.

> The policy laid out in this fateful document was tantamount to a declaration of war, and it was one which Evans had no legal authority to make.

> As for issuing such a proclamation as Superintendent of Indian Affairs, not in any stretch of the imagination could the laws that were in place at the time be interpreted as permitting a superintendent to send cadres of armed citizens to exterminate and loot unidentified Indian people.

In the direct aftermath of these events Colonel John Chivington declared martial law on August 23, 1864, at the request of Denver businessmen who "hoped to promote enlistments of 100-day men to rid our territory of all hostile Indians."

According to Gary Roberts, Evans chillingly "told Wynkoop matters were out of his hand, and that the Indians needed to be punished more to insure peace. More than once Evans asked, 'What will I do with the 3rd Regiment if I make peace?' He told Wynkoop, 'The 3rd Regiment was raised to kill Indians, and kill Indians it must.'" Evans asserted that his credibility in Washington would be lost if, having agitated so stridently for war, he now made peace.[4]

August 1864 - November 1864: Cheyenne and Arapaho Indians Repeatedly Seek Peace

In the period from August 1864 - November 1864, the Cheyenne and Arapaho Indians repeatedly sought peace.

August 29, 1864: Cheyenne and Arapahos Call for Peace Talks

George Bent, son of trader William Bent and his Cheyenne wife, Owl Woman, and Edmund Guerrier, another mixed blood, wrote letters to Indian Agent S.G. Colley and the commander of Fort Lyon, Major Wynkoop, on behalf of Chief Black Kettle and other chiefs, seeking peace talks in response to Governor Evans Proclamation. Com'r Of Indian Affairs Cole was Indian Agent Colley's cousin which provided an avenue for direct communication of Indian issues.

September 4, 1864: Governor Evans Informed by Indian Agent Colley that Cheyenne and Arapaho Desire Peace

On September 4, 1864, Governor Evans, Superintendent of Indian Affairs, was informed in writing of the Cheyenne and Arapaho's plea for peace:

> Two Cheyenne Indians and one squaw have just arrived at this post. They report that nearly al (sic) of the Arapahoes, most of the Cheyennes, and two large bands of Ogallala and Brule Sioux are encamped near

the "Bunch of Timbers" some 80 to 100 miles northeast of this place; that they have sent runners to the Comanches, Apaches, Kiowas, and Sioux requesting them to make peace with the whites. They brought a letter purporting to be signed by Black Kettle and other chiefs, a copy * [Not Found] of which is here inclosed. They say that the letter was written by George Bent, a half-breed son of W.W. Bent, late U.S. Indian agent for this agency. They also state that the Indians have seven prisoners. One says four women and three children, the other states three women and four children. Major Wynkoop has put these Indians in the guard house, and requested that they be well treated in order that he may be able to rescue the white prisoners from the Indians. S. G. Colley, U.S. Indian Agent, Upper Arkansas.[5]

September 14, 1864: Governor Evans Forwards Agent Colley's Letter that Cheyenne and Arapaho Desire Peace to Colonel Chivington

September 14, 1864, Colonel J. M. Chivington, Commanding District of Colorado:

I herewith enclose for your information a copy of a letter received from Major Colley, U.S. Indian agent, Upper Arkansas Agency, dated September 4, 1864, Fort Lyon, stating the location of the Arapahoes and portions of other tribes of Indians, and inclosing a proposition for peace from Black Kettle and other chiefs. Jno. Evans, Governor of Colorado Territory.[6]

September 18, 1864: Major Wynkoop Reports Meeting with Cheyenne and Arapaho regarding Peace to Acting Assistant Adjutant-General, District of Upper Arkansas

Fort Lyon, Colorado Ter., September 18, 1864.
Lieutenant J. E. Tappan, Acting Assistant Adjutant-General, District of Upper Arkansas:

They came, as they stated, bearing with them a proposition for peace from Black Kettle and other chiefs of the Cheyenne and Arapahoe Nations. Their propositions were to the effect that they, the Cheyennes and Arapahoes, had in their possession seven white prisoners whom they offered to deliver up in case that we should come to terms of peace with them. They told me that the Cheyennes, Arapahoes, and Sioux were congregated for mutual protection, at what is called "Bunch of Timber," on headwaters of the Smoky Hill, at a distance of 140 miles northeast of this post numbering altogether about 3,000 warriors, and desirous to make peace with the whites. I told them I was not authorized to conclude terms of peace with them, but if they acceded to my proposition I would take what chiefs they might choose to select to the Governor of Colorado Territory and state the circumstances to him, and that I believed it would result in what it was their desire to accomplish, viz, peace with their white brethren. I had reference particularly to the Cheyenne and Arapahoe tribes ... they brought and turned over into my possession four white prisoners, all that was possible at the time being for them to turn over, the balance of the seven being, as they stated, with another band far to the northward ... I have the principal chiefs of the two tribes with me, and propose starting immediately to Denver City, Colorado Ter., to put into effect the proposition made aforementioned by me to them. E. W. Wynkoop, Major First Cavalry of Colorado, Commanding Post. (Emphasis added).[7]

September 28, 1864: Governor Evans Meets with Cheyenne and Arapaho Peace Party; Rejects Peace Offer Alleging State of War with Military in Control

September 1864 The Cheyenne and Arapaho seeking peace, traveled to Denver for a meeting with Governor and Superintendent of Indian Affairs Evans seeking peace. Governor Evans and Colonel Chivington met with the Cheyenne and Arapaho Chiefs at Camp Weld, near Denver.

September 28, 1864 Meeting at Camp Weld

> We have come with our eyes shut, following [Major Wynkoop's] handful of men like coming through the fire. All we ask is that we have peace with the whites. We want to hold you by the hand. You are our father. We have been traveling thro' a cloud. The sky has been dark ever since the war began. These braves who are with me are all willing to do what I say. We want to take good tidings home to our people, that they may sleep in peace. I want you to give all the chiefs of these soldiers to understand that we are for peace, and that we

> have made peace, that we may not be mistaken by them for enemies. I have not come here with a little wolf bark, but have come to talk plain with you. We must live near the buffalo or starve. When we came here we came free, without any apprehension to see you, and when I go home and tell my people that I have taken your hand, and the hand of all the chiefs here in Denver, they will feel well, and so will all the different tribes of Indians on the Plains, after we have eaten and drank with them.⁸

Evans accused the leaders—men who had already signed the Fort Wise Treaty and who had now come to him at great personal risk—of being allied with the Lakota and having committed depredations...

Several of the Indians in attendance responded, asserting, "This is a mistake. We have made no alliance with the Sioux, or any one else."

As the meeting report shows, the Cheyenne and Arapaho also pointed out that they did not know the reasons for the fighting launched by Chivington's forces in the three battles of the spring, with White Antelope raising this question to Evans, who simply ignored it.

Toward the end of the meeting, Evans claimed that he was obligated to turn the Cheyenne and Arapaho over to the Army, given his claim that the settlers and Indian peoples were at war: *"Another reason that I am not in a condition to make a treaty, is that war is begun, and the power to make a treaty of peace has passed from me to the Great War Chief,"* he asserted. (Emphasis added).⁹

September 29, 1864: Governor Evans Sends Letter to Agent Colley regarding Meeting with Cheyenne and Arapaho Peace Party; That, as Governor, He Rejected Peace Offer due to U.S. State of War

Denver, September 29, 1864. S. G. Colley, U.S. Indian Agent:

> The chiefs brought in by Major Wynkoop have been heard. I have declined to make any treaty with them, lest it might embarrass the military operations against the hostile Indians of the plains. *The Arapahoe and Cheyenne Indians being now at war with the United States Government must make peace with the military authorities.* Of

course this arrangement relieves the Indian Bureau of their care until peace is declared with them, and as their tribes are yet scattered, and all except Friday's band are at war, it is not probable that it will be done immediately. You will be particular to impress upon these chiefs the fact that my talk with them was for the purpose of ascertaining their views and not to offer them anything whatever. They must deal with the military authorities until peace, in which case alone they will be in proper position to treat with the Government in relation to the future. Jno. Evans, Governor Colorado Ter. and ex- officio Supt. of Indian Affairs. (Emphasis added).[10]

September 29, 1864: Major-General Curtis Asserts Indians Don't Want Peace and Are Trying to Avoid Winter Campaign

Fort Leavenworth, September 29, 1864. To Agent Colley from Major-General Curtis:

General Mitchell is hunting Indians up the Platte, and General Blunt south of Arkansas also searching for them. Try and give them any information you think reliable. The chiefs you named are not reliable, and desire to save their friends, who are near the Arkansas, by extravagant reports of forces elsewhere. They ought to be made to go and show our enemies. Their chiefs are all implicated in the attacks where they have depredated. *All they fear is winter approaching and therefore they desire peace, which they cannot have at present.* S. R. Curtis, Major-General. (Emphasis added).[11]

October 14, 1864: Colonel Chivington Orders Capt. Nichols, Colorado Third Regiment, to Kill All Indians His Command Encounters

Headquarters District of Colorado, Denver, October 14, 1864.
Captain D. H. Nichols, Third Regiment Colorado Cav., Valley Station, Colorado Ter.:

Captain: Be vigilant. *Kill all the Indians you come across.* Strengthen your squads at stations below you to Julesburg. Ammunition leaves by tomorrow's coach.
J. M. Chivington, Colonel, Commanding District. (Emphasis added).[12]

October 15, 1864: Commissioner Dole Orders Governor Evans to Negotiate for Peace with Indians when They Offer, Regardless of U.S. State of War

> Sir: I have the honor to acknowledge the receipt of your letter of the 29th ultimo, stating that at a council held with certain Arapahoes and Cheyenne Indians, you informed them, in answer to their expressed desire for peace, that you had no treaty to make with them, that they must make terms with the military authority. In reply, I have to say that while I approve of your course as a matter of necessity, while these Indians and the military authorities are at war, and the civil authority is in abeyance, yet, as *superintendent of Indian affairs, it is your duty to hold yourself in readiness to encourage and receive the first intimations of a desire on the part of the Indians for a permanent peace, and to cooperate with the military in securing a treaty of peace and amity.*
>
> I cannot help believing that very much of the difficulty on the plains might have been avoided, if a spirit of conciliation had been exercised by the military and others. (Emphasis added).[13]

November 4, 1864: Major Wynkoop Relieved of Command

Orders relieving Major Wynkoop of command and directing him to report to district headquarters at Fort Riley in Kansas are issued.

I. Major E. W. Wynkoop, First Cavalry of Colorado, is hereby relieved from the command of Fort Lyon, Colorado Terr., and is ordered to report without delay to headquarters District of the Upper Arkansas, for orders. II. Major Scott J. Anthony, First Cavalry of Colorado, will proceed to Fort Lyon, Colorado Terr., and assume command of that post.[14]

November 15, 1864: Majors Anthony and Wynkoop Meet with Cheyenne and Arapaho Who Continue to Press for Peace

Major Anthony (New Commander at Fort Lyon) and Major Wynkoop (Relieved of Fort Lyon Command) met with about 60 Cheyenne and Arapaho chiefs and headmen at Fort Lyon.

Major Anthony advised the Cheyenne to return to their camps at Sand Creek and allowed the Arapaho under Little Raven to move down the Arkansas about 60 miles and there wait until he received further instructions from his superior officers. (Emphasis added).[15]

November 15, 1864: Commissioner Dole Reports to Secretary of Interior that Cheyenne and Arapaho Urge Peace - Military Says Further Punishment Needed

> ...on the 4th of September Agent Colley forwarded to the superintendent a letter signed by several of the Cheyenne chiefs, proposing terms of peace. On the 28th an interview took place between Governor Evans and these chiefs, at which, it appears, from the annual report of that officer, they seemed earnest for peace; but the governor deemed it his duty, under the existing circumstances, to decline acceding to their terms, or indeed to make any terms with them, and the interview ended with leaving the chiefs referred to, or any others who might be disposed towards peace, to communicate with the military authorities. This course seems, from the paper accompanying Governor Evans's report, to have commended itself to Major General Curtis as the proper one to be pursued, that *officer deeming it necessary, in order to a permanent peace and the future good behavior of the Indians, that they should receive further punishment;* ... *Governor Evans advocates the policy of a winter expedition against the offending tribes.* (Emphasis added).[16]

November 16, 1864: Major Anthony Reports to Headquarters that Cheyenne and Arapaho Appealing for Peace

Headquarters, Fort Lyon, Colorado Ter., November 16, 1864.

> SIR: I have the honor to report that since my last report on the 7th [6th] instant the Cheyenne Indians, numbering about 200, under their head chief, Black Kettle, have sent into the post a request to meet me for a council. I met them and had a talk. They profess friendship for the whites, and say they never desired war, and do not now. They were very desirous of visiting the post and coming in with their whole band. I would not permit this, *but told them they might camp on Sound [sic] [Sand] Creek, twenty-five miles northeast of the*

post, until the pleasure of the commanding officer of the district could be learned. They appear to want peace, and want some one authorized to make a permanent settlement of all troubles with them to meet them and agree upon terms. I told them that I was not authorized as yet to say that any permanent peace could be established, but that no war would be waged against them until your pleasure was heard. *I am satisfied that all of the Arapahoes and Cheyennes who have visited this post desire peace* ... Neither of these tribes are satisfied with me for not permitting them to visit the post, and cannot understand why I will not make peace with them. *My intention, however, is to let matters remain dormant until troops can be sent out to take the field against all the tribes.* Scott J. Anthony, Major First Cavalry of Colorado, Commanding Post. (Emphasis added).[17]

November 28, 1864: Major Anthony Reports Arrival of Colorado Third Regiment at Fort Lyon: 1000 Soldiers

Fort Lyon, Colorado Terr., November 28, 1864. Lieutenant A. Helliwell, Acting Assistant Adjutant-General, Fort Riley, Kans.:

SIR: I have the honor to report that Colonel John M. Chivington, First Cavalry of Colorado, arrived at this post this day with 1,000 men of the Third Regiment Colorado Cavalry (100-day's men) and two howitzers, on expedition against Indians. This number of men has been required for some time, and is appreciated by me now, as I believe *the Indians will be properly punished— what they have for some time deserved.* I go out with 125 men and two howitzers to join his command. Scott J. Anthony, Major First Cavalry of Colorado, Commanding Post. (Emphasis added).[18]

November 28, 1864: Major General Curtis Reports to Brigadier General Carleton that Cheyenne and Arapaho Are Begging for Peace

Headquarters Department of Kansas, Fort Leavenworth,
November 28, 1864. Brigadier General J. H. Carleton, Commanding Department of New Mexico:

General: ...*The Arapahoes and Cheyennes have come into Lyon begging for peace,* turning over prisoners, horses, &c., for that purpose. The hardest kind of terms are demanded by me and conceded by some of these Indians. They insist on peace or absolute sacrifice, as I choose. Of course, they will have to be received, but *there still remains some of these tribes and all the Kiowas to attend to, and I have proposed a winter campaign for their benefit. This, if successful, must be secret* and well arranged beforehand. I have written the War Department, and Governor Evans, of Colorado, has gone to Washington to urge my plans. S. R. Curtis, Major-General. (Emphasis added).[19]

November 29, 1864: Sand Creek Massacre - Colonel Chivington Reports Killing 400-500 Indians and Leaders; Third Regiment Colorado Cavalry Scalped Dead Indians; Mutilated Their Bodies; Removed Private Parts as War Trophies

On November 29, 1864, from in the field at the South Bend of the Big Sandy, John M. Chivington, First Colorado Cavalry, reported:

> In the last ten days my command has marched 300 miles, 100 of which the snow was two feet deep. After a march of forty miles last night I, at daylight this morning, attacked Cheyenne village of 130 lodges, from 900 to 1,000 warriors strong; *killed Chiefs Black Kettle, White Antelope, Knock Knee, and Little Robe [Little Raven], and between 400 and 500 other Indians*, and captured as many ponies and mules. Our loss, 9 killed, 38 wounded. All died nobly. *Think I will catch some more of them eighty miles, on Smoky Hill.* Found white man's scalp, not more than three days' old, in one of lodges. (Emphasis added).[20]

December 7, 1864: Colonel Chivington's Second Report to Governor Evans: Killed 500 Indians, Still in Pursuit of Cheyenne and Arapaho

December 7, 1864. Governor John Evans

> Had fight with Cheyennes forty miles north of Lyon. I lost 9 killed and 38 wounded. *Killed 500 Indians*; destroyed 130 lodges; took 500 mules and ponies. Marched 300 miles in ten days; snow two feet deep for 100 miles. *Am still after them.* J. M. Chivington, Colonel, Commanding District of Colorado and First Indian Expedition. (Emphasis added).[21]

Return of Colorado Third Regiment to Denver

Rocky Mountain News, December 22, 1864, Arrival of the Third Regiment—Grand March Through Town

The return of the Third regiment boys from the victorious field of Indian warfare was the grand feature of today. Those ten companies, (the Eleventh and twelfth of the regiment being stationed at the Junction Valley Station, on the Platte, protecting that route, and for a few months past,) who have stood the severity of the season, the snow storms of Bijou Basin, the fatigues of forced marches, and the deprivation of all comforts both by day and night—camping where the hostile savage was expected to be met, or following the red assasins (sic) to their strongholds in the interior of the desert—were the admired of all observers, on their entry into town this morning.

Headed by the First Regiment Band, and by Colonels Chivington and Shoup, Lieut. Col. Bowen and Major Sayr, the rank and file of the "bloody Thirdsters" made a most imposing procession, extending, with the transportation trains, from the upper end of Ferry street, through Larimer, G and Blake, almost back to Ferry street again. As the "bold sojer boys" passed along, the sidewalks and the corner stands were thronged with citizens saluting their old friends: and the fair sex took advantage of the opportunity, wherever they could get it, of expressing their admiration for the gallant boys, who donned the regimentals for the purpose of protecting the women of the country by ridding it of red skins. Although covered o'er with dust, and suffering from the hardships of the tended field, the boys looked bully, and the general appearance of the whole was soldierly and service-like.[22]

Report on Sand Creek Massacre by Indian Agent Leavenworth

I have the honor to enclose herewith papers relating to the late massacre of friendly Indians by Colonel J.M. Chivington,* near Fort Lyon. It is impossible for me to express to you the horror with which I view this transaction; it has destroyed the last vestige of confidence between the red and white man. *Nearly every one of the chiefs and headmen of the Arapahoe and Cheyenne tribes who had remained true*

> to the whites, and were determined not to fight the whites, were cruelly murdered when resting in all the confidence of assurances from Major Wyncoop, and I also believe from Major Anthony, that they should not be disturbed. ... When Major Wyncoop went to Denver with the chiefs of tribes under his charge, why did Governor Evans refuse to act in any way, for or against them ... they were determined not to fight the whites ... I'm making every effort possible to find the Comanches and Kiowas; but I have little hope of succeeding. J. H. Leavenworth, U.S. Indian Agent (Emphasis added).
> *The papers referred to above were not received.[23]

Sand Creek Massacre Reported as "Disastrous and Shameful Occurrence"

> Most disastrous and shameful occurrence of all, the massacre of a large number of men, women and children of the Indians of this agency by the troops under command of Colonel Chivington, of the United States volunteer cavalry of Colorado. ... Several hundred of them had come in to a place designated by Governor Evans as a rendezvous for those who would separate themselves from the hostile parties, these Indians were set upon and butchered in cold blood by troops in the service of the United States.[24]

Governor Evans Culpability in Sand Creek Massacre - University of Denver's John Evans Study Committee

> Evans abrogated his duties as superintendent, fanned the flames of war when he could have dampened them, cultivated an unusually interdependent relationship with the military, and rejected clear opportunities to engage in peaceful negotiations with the Indian peoples under his jurisdiction. Furthermore, he successfully lobbied the War Department for the deployment of a federalized regiment who executed the worst of the atrocities during the massacre.[25]

May 30, 1865: U.S. Condemns Sand Creek Massacre

On May 30, 1865, the military commission investigation into the Sand Creek Massacre concluded, resulting in condemnation from Judge Advocate General Joseph Holt. The report was published.[26] The U.S. decided to offer reparations to the afflicted parties in exchange for peace.

April 28, 1865: Instructions to Treaty Commission Appointed to Negotiate for Arapaho and Cheyenne Colorado Land - Offer No Money, No Specific Land for New Reservation

By the Spring of 1865, President Abraham Lincoln appointed Vital Jarrot as the Indian Agent to the Upper Platte Agency. He had served in the leading role of Adjutant General during the Black Hawk War in 1832 in which Lincoln served as a volunteer.[27]

On April 28, 1865, Jarrot was notified by Charles Mix, Acting Commissioner, that he was to negotiate with the Arapaho, Cheyenne and Sioux affiliated with them and Cheyenne for a cession of their lands. His instructions were as follows:

> Agreements to pay money will not be approved. If a treaty is made, it will be one of occupancy only: no title to lands will be acknowledged in the Indians of the country they abandon, nor will any be conferred upon them in the country they are to inhabit; Just an article may be inserted providing that the whites will be excluded from settlement in the country assigned to them.[28]

October 11-13, 1865: U.S. Treaty Delegation, Arapaho and Cheyenne Still Recovering from Sand Creek Massacre, Not Ready to Agree to Relinquish Land in Colorado

On October 13, 1865, the surviving Arapaho and Cheyenne chiefs met with government treaty commissioners. The Arapaho didn't want to agree on land at the time—few were present, the rest were up north. They were still reeling from the Sand Creek Massacre:

> Little Raven: There is something very strong for us-that fool band of soldiers that cleared out our lodges, and killed our women and children. This is strong (hard) on us. *There, at Sand creek, is one chief, Left Hand; White Antelope and many other chiefs lie there; our women and children lie there.* Our lodges were destroyed there, and our horses were taken from us there, and *I do not feel disposed to go right off in a new country and leave them.* (Emphasis added).[29]

October 13, 1865: Treaty Council with Arapaho and Cheyenne - Unfortunately for You, Gold Discovered in Your Country

Treaty Council held in camp on the Little Arkansas River, October 13, 1865:

> We all fully realize that it is hard for any people to leave their homes and graves of their ancestors; but, *unfortunately for you, gold has been discovered in your country, and a crowd of white people have gone there to live, and a great many of these people are the worst enemies of the Indians*—men who do not care for their interests, and who would not stop at any crime to enrich themselves. These men are now in your country—in all parts of it—and there is no portion where you can live and maintain yourselves but what you will come in contact with them. The consequences of this state of things are that you are in constant danger of being imposed upon, and you have to resort to arms in self defense. ... We want to give you a country that is full of game and good for agricultural purposes, and where the hills and mountains are not full of gold and silver. In such a country as this the government can fully provide for your wants ... We are sorry that we have bad people among us, as you are sorry that you have bad people among you; but this is unfortunately the case with all people, and however severe we make laws it is impossible to prevent crime. *You may accede to our wishes, and be happy and prosperous, or you may refuse to make a treaty, and be ruined in health and happiness.* (Emphasis added).[30]

1867: Medicine Lodge Treaties - Cheyenne and Arapaho Treaty Establishing Reservation in Indian Territory

The Medicine Lodge Treaties in 1867 were a series of three treaties between the U.S. and the Comanche, Kiowa, Plains Apache, Southern Cheyenne, and Southern Arapaho nations. By treating with multiple tribes at once, the appointed Peace Commission's goal was to "establish security for person and property along the lines of railroad now being constructed to the Pacific."

The U.S. had the upper hand as the military had already established forts in the region, the tribes were fractured along lines of peace and warfare, and they needed annuities to survive, given the depletion of their subsistence base.

On October 28, the Cheyenne and Arapaho chiefs signed a treaty creating a reservation in western Indian Territory. Capt. Barnitz of the 7th U.S. Cavalry, who recorded the speeches during the negotiations, expressed his misgivings.

> *They have no idea that they are giving up, or that they have ever given up the country which they claim as their own... The treaty amounts to nothing*, and we will certainly have another war sooner or later with the Cheyennes, at least, and probably with the other Indians... (Emphasis added).

The eastern plains of Colorado were cleared of Indians by 1870, primarily because superior military power and the physical removal to Indian Territory eliminated the presence of these peoples.[31]

Notes:

1. The War of the Rebellion: A Compilation of the Official Records of the Union and Confederate Armies, United States War Department, 1891. Series I, Vol. XXXIV, Part IV, CORRESPONDENCE, ETC.—UNION, pp. 402-404.

2. Report of the Commissioner of Indian Affairs to the Secretary of the Interior, United States. Office of Indian Affairs. Colorado Superintendency, 1864, pp. 218-219.

3. Report of the Commissioner of Indian Affairs to the Secretary of the Interior, United States. Office of Indian Affairs. Colorado Superintendency. 1864, pp. 230-231.

4. Report of the John Evans Study Committee, University of Denver, November 2014, Denver, pp. 63, 64, 65, 66, 69.

5. The War of the Rebellion: A Compilation of the Official Records of the Union and Confederate Armies, United States War Department, 1891. Series I, Vol. XLI, Part III, Chapter LIII, CORRESPONDENCE, ETC. - UNION, pp. 195-196.

6. Ibid., p. 195.

7. Ibid., p. 242.

8. Condition of the Indian Tribes: Report of the Joint Special Committee, Appointed Under Joint Resolution of March 3, 1865, United States, Congress. Joint Special Committee to Inquire into Condition of the Indian Tribes, Kraus Reprint Company, p. 87.

9. The Sand Creek Massacre Weld Council Transcript. https://www.kclonewolf.com/History/SandCreek/sc-documents/sc-weld-council.html (accessed online October 2, 2021).

10. The War of the Rebellion: A Compilation of the Official Records of the Union and Confederate Armies, United States War Department, 1891. Series I, Vol. XLI, Part III, Chapter LIII, CORRESPONDENCE, ETC. - UNION, p. 495.

11. The War of the Rebellion: A Compilation of the Official Records of the Union and Confederate Armies, United States War Department, 1891. Series I, Vol. XLI, Part III, Chapter LIII, CORRESPONDENCE, ETC. - UNION, p. 525.

12. Ibid., p. 876.

13. Report of the Commissioner of Indian Affairs to the Secretary of the Interior, United States. Office of Indian Affairs. 1864, p. 256.

14. The War of the Rebellion: A Compilation of the Official Records of the Union and Confederate Armies, United States War Department, 1891. Series I, Vol. XLI, Part IV, Chapter LIII, CORRESPONDENCE, ETC. - UNION, p. 433.

15. Ibid., p. 876.

16. Report of the Commissioner of Indian Affairs to the Secretary of the Interior, United States. Office of Indian Affairs. 1864, p. 23.

17. The War of the Rebellion: A Compilation of the Official Records

of the Union and Confederate Armies, United States War Department, 1891. Series I, Vol. XLI, Part III, Chapter LIII, CORRESPONDENCE, ETC. - UNION, p. 914.

18. Ibid., p. 708.

19. Ibid., p. 709.

20. The War of the Rebellion: A Compilation of the Official Records of the Union and Confederate Armies, United States War Department, 1891. Series I, Vol. XLI, Part I, LOUISIANA AND THE TRANS-MISSISSIPPI, Chapter LIIIO, p. 948.

21. The War of the Rebellion: A Compilation of the Official Records of the Union and Confederate Armies, United States War Department, 1891. Series I, Vol. XLI, Part IV, LOUISIANA AND THE TRANS-MISSISSIPPI, Chapter LIII, CORRESPONDENCE, ETC.- UNION, p. 797.

22. https://kclonewolf.com/sand-creek-documents-rmn-3rdreg-arrival.html (accessed online June 28, 2024).

23. Report of the Commissioner of Indian Affairs to the Secretary of the Interior, United States. Office of Indian Affairs. Central Superintendency. 1865, p. 387.

24. Report of the Commissioner of Indian Affairs to the Secretary of the Interior, United States. Office of Indian Affairs. 1865, p. 24.

25. Report of the John Evans Study Committee, University of Denver, November 2014, Denver, p. iii.

26. https://www.nps.gov/sand/learn/timeline.htm (accessed online June 21, 2024).

27. Patrick J. Jung, The Black Hawk War of 1832 (Norman: University of Oklahoma Press, 2007).

28. Report of the Commissioner of Indian Affairs to the Secretary of the

Interior, United Sates. Office of Indian Affairs. 1865, p. 431.

29. Report of the Commissioner of Indian Affairs to the Secretary of the Interior, United States. Office of Indian Affairs. 1865, p. 525.

30. Report of the Commissioner of Indian Affairs to the Secretary of the Interior, United States. Office of Indian Affairs. 1865, p. 523.

31. Athearn, Frederic J. Land of Contrast: A History of Southeast Colorado. Colorado Bureau of Land Management, Cultural Resource Series No. 17, 1985, p. 79.

6

Retaliatory American Indian Military Campaigns

After the Sand Creek Massacre of the Cheyenne and Arapaho on November 29, 1864, a number of Colorado and Kansas tribes allied to conduct hostilities against the U.S. Army and white settlers. Many of the Cheyenne survivors had fled north to the Republican River, where a large contingent of "Dog Soldiers" were camped.

Among the Cheyenne Indians one of the most important military societies was the Dog Soldiers, of which Tall Bull was chief. It was considered a great honor to belong to this band of warriors. In battle, a Cheyenne Dog Soldier would stake his dog rope in the ground. Dog ropes were made out of rawhide leather and decorated with porcupine quills and feathers. One end was tied to a red wooden stake. During combat, a Cheyenne Dog Soldier would plant the stake in the ground as a sign of perseverance and standing one's ground. The area over which the Dog Soldier could fight was limited to the length of the rope. Dog Soldiers would not remove the stake until their people had safely retreated or a comrade removed it, so it was used as a last resort.

On January 1, 1865, the Indians met at present-day St. Francis, Kansas, to plan a concerted strategy against the invasive settlement and trespass of white settlers on their land. In the meeting were the Cheyenne Dog Soldiers, the Northern Arapaho, and two Bands of Lakota Sioux, including the Brule, under Chief Spotted Tail, and the Oglala, under War Leader Pawnee Killer. The U.S. had failed to provide any protection of Indian lands and lives resulting in these Indians having to fight against insurmountable odds.

As many as 2,000 Cheyenne, Sioux, and Arapaho warriors shifted their camps closer to the South Platte River, where it cut through the northeast corner of Colorado. In the midst of this area was Fort Rankin (later Fort Sedgwick), an Overland Trail stagecoach station and the station town of Julesburg.

These warriors would lead a campaign between the 1st Battle of Julesburg in January 1865 and the 2nd Battle of Julesburg on February 2, 1865, over a 150 mile stretch of the Overland Trail near the South Platte River in Northern Colorado.[1]

January 6, 1865: Battle of Fort Rankin: Capt. O'Brien's 60-Man Cavalry Ambushed by 1000 American Indian Warriors; 14 U.S. Soldiers and Four U.S. Civilians Killed

> On January 6, 1865, a small party of Indians hit a wagon train and killed 12 men. In the early morning hours of January 7th, the Indians attacked Fort Rankin. While the majority of the Indians concealed themselves in some sandhills a short distance from the Fort, Cheyenne Chief Big Crow and about ten of his warriors charged the Fort and then quickly retreated as a decoy. In response, Capt. Nicholas O'Brien led a 60-man cavalry troop out of the Fort to chase the would-be attackers.
>
> About three miles from the Fort, up to 1000 warriors were hidden in the nearby bluffs. Some Indian warriors fired prematurely, alerting Capt. O'Brien. His troops fled back to the Fort with the Indians in pursuit, cutting off some of the soldiers before they reached safety. Of those who didn't reach the Fort, they dismounted to defend themselves. In the battle, 14 soldiers and four civilians were killed. Capt. O'Brien and the rest of his men made it back to the Fort.
>
> As the remaining troops prepared to defend the Fort against further attack, the Indians looted the stage station, store, and warehouse at Julesburg. Julesburg was only 200 miles east of Denver. It was an important waystation for immigrants and settlers traveling along the Platte River on the Oregon Trail, which built up around the home station for the Overland Trail Stagecoach Lines.

In response to the attack on Fort Rankin, General Robert Byington Mitchell gathered 640 cavalry, a battery of howitzers, and some 200 supply wagons at Cottonwood Springs, which was located near present-day North Platte, Nebraska. He then marched southwest to find and punish the Indians who had attacked Fort Rankin and Julesburg. On January 19th, he found their deserted camp and returned to his base.²

In the meantime, the Indians raided ranches and stagecoach stations up and down the South Platte River Valley. The Sioux struck east of Julesburg, the Cheyenne west of Julesburg, and the Arapaho in between. George Bent, the mixed-race son of William Bent, the founder of Bent's Fort, and his Cheyenne wife, was with this group of Indians. He would later say that at night "the whole valley was lighted up with the flames of burning ranches and stage stations, but the places were soon all destroyed, and darkness fell on the valley."

Just weeks after the first attack at Julesburg, the warriors returned in force on February 2, 1865, where they once again looted the town and, this time, burned it to the ground. They also looted some wagon trains. The 15 soldiers and 50 civilians sheltered at nearby Fort Rankin did not venture outside the Fort's walls. As the fire and smoke poured from the settlement, Capt. O'Brien and 14 of his men, who had been away from the Fort, returned to Julesburg. O'Brien scattered the Indians with a round from his field howitzer, and the Indians fled.²

1868: Battle of Beecher Island: Tenth Cavalry Rout Allied Forces of Northern Cheyenne, Arapaho, and Oglala after Their Week-Long Siege of Colonel Forsyth's Command

The Battle of Beecher Island was fought on September 17, 1868, on the Arikaree River, near present-day Wray, Colorado. Fifty-one scouts and frontiersmen under the command of Colonel George A. Forsyth engaged the combined forces of the Northern Cheyenne, Arapaho, and Oglala after hunting them for several days due to their attacks on settlers. The advantage of the frontiersmen was a new firearm, the Spencer Seven repeating rifle; it shot seven times without re-loading. Unaware of this new rifle, the Indians tried making a direct charge on the frontiersmen, but were cut down. The frontiersman took cover on a sandbar island. The battle changed to a siege; starvation was the Indian plan. The frontiersmen lay in their sand pits for a whole week, drank river water, and ate horse meat. Two of their scouts were able to escape and go for help. Three military rescue parties departed following different routes due to the uncertainty of Forsyth's location. The Battle had the makings of a disaster until the Tenth Cavalry and other units arrived and routed the Indians.[3]

1869: Battle at Summit Springs; U.S. Army Force of About 300 Attack Cheyenne Encampment

In response to a series of Cheyenne Indian raids in north-central Kansas in 1868 and 1869, after the Washita Massacre, Colonel Eugene Carr, with 244 men of the 5th U.S. Regiment of Cavalry and 50 Pawnee Scouts led by Major Frank North, were given orders to clear the Republican River country of all Indians. On July 11, 1869, Carr's force came upon an unsuspecting Cheyenne camp and attacked at 3 p.m., from three sides at once.[4] The Indian camp contained 84 lodges housing approximately 450 people. Even though the battle took place in the middle of the afternoon it came as a complete surprise to the Indians.[5]

The diary of Major Frank North reads: Took the whole village of about 85 lodges. *Killed about sixty Indians.* Took seventeen prisoners and about three hundred ponies and robes, etc., innumerable. (Emphasis added).

By capturing the Dog Soldiers' village, many of the ponies, and practically all of their supplies and equipment, Carr's offensive effectively ended Cheyenne resistance on the Southern Plains.

One story told by Major North is worth repeating:

> As the mounted horsemen galloped toward the hide-covered lodges a young boy, later identified as 12-year-old Little Hawk, was caught between the advancing Cavalry and the horses that he had been herding. The horses he was guarding were spooked by the advancing troops and began to scatter. Although the boy could have made his escape he mounted his own pony, gathered up the horses that had broken away and drove them into the camp ahead of the charging troops. ... at the edge of the village he turned and joined a band

of warriors that were trying to hold us back, while the women and children were getting away, and there he died like a warrior. No braver man ever existed than that 15 year old boy. His actions so impressed Capt. Luther North that he recorded the events in his book "Man of the Plains."[6]

The lodges and all the contents of the village, except such articles as the soldiers desired to keep were burned. In an article for the Colorado Historical Society, Clarence Reckmeyer wrote:

> On a plate ... is shown a tobacco pipe the description of which reads: "Tall Bull's tobacco pipe, ornamented with feathers and scalp locks." Tall Bull was chief of a band of outlaw Cheyenne and Sioux. He was killed at the Battle of Summit Springs, Colorado. *[N]early a wagon load of Indian trophies were hauled from the battlefield to Fort Sedgwick.* (Emphasis added).[7]

An anonymous Indian artist's sketchbook captured at Summit Springs, which portrays Indian life and war with the bluecoats, is now in the Colorado History Museum in Denver.[8]

A joint resolution of the Nebraska legislature approved February 23, 1870, reads in part as follows:

> The thanks of the people of Nebraska are hereby tendered to Brevet Major General Carr and the officers and soldiers under his command of the 5th U.S. Cavalry, for their heroic courage and perseverance in their campaign against hostile Indians, driving the enemy from our borders and achieving a victory at Summit Springs, Colorado Territory. The thanks of this body and the people of the State of Nebraska are hereby also tendered to Major Frank J. North and the officers and soldiers under his command of the 'Pawnee Scouts' for the heroic manner in which they have assisted in driving hostile Indians from our frontier settlements.[9]

A resolution adopted by the Colorado legislature on January 25, 1870, reads as follows:

> Whereas, The prosperity of this territory has been greatly retarded

during several years past by Indian warfare, preventing immigration, and greatly paralyzing industry; and whereas, defenseless women and children of our pioneer settlements have been murdered by savages, or subjected to captivity worse than death; and whereas, a detachment of U.S. troops under General Carr, on the twelfth [11th] of July last, at Summit Springs, in this territory, after a long and tedious pursuit, achieved a signal victory over a band of Dog Indians, retaking considerable property that had been stolen, and recapturing a white woman held captive. Resolved, That the thanks of the people of Colorado, through the council and house of representatives of the legislative assembly of the territory of Colorado, be extended to Brevet Major General Eugene A. Carr, of the U.S. Army, and the brave officers and soldiers of his command for their victory thus achieved. Resolved, That the secretary of the territory be required to have a copy of these resolutions prepared upon parchment, and transmitted to General Carr.[10]

Notes:

1. https://thejulesburgproject.org/ (accessed online February 4, 2023). https://www.legendsofamerica.com/battle-of-julesburg-colorado/ (accessed online June 21, 2024); https://www.legendsofamerica.com/julesburg-colorado/ (accessed online June 21, 2024).

2. Kathy Alexander/Legends of America, September 2022. https://www.legendsofamerica.com/battle-of-julesburg-colorado/ (accessed online June 21, 2024).

3. By Addison Erwin Sheldon, 1913. Compiled and edited by Kathy Alexander/Legends of America, updated July 2023. https://www.legendsofamerica.com/co-beecherisland/ (accessed online February 4, 2023).

4. Kathy Alexander. https://www.legendsofamerica.com/battle-summit-springs-colorado/ (accessed online February 4, 2023).

5. https://www.ghosttowns.com/states/co/summitspringsbattlefield.html (accessed online February 4, 2023).

6. The Battle of Summit Springs, Clarence Reckmeyer, The Colorado Magazine, The State Historical Society of Colorado, Vol. VI, No. 6, November 1929.

7. Id.

8. Id.

9. Session of the Legislative Assembly of the State of Nebraska, St. A.S. Balcombe, Printer to the State, 1871, p. 50.

10. https://www.ksgenweb.org/archives/statewide/history/roenigk/chpt32.htm (accessed online February 4, 2023).

7

1887: "Colorow's War"– False Nomenclature to Hide Murder of and Forced Removal of Utes Lawfully Hunting on Ceded Land

Colorow was born a Comanche who was adopted and raised by the Mouache Utes.

The Brunot Agreement of 1873 had stated: *"The United States shall permit the Ute Indians to hunt upon [Ute land ceded to Colorado] so long as game lasts, and the Indians are at peace with the white people."* (Emphasis added).

Under this reserved right, Colorow and his band of about 200 hunted and fished in western Colorado. (Emphasis added).

> Much of this land remained as public domain. Whites used it for grazing their livestock. They opposed the Utes using it for hunting. Local sheriffs attempted to arrest them for poaching and some were accused of stealing horses.
>
> In August of 1887, a new sheriff of Garfield County, James Kendall, proceeded to Chipeta's camp, southeast of Meeker, to order her away. She told him in plain English that she had a right to stay according to the treaty. Undeterred, the sheriff intimidated her to the point where she took the women, children, and old men and hid in the shrubs. The posse left, then returned, ransacking and burning her camp.

A mixed force of sheriffs' posses, cowboys and state militias that included volunteers from Glenwood Springs, Leadville and Aspen then pursued Colorow's band in a two-week campaign that newspapers dubbed the "Colorow War."[1]

White Military Forces Arrayed against Colorow's Band Utterly Disproportionate to Utes Fighting Warriors

> *"The whites numbered 180 men, 100 being militia, the remainder being cow-boys and others. The Indians numbered not more than 25 fighting men."*[2]

Many different versions of this conflict exist. General George Crook's Military Report is set forth below.

1887: Brigadier-General George Crook's Report on Ute Troubles Caused by White Aggression against Lopsided Small Force of Indians Who Had No Desire to Fight

> *These troubles arose from attempts made by Colorado officials to serve warrants on certain Ute Indians for alleged stealing of horses and for violation of the State game laws. Application was made to the proper State officials for exact data concerning the indictments found against the two Indians, Cibilo and Big Frank, for stealing horses, but up to this present date the information requested has not been furnished.* (Emphasis added).
>
> On ... August 9, with a posse of seventeen men, he [Sheriff Kendall] went to a Ute camp on the North Fork of White River to serve the warrants. He entered the camp without molestation... The Indians expected nothing of his intentions. *Apparently without attempting to explain their objects or motives the whites suddenly seized several of the Indians. ... The Indians succeeded in breaking away and in recovering some of their weapons, at the same time running for the cover of the brush. At this juncture the posse fired on them, wounding Big Frank and two others....*
>
> [In a subsequent meeting requested by Colorow], Colorow agreed to

leave the country as soon as was possible. He required fifteen days for this purpose, as it would be necessary for him to gather his herds of horses and sheep, and drive them to the reservation, which was over 100 miles distant... Colorow began at once to collect his herds...

[Sheriff Kendall though] increased his posse until it numbered about fifty men ... and on the 20th again started in pursuit of Colorow's band, disregarding the assurances that had been given the Indians that they would be allowed fifteen days in which to go to their reservation, and stating that this time was only desired by Colorow in order to get re-enforcements and prepare for war.

On the same day a letter from Kendall was received by the commanding officer of the troops at Meeker, requesting that a force of one hundred men be sent down the White River to the Blue Mountains for the purpose of intercepting the Indians, who were retreating before him to the northward of Meeker in the direction of the Ute Reservation.

[At about 7 a.m. Sheriff Kendall's posse struck the Indians in a surprise attack], as the latter were preparing their breakfast. They believed themselves perfectly secure; no sentinels or runners were guarding the approaches to the camp, and the whites attained a position on the bluff without alarming the Indians. Kendall's party at once opened fire. The surprise was complete. The Indians took refuge in the brush, and returned the fire for about three and a half hours, covering in this way the removal of their wounded and the women and children....

The whites numbered 180 men, 100 being militia, the remainder being cow-boys and others. The Indians numbered not more than 25 fighting men. The whites justify their attack on the ground that the Indians broke faith with them in moving their camp as above related.

On the day upon which this affair occured, Lieut. G. R. Burnett, Ninth Cavalry, with 12 colored troopers, was at the Ouray (Uncompahgre) Agency ... In the afternoon of this day, however, a runner came to the agency bearing the news of the attack upon Colorow ...The Indians became at once greatly excited, and urged Lieutenant Burnett to go with them to meet the Colorado troops and prevent an invasion of their reservation. He assumed the responsibility, without waiting for orders. ... By the influence of Lieutenant Burnett, Agent Byrnes and Interpreter Curtis, the Indians, including Colorow's band, were induced to go to the agency, where they arrived August 27.

... From the outset the Indians were, with but one slight interruption, pursued incessantly; in every case the whites were the aggressors, and fired first. Colorow had no desire whatever to fight, and made use of his weapons in self defense only, for the protection of his women and children and his herds....

There can be no doubt, and it was so stated by Brigadier-General Reardon, that his presence [Lt. Burnett] saved the lives of Kendall's entire party and prevented a serious outbreak....

There is no doubt but that the warrants could have been served without difficulty had the service been properly undertaken. (Emphasis added).[3]

1887: Major-General Alfred H. Terry's Report to Adjutant-General on Colorow Conflict

I do not think that any comment upon this report, or upon the painful facts that it discloses, can be necessary. These facts speak for themselves. Moreover it is not within my province to criticise the actions of the civil authorities whose part in these transactions is set forth. I may, however, be permitted to say that if General Crook has not been deceived, the methods pursued by the civil authorities of Garfield County were, to say the least, unusual.

I do not understand that the burning of the unoccupied habitations of persons, for the arrest of whom warrants have been issued, and the burning of the habitations of their friends and neighbors, or the opening of rifle fire without warning, upon an unsuspecting body of men, women, and little children, among whom persons for whose arrest warrants have been issued are supposed to be, are usual steps in the service of process. (Emphasis added).[4]

Without General Crook's Military Report, Totally False 'Historical' Versions, Concealing Murder of and Forced Removal of Utes, Lawfully

Hunting on Ceded Land, Would Prevail

The white 'historical' versions of the conflict blamed Colorow and even named it "Colorow's War." Colorow desired only peace.

> Through the 1910s, some Utes, including those led by Chief Colorow, ventured off the reservation to hunt in Colorado, which sometimes resulted in violent skirmishes with whites.[5] Indeed by 1895, off-reservation hunting by Utes was so extensive as to raise concerns about the extermination of elk, deer, and other game.[6]

This white 'historical' version fails to note that the Utes were exercising their lawful right to hunt in the ceded area. White opposition led to the "violent" aggression against the Utes.

Another white historical version stated as follows:

> In 1887 a group of Uncompahgre and White River Utes left the Uinta Basin to hunt and fish in western Colorado. Local sheriffs attempted to arrest them for poaching and some were accused of stealing horses. The Ute people resisted; this brought about growing white hysteria in western Colorado, and the Colorado militia was ordered to put an end to the so-called "Colorow War." Outnumbered and destitute, the Ute hunting party finally capitulated and was accompanied back to the Uinta Basin by soldiers from Fort Duchesne.[7]

This version also fails to note that that the Ute response was wholly in self-defense. The Ute hunting party did not capitulate. As they were trying to return to their Reservation for which they had been given fifteen days, they were rescued by Lieut. G. R. Burnett, Ninth Cavalry, with 12 colored troopers.

Without the military version of General Crook, it would have appeared Colorow was in the wrong. Again,

> ... *From the outset the Indians were, with but one slight interruption, pursued incessantly; in every case the whites were the aggressors, and fired first. Colorow had no desire whatever to fight, and made use of his weapons in self defense only, for the protection of his women and children and his herds.*[8]

Notes:

1. https://aspenjournalism.org/ute-removal-policy-comes-to-a-head-in-the-1887-colorow-war/ (accessed online June 30, 2024).

2. Annual Reports of the War Department, Part 1, U.S. Government Printing Office, 1887, p. 366.

3. Annual Reports of the War Department, Part 1, U.S. Government Printing Office, 1887, pp. 366-368.

4. Annual Reports of the War Department, Part 1, U.S. Government Printing Office, 1887, p. 368.

5. 95 Denv. L. Rev. (2018), p. 397. Virginia McConnell Simmons, The Ute Indians of Utah, Colorado, and New Mexico (2d Ed. 2000), pp. 204-206.

6. 95 Denv. L. Rev. (2018), p. 397. 4 Frank Hall, History of the State of Colorado from 1858 to 1890 (1895), p. 66.

7. Barton, John D. "A history of Duchesne County." (1998), pp. 61-62.

8. Annual Reports of the War Department, Part 1, U.S. Government Printing Office, 1887, pp. 366-368.

8

Utes–Treaties and Agreements with U.S.

The government of the Ute peoples cannot be understood without a brief reference to the treaties and agreements entered into between the U.S. government and the various Ute Bands that wantonly diminished the Ute tribal land base.

September 15, 1865: Superintendent Taylor, Upper Platte; Obstruction of Mining Prejudicial to U.S.

Edward B. Taylor, Superintendent, Upper Platte, advised that obstruction to the development of the mines in this region should be avoided:

> *The precious metals, our sole reliance to liquidate the accruing interest upon the national debt*, are derived chiefly from the mining districts of Colorado, Oregon, California, Nevada, Idaho, and Montana, and any barrier which obstructs emigration to these mines, and retards their development, must prove highly prejudicial to the financial prosperity of the country. (Emphasis added).[1]

William Vickers, an adviser to Governor Pitkin, wrote in the *Denver Tribune*:

> The Utes are actual, practical Communists and the Government should be ashamed to foster and encourage them in their idleness and wanton waste of property. Living off the bounty of a paternal but idiotic Indian Bureau, they actually become too lazy to draw their rations in the regular way but insist on taking what they want wherever they find it. Removed to Indian Territory, the Utes could be fed and clothed for about one half what it now costs the government.[2]

1866: Gold, Silver and Coal Discovered on Ute Land; Fertile Land, Timber, Water Power, All Requirements for Profitable Occupation

The Central Superintendency reported the following:

> Colorado Territory. *Last summer gold, silver, and coal were discovered in this section, which is reported to have many fertile valleys, abundance of timber and water powers, a fine climate, and all the requirements for profitable occupation. Many parties are preparing to invade this new land early in the spring* ... It is important that a treaty be made with the Grand River and Uintah bands at as early a day as possible. *I need scarcely allude to the necessity of limiting, as far as possible, the amount which the government will be called upon to pay for a cession* of the right of occupancy of the land by the Indians, but deem it of importance that, so far as possible, no promises of money annuities shall be made, but that all payments shall be made in stock animals, implements, goods adapted to their wants, and for other beneficial objects. (Emphasis added).[3]

1868: Ute Treaty of 1868 - Utes Cede Central Rockies

The Ute Treaty of 1868, also known as the "Kit Carson Treaty," was negotiated between agents of the U.S., including Kit Carson, and leaders of seven bands of Utes living in Colorado and Utah. The treaty created for the Utes a massive reservation on Colorado's western slope in exchange for ceding the central Rockies to the U.S. For the miners, it opened a huge portion of the mineral-rich Rocky Mountains to development. A reservation was created in northeast Utah for the Uintah Utes.

In 1870 Governor Edward M. McCook wrote a letter declaring:

> "I have never been able to comprehend the reasons which induced the Colorado officials and the General Government to enter into a treaty setting apart one-third of the whole area of Colorado for the exclusive use and occupation of the Ute nation." He claimed: "The greater part of this country is the best agricultural, pastoral, and mining land on the continent ... The Ute reservation includes mines which will pay $100 per day to the man, grasses are luxuriant and

inexhaustible, and a soil richer and more fruitful than any other in the Territory." McCook closed his letter with an appeal to the ideals of Manifest Destiny: *"I believe that God gave to us the earth, and the fullness thereof, in order that we might utilize and enjoy His gifts. I do not believe in donating to these indolent savages the best portion of my Territory."* (Emphasis added).[4]

1872: Colorado Citizens Demand Utes Cede Mineral-Rich San Juan Mountains

By 1872, the discovery of silver in the San Juan Mountains of southwestern Colorado caused the settlers in Colorado to agitate for revision of the 1868 Ute Treaty. The Colorado delegation to Congress complained that this vast amount of land was underutilized by the lazy Ute people.[5]

In 1872, a government commission was appointed with instructions to negotiate a treaty with the Ute Indians for a reduction of their immense reservation covering the rich mineral-bearing section known as the "San Juan country."[6] The terms proposed to the Indians were unsatisfactory to them, and the negotiations terminated in September. Eventually, they agreed to cede the area which included the principal mines.[7]

> The Brunot Agreement of 1873 was ratified by the U.S. in 1874, and is most often remembered by Utes as the agreement when their land was fraudulently taken away. The Utes were led to believe that they would be signing an agreement that would allow mining to occur on the lands located only in the San Juan Mountain area, the site of valuable gold and silver ore. About four million acres of land not subject to mining would remain Ute territory under ownership of the tribe. However, they ended up forcibly relinquishing the lands to the U.S.[8]

Brunot's actions are remembered to this day.

> May 17, 2024: It was over 140 years ago that Felix Brunot, Chairman of the Board of Indian Commissioners, made promises and assurances to the Utes about protecting tribal interests while secretly hiding his intentions to turn over 3.7 million acres of land reserved to the Utes in the Treaty of 1868 to mining interests. Despite evidence of his

wrongdoing, Congress approved the agreement he reached in 1874, resulting in the loss of Ute land to state jurisdiction.[9]

With completion of the agreement, the San Juan Mountains saw a mining rush that resulted in many towns being established in 1874 and 1875, including Silverton. When the boundaries of the ceded lands were surveyed, the surveyor failed to exclude Uncompahgre Park, and it was quickly settled, much to the dissatisfaction of the Utes. Seeing the abundant farm and grazing land that surrounded the ceded territory, the Colorado citizenry became even more covetous of the Utes' land, making it only a matter of time before most of the Utes were forced from their Colorado homeland.[10]

1873: Incalculable Value of San Juan Mountains Ceded by Utes

> The country ceded by the Utes, including, as it does, probably the most extensive and richest mining district in the United States, embraces about four million acres of land, of very little value to Indians, being unfit for agricultural purposes and devoid of game, but of almost incalculable value to Colorado and the nation.[11]

1877: Stay Friendly with Utes

> Every day it becomes of higher importance that friendly relations should be maintained with the Utes, for it is in their power to stop, for a time at least, the development of the great San Juan mining district, which borders on the reservation. Los Pinos, Co., Agent W. D. Wheeler.[12]

Notes:

1. Report of the Commissioner of Indian Affairs to the Secretary of the Interior, United States. Office of Indian Affairs, Central Superintendency. 1865, p. 400.

2. Dee Brown, Bury My Heart at Wounded Knee: An Indian History of the American West (London: Vintage, 1991), p. 376.

3. Report of the Commissioner of Indian Affairs to the Secretary of the

Interior, United States. Office of Indian Affairs, Central Superintendency. 1866, pp. 158-160.

4. Report of the Commissioner of Indian Affairs to the Secretary of the Interior, United States. Office of Indian Affairs. 1870, p. 163.

5. Santala, Russel Dale. The Ute campaign of 1879: a study in the use of the military instrument. US Army Command and General Staff College, 1994, p. 44.

6. Hall, Frank. History of the State of Colorado from 1858 to 1890. Vol. 4, Blakely Printing Company, 1895, p. 189.

7. Hall, Frank, pp. 60-61.

8. https://www.southernute-nsn.gov/history/ (accessed online June 21, 2024).

9. Durango's secret efforts to annex Reservation lands. Southern Ute Indian Tribe, May 17, 2024. https://www.sudrum.com/top-stories/2024/05/17/durangos-secret-efforts-to-annex-reservation-lands/ (accessed online June 23, 2024).

10. https://coloradoencyclopedia.org/article/brunot-agreement (accessed online June 21, 2024).

11. Report of the Commissioner of Indian Affairs to the Secretary of the Interior, United States. Office of Indian Affairs. 1873, p. 258.

12. Report of the Commissioner of Indian Affairs to the Secretary of the Interior, United States. Office of Indian Affairs. 1877, p. 45.

9

CITY AND RAILROAD DEVELOPMENT LEAD TO COLORADO STATEHOOD

Colorado Water and Railroad Developers

Early arrivals such as Walter Cheesman, David Moffat, and James Archer led efforts to bring reliable and safe water service to Denver. They provided the financing for constructing and maintaining extensive ditch systems.

In 1868 Cheesman, John Evans and David H. Moffat began work to build the Denver Pacific Railroad to Cheyenne, Wyoming. Cheesman planned for the construction of the Union Station, and he was active in the building of the Denver Boulder Valley Railroad and South Park Road. He bought real estate, established financial institutions, and helped develop mines.

In 1870, he became a principal in a company to provide water to Denver. With David Moffat and Thomas Hayden, they consolidated two water plants into the monopolistic Denver Union Water Company in 1894, which grew to a $25 million organization. Cheesman built dams, reservoirs, and filtration and distribution systems.

1867: American Express Co., Shoot Indians

Upper Arkansas Agency, Fort Larned, Kansas, May 27, 1867

Thomas Murphy, the Superintendent of Indian Affairs, on May 27 issued a complaint to his superior Commissioner Taylor. He wrote:

I have the honor to transmit herewith a circular issued by the superintendent of the American Express Company to their employes on the Smoky Hill route from Fort Harker to Denver City. "If Indians come within shooting distance, shoot them; show them no mercy, for they will show you none."

... According to existing treaty stipulations the Cheyennes, Arapahos, and Apaches have permission to live in and roam over the country lying between these two rivers until the President orders their removal to reservations selected for them. If the government countenances these arbitrary acts of military commanders and superintendents of express companies in violating treaties, it is unreasonable to expect that the Indians will keep their part of these treaties. If this condition of affairs is permitted to exist much longer, every effort that has been made during the past two years by the civil officers of the government to promote peace and friendship among those Indians, and to prevent depredations, will have been utterly in vain, and it is but reasonable to expect that an Indian war of gigantic proportions will ensue, which will astonish the American people and cost millions of treasure. In view of these facts, I respectfully request that you will take such immediate steps as in your judgement will the soonest and most effectually put a stop to these arbitrary and cruel orders.[1]

1867: Central City—Bounty for "Indian Scalp with Ears"

The citizens of Central City have raised $5,000 to pay for Indian scalps, and offer $25 each for "scalps with the ears on."[2]

1871: Denver Pacific Railway Completed to Colorado

This railway was the first to open railroad transportation to Colorado. It extended from Cheyenne, Wyoming Territory, to Denver, Colorado-a distance of 106 miles, connecting with the Union Pacific railroad at Cheyenne, the Kansas Pacific and Colorado Central at Denver, and the Denver and Boulder Valley at Hughes.

> The advantages and benefits accruing to Colorado, from the completion of this road, are incalculable. New life has been infused into her mining and agricultural industries, and vigorous vitality given

to all business enterprises. By this the tariff on freight and passenger transportation has been so reduced, from the high rates which were peculiar to stage and wagon lines, that it seems comparatively trifling. This has stimulated large immigration and vast shipments of merchandise, which have increased the revenues of the Territory, and decreased the expense of conducting all business and mining enterprises, and the cost of living generally.

Along the line of the road, nearly its entire extent, are some of the best farming lands in the Territory, which have been already considerably improved by colonists and settlers; and, at different points, beds of lignite have been discovered, which promise to be valuable.

A portion of the Denver Pacific Railway lands were opened for sale January 1, 1868, and the company has already sold over 600,000 acres, and the sales would have been much larger, but that a large portion of the lands in western Kansas and Colorado have never been surveyed by the Government until the present year (1870). The lands are sold for cash, or part cash and part notes, the latter bearing interest at six per cent. per annum and payable in from one to five years.[3]

City Developers, Durango, Colorado

General William J. Palmer, president of the Denver & Rio Grande Railway railroad, along with William A. Bell and John A. Porter formed the Durango Trust to establish the town site and buy and sell property. As investors in the New York and San Juan Mining and Smelting Company, they built a smelter in Durango, purchased a limestone quarry and several nearby coal mines. On July 8, 1882, the Denver & Rio Grande Railroad made its way into Silverton. In that year, the "Silvery San Juan" produced $20,000,000 worth of ore.

1876: Colorado Statehood

Colorado became a state in 1876. Colorado's "Centennial" Constitution was accepted by voters on July 1, 1876.[4]

Notes:

1. Report of the Commissioner of Indian Affairs to the Secretary of the Interior, Accompanying Papers. REPORT TO THE PRESIDENT BY THE INDIAN PEACE COMMISSION, JANUARY 7, 1868. United States. Office of Indian Affairs. 1868, p. 38.

2. The Burlington Weekly Sentinel, June 28, 1867; The Chicago Evening Post, June 26, 1867.

3. Source: Rocky Mountain Directory and Colorado Gazetteer for 1871, transcribed by J.S.

4. Romero, Tom I. "Wringing Rights Out of the Mountains: Colorado's Centennial Constitution and the Ambivalent Promise of Human Rights and Social Equality." Alb. L. Rev. 69 (2005): 569.

10

PUSH TO REMOVE ALL UTES FROM COLORADO

Commissioner of Indian Affairs Smith: End Indian Fiction of Sovereignty

As the 1870s progressed, federal officials further recommended that the entirety of the indigenous population be "brought within the protection and restraint of ordinary law" and that civilized Indians be permitted to adopt American citizenship. In his 1874 report, Indian Affairs Commissioner Smith argued that such measures would benefit the Native population, *reflect the fact that their tribal government structures had collapsed*, and put an end to the "fiction of sovereignty" by which the tribes were described as independent nations. Commissioner. J.Q. Smith. (Emphasis added).[1]

The Fiction in Indian Relations

A radical hindrance is in the anomalous relation of many of the Indian tribes to the Government, which requires them to be treated as sovereign powers and wards at one and the same time. The comparative weakness of the whites made it expedient, in our early history, to deal with the wild Indian tribes as with powers capable of self-protection and fulfilling treaty obligations, and so a kind of fiction and absurdity has come into all our Indian relations. We have in theory over sixty-five independent nations within our borders, with whom we have entered into treaty relations as being sovereign peoples; and at the same time the white agent is sent to control and supervise these foreign powers, and care for them as wards of the

> Government. ... So far, and as rapidly as possible, all recognition of Indians in any other relation than strictly as subjects of the Government should cease. ... Commissioner. J.Q. Smith. (Emphasis added).[2]

Captain Pratt chaired the Sioux Commission appointed to negotiate with the Sioux for a reduction of their lands. He stated forcefully: *"[T]he domination of the chiefs should be broken up."* (Emphasis added).[3]

Again, Com'r Morgan reiterated this policy in 1890:

> It has become the settled policy of the Government to break up reservations, *destroy tribal relations*, settle Indians upon their own homesteads, incorporate them into the national life, and deal with them not as nations or tribes or bands, but as individual citizens. The American Indian is to become the Indian American. (Emphasis added).[4]

1877: Commissioner of Indian Affairs Hayt Recommends Removing All Indians in Colorado and Arizona to Indian Territory to Facilitate Mining and Farming by Whites

Commissioner E. A. Hayt reported to the Secretary in 1877 that all Indians in Colorado and Arizona should be removed to the Indian Territory in what is now Oklahoma. Miners, in search of gold and silver, could claim lands without regard to Indian reservations established by the U.S. by treaty or legislative authority. He further stated that all of the arable land was required by white settlers and feeding them was of paramount importance.[5]

Com'r Ezra Hayt:

> The reason I favored it [transfer of the Utes to Indian Territory] is this: The Indian Territory has enough fertile land to enable those Indians to settle down comfortably. It has a superabundance of fertile land. Again, the country is not broken, ridged, and labyrinthine like this region in Colorado; it is a country where the Army could use artillery; and wherever our troops can use artillery the Indians know very well that it is useless for them to go upon the warpath, so that, as a defensive measure, I think it would be wise to take them out of

their fortresses and put them where they will be less formidable ... I think, then, if we wish to avoid expensive wars and to save the lives of our soldiers, it is very desirable to put these Indians out of their fortresses in Colorado.[6]

1878: Colorado Legislators Petition for Removal of All Utes

At this time, articles headlining "The Utes Must Go" were being prepared by members of the staff of Gov. Frederick W. Pitkin. Pitkin was a former miner who used his wealth (acquired from a gold mine in the San Juan Mountains of Colorado) to influence the revision of the Ute treaty in 1873 and to become the first governor of Colorado on its statehood in 1876. His view of the Utes was an expression of the statewide view among whites that they were an impediment to the development of the richest part of the state and should be removed to the Indian Territory or elsewhere.

> On February 4, 1878, the Colorado delegation introduced the first of three bills designed to remove the Utes from Colorado. House Resolution 351 was typical of the three. It empowered the Secretary of the Interior to negotiate with the Utes and "establish by law the extinguishment of title to their lands, removal from their present locations and consolidation on certain reservations."[7]

Early in 1879, an editorial in the Denver Times stated what had become obvious to most white Colorado residents. Since the 1873 Brunot Agreement, pressure had continued to mount for the removal of the Utes from Colorado.

> Either they [the Utes] or we go, and we are not going. Humanitarianism is an idea. Western empire is an inexorable fact. He who gets in the way of it will be crushed.[8]

1879: Colorado Gov. Pitkin's Message to State Legislature: Need to Remove Indians

> Along the western borders of the state and the Pacific lies a vast tract occupied by the tribe of Ute Indians as their reservation. It contains about 12 million acres and is nearly three times as large as the State of Massachusetts. It is watered by large streams and rivers and contains

many rich valleys and a large number of fertile plains. The climate is milder than most localities of the same altitude on the Atlantic slope. Grasses grow there in great luxuriance and nearly every kind of grain and vegetables can be raised without difficulty. *This tract contains nearly one-third of the arable land of Colorado, and no portion of the State is better adapted for agricultural and grazing purposes than many portions of this reservation.* ... The number of Indians who occupy this reservation is about three thousand. If the land was divided up between individual members of the tribe, it would give every man, woman and child a homestead of between three and four thousand acres. It has been claimed that the entire tribe have had in cultivation about fifty acres of land and from some personal knowledge of the subject, I believe that one able-bodied white settler would cultivate more land than the whole tribe of Utes. These Indians are fed by the government, are allowed ponies without number, and except when engaged in an occasional hunt, their most serious employment is horse racing. If this reservation could be extinguished and the land thrown open to settlers, it would furnish homes to thousands of people of the State who desire homes. (Emphasis added).[9]

1879: Nathan Meeker Wrong Person to Appoint as Indian Agent at White River Agency, or Any Other Indian Agency

Nathan C. Meeker was the wrong person to appoint as the White River Indian Agent. He had no experience working with Indians and the White River Utes resented his paternalistic attitudes. He expressed his unfavorable opinions about the Utes in the press and to Nevada's popular Senator Teller:

> In an article in the *Greeley Tribune* on January 29, 1879, Meeker had written: "The habits of this sui generis [unique] American aristocracy seem almost identical with those of the European. Neither will work, neither attach any value to learning, both have the lower classes do work for them, both find occupation and happiness in gambling and horseracing, and the women in both are of no account."[10]

Utes, led by their Chief Jack, went to see Governor Pitkin in Denver where they asked him to remove Meeker.[11]

Meeker believed the Indians must be brought down to the level of basic survival in order to guide them to civilized and agrarian lifestyles. He reported to Colorado's influential Senator Teller, "I propose to cut every Indian down to the bare starvation point if he will not work."[12] He also wrote the following in an article published in the American Antiquarian Newsletter, 1878:

> They are savages, having no written language, no traditional history, no poetry, no literature... a race without ambition, and also a race deficient in the inherent elements of progress. Vermin abound on their persons...

The Utes suspected him of direct involvement with the anti-Ute movement in the State.[13]

Statements, such as Colonel Richard Irving Dodge's, were common:

> Christian-appointed agents were a fitting climax to the preposterous acts which for a century have stultified the governmental control and management of Indians. To appoint Nathan Meeker, however faithful, honest, and christian in bearing he, might be, to an agency in charge of a set of wild brigands like the Utes, is simply to invite massacre.[14]

On September 10, 1879, Meeker requested a telegram be sent to Commissioner Hayt requesting troops to repress a threatened uprising by the White River Utes after a Ute pushed him during an argument. The message reached Commissioner Hayt on September 13, 1879. General Sherman approved the request for troops and instructed Major General Phillip H. Sheridan to order "the nearest military commander" to send troops to White River.

Brigadier General George Crook, gave the following order to the forces at Fort Steele: You will move with a sufficient number of troops to White River Agency under special instructions. The special instructions that General Crook spoke of were to contact the agent on the scene and "develop" the situation.[15]

Major Thomas T. Thornburg began his march to the White River Agency on September 22, 1879, with a total of 153 soldiers and 25 civilians. On

September 25, 1879, Major Thornburgh wrote to Agent Meeker seeking instructions. Thornburgh continued his march toward the Agency. En route, a delegation of eleven Utes met with Thornburgh, voicing their concern over the arrival of troops and denouncing Agent Meeker.

September 29, 1879: Battle at Milk Creek; Utes Attack White River Agency

On September 27, 1879, Meeker sent a letter to Major Thornburgh:

> ...*the Indians are greatly excited*, and wish you to stop at some convenient camping place, and then that you and five soldiers of your command come into the Agency, when a talk and a better understanding can be had. ... ... *The Indians seem to consider the advance of the troops as a declaration of real war.* ... The first object is to allay apprehension. (Emphasis added).[16]

Fearing trouble, Major Thornburgh unilaterally decided that instead of sending a small group to meet with Meeker as Meeker and the Indians personally requested of him, he would enter the Reservation with all of his soldiers. He sent Agent Meeker the following message:

> I have, after due deliberation, decided to modify my plans ... I shall move with my entire command to some convenient camp near, and within striking distance of your agency, reaching such point during the 29th. ... I have carefully considered whether or not it would be advisable to have my command at a point as distant as that desired by the Indians ... and have reached the conclusion that I am not at liberty to leave [my command] at a point where it would not be available in case of trouble.[17]

When Thornburgh's command reached Milk Creek, twenty-five miles from the agency, and entered the Reservation, a large body of Indians confronted it ... For seven days, Thornburgh was besieged by the Utes. Major Thornburgh and thirteen of his men were killed.[18] Fearing outright war by the U.S., other Utes attacked the Indian Agency, killing Agent Meeker, his 10 male employees and taking five women and children captive. Troops proceeded to Colorado from all directions.

Sample News Headlines from Colorado Newspapers (1878–1879):

1878

2 January "Indian Hostilities"
3 March "Utes on Rampage, Whites Fear Uprising"
5 March "Utes Kill Cattle on Snake River"
18 April "Ute Massacre in Pagosa Springs"
23 April "Rumors of Ute War"
28 April "Utes' Gold Locations Secret from Whites"
24 May "Utes Rebellious Through Neglect of Indian Bureau"
21 July "Movements of Ute Indians"
3 August "Utes Kill Joe McLane, Stockmen Seek Revenge"
1 September "Ute Uprising Feared in Grand County"
12 September "Utes in Trouble over Murder of Settlers"[19]

1879

1 January "Utes Make Trouble in Middle Park"
27 June "Utes Threaten Miners in North Park"
9 July "Ute Hostile Attitude Excites State Officials"
6 July "Shall We Kill or Starve the Indians? [editorial]"
6 August "The Indians Must Go"
14 August "Utes Arrested and Charged with Arson"
10 September Letter to the editor from Meeker complaining of his treatment by the Utes.[20]

October 1879: *Leadville Chronicle*

> [T]he savages are sweeping through the outlying settlements of the State, murdering miners and ranchmen ... Some man is needed who will out Chivington—some man who will duplicate Sand Creek... Murder is the Indian game. Give them enough of it.

Governor Pitkin's Order: Bring In, Dead or Alive, All Hostile Indians

On October 13, 1879, the newspapers reported on the Meeker Agency incident. The headlines blazed, "A SCENE OF SLAUGHTER." Governor Pitkin denounced the attack in no uncertain terms, and incidentally pointed out that 12,000,000 acres could be opened with the removal of the Utes. [Frederick Pitkin, quoted in the Denver Daily News, October 13, 1879.] Herein lay the perfect opportunity to be rid of the Indians for good.[21]

The Governor mustered two companies of the Colorado militia: His War Order No. 1 was to "bring in, dead or alive, all hostile Indians found off the reservation ... consider all Indians off the reservation hostile, and bring them in, dead or alive, and we will determine their docility afterward."[22]

Pitkin commented to the press: "It will be impossible for the Indians and whites to live in peace hereafter ... This attack had no provocation and the whites now understand that they are liable to be attacked in any part of the state ... *My idea is that, unless removed by the government they must necessarily be exterminated.*" (Emphasis added).[23]

1880: After Thornburgh/Meeker Incidents Utes Forced Out of Colorado

After the Thornburgh/Meeker hostilities, Otto Mears accompanied Chief Ouray and an Indian delegation ordered to Washington, where an agreement dispossessing them of their Colorado reservation was forced upon them. Congress passed the Act of June 15, 1880, 21 Stat. 199, ceding to the U.S. all of "the present Ute Reservation," which would be restored to the public domain for sale. An Executive Order of 1882 restored the lands to the public domain. The settlement of the valleys of the Gunnison, the Grand and the White Rivers by white settlers was then possible.

The commission appointed to superintend the physical removal and settlement of the Utes questionably found that land at the junction of the Uncompahgre and Grand River, in Colorado, was unsuitable for the Indians, *being neither adapted to agricultural nor pastoral pursuits*. and instead removed them to the Territory of Utah. The Uncompahgre Utes of the Uncompahgre Valley (near today's Montrose) and the northwest White River Utes (near today's Meeker) were directed to evacuate their territories and move to the Uintah and Ouray reservations in northeast Utah or face extinction; at the same time, the Southern Utes were confined to a reservation on a fraction of their original southwest Colorado territory.

Otto Mears acted as translator for the Ute Commission, even though his financial interest was in laying out Colorado's roads and railroad spurs in the former western Ute territories.[24]

In late August 1881 the commissioners said it was time for the move to begin.

> The September Uncompahgre evacuation described by Capt. James Parker of the 4th Cavalry was as follows: Brevet Brigadier General Mackenzie informed the chiefs: "If you have not moved by nine o'clock tomorrow morning, I will be at your camp and make you move."

> Parker added, "The next morning after sunrise we saw a thrilling and pitiful sight. The whole Ute Nation on horseback and foot was streaming by." As they passed Parker's troops, "their gait broke into a run. Sheep were abandoned, blankets and personal possessions strewn along the road, women and children were loudly wailing." ... they arrived at their destination on September 13, having accomplished the two hundred-mile journey in less than two weeks.[25]

Throughout the state of Colorado there was rejoicing. *The Ouray Times* said:

> Sunday morning the Utes bid adieu to their old hunting grounds and folded their tents, rounded up their dogs, sheep, goats, ponies and traps, and took up the line of march for their new reservation, followed by General McKenzie and his troops. This is an event that has been long and devoutly prayed for by our people. How joyful it sounds, and with what satisfaction one can say, "The Utes have gone". The great menace to the advancement and development of this grand southwestern country is no more. Eastern people can now come to this section in the most perfect security. Besides it throws open to the dominion of white men one of the most fertile and beautiful valleys in all Colorado; a valley that will be to those who are so fortunate as to become owners of its broad acres, a happy land of Canaan.[26]

1881: Whites Pour onto Land Left by Uncompahgre Utes with No Shred of Common Decency

General Pope wrote of the occasion:

> ... the whites who had collected, in view of [the Utes] removal were so eager and unrestrained by common decency that it was absolutely necessary to use military force to keep them off the reservation until the Indians were fairly gone...[27]

Capt. James Parker of the 4th Cavalry, reported that "in three days, the rich land of the Uncompahgre was all occupied, towns were being laid out and lots being sold at high prices."[28]

Ute Commission - Those Engaged in Meeker Murders, Not Now in U.S. Custody, Are Dead or Have Fled Outside U.S.

The Ute Commission reported that they were unable to find or capture any of the Utes that committed the Thornburgh/Meeker attacks and that they were either dead, or had fled the country. The President authorized payment to the Utes for their Colorado lands. The Southern Utes received $25,000, the Uncompahgre $37,500 and the White River Utes $12,500, coupled with rations and annuities.[29]

Utes Blame Otto Mears for Removal to Utah; Co joe, Ute Sub-Chief, Tries to Assassinate Him

When Mears delivered money owed by the U.S. to Ouray's Widow, Chipeta, he was forced to flee in the night to avoid being killed by a leader of Chipeta's band, Co joe, a sub-chief, claiming it was through Mears they were forced to leave Colorado.[30]

1890: Commissioner Morgan - Southern Utes to Stay in Colorado

Colorado continued to advocate for removal to Utah of the one remaining Indian tribe in Colorado, the Southern Utes. Utah objected in no uncertain terms..

> The legislative assembly of [Utah] Territory [stated] the presence of these Indians would be a menace and a hindrance to the settlement of the country... Utah has now her share of Indians, and should not be made to receive more at the selfish behest of a neighboring State.[31]

They did not succeed and the Commissioner noted Colorado should not be too overly concerned:

> ... the Southern Utes are the only Indians now remaining in Colorado, and they number less than two thousand. Minnesota, Michigan, and Wisconsin each have over three times as many, Montana five, and California six times as many, North Dakota and South Dakota four and ten times as many, respectively, and the State of Washington five times as many; so that in the distribution of our Indian population, to those who regard their presence as a detriment, Colorado seems to have been much more fortunate than many of her sister States.[32]

Notes:

1. Report of the Commissioner of Indian Affairs to the Secretary of the Interior, United States. Office of Indian Affairs, 1874, p. 15.

2. Report of the Commissioner of Indian Affairs to the Secretary of the Interior, United States. Office of Indian Affairs, 1874, p. 15.

3. Report of the Commissioner of Indian Affairs to the Secretary of the Interior, United States. Office of Indian Affairs, Report of the Sioux Commission, 1878, pp. 655-656.

4. Report of the Commissioner of Indian Affairs to the Secretary of the Interior, United States, Office of Indian Affairs, 1890, p. VI.

5. Report of the Commissioner of Indian Affairs to the Secretary of the Interior, United States. Office of Indian Affairs, 1877, p. 6.

6. U.S. Congress, House, The Committee on Indian Affairs, Testimony In Relation To The Ute Indian Outbreak, 102.

7. Santala, Russel Dale. The Ute campaign of 1879: a study in the use of the military instrument. US Army Command and General Staff College, 1994, p. 47.

8. Carl, Ubbelohde, Maxine Benson, and Duane A. Smith, A Colorado History (Boulder, Colorado: Pruett Publishing, 1988), 190.

9. Steinel, Alvin Theodore. History of Agriculture in Colorado: A Chronological Record of Progress in the Development of General Farming, Livestock Production and Agricultural Education and Investigation, on the Western Border of the Great Plains and in the Mountains of Colorado, 1858 to 1926. State agricultural college, 1926, p. 99.

10. Mehls, Steven F. The new empire of the Rockies: A history of northeast Colorado. No. 16. Bureau of Land Management, 1984. Athearn, Robert G. The Coloradans (Albuquerque: University of New Mexico Press, 1976).

11. U.S. Congress, House, The Committee on Indian Affairs, Testimony in Relation to the Ute Indian Outbreak, p. 10.

12. Parkhill, Forbes. The Wildest of the West. "The Meeker Massacre." Denver: Sage, 1957, p. 235.

13. Brown, Dee. Bury My Heart at Wounded Knee: An Indian History of the American West (London: Vintage, 1991).

14. Sherry L. Smith, The View from Officers' Row: Army Perceptions of Western Indians (Tucson: University of Arizona Press, 1990), 95.

15. Santala, Russel Dale. The Ute campaign of 1879: a study in the use of the military instrument. US Army Command and General Staff College, 1994, p. 5.

16. Santala, Russel Dale. The Ute campaign of 1879: a study in the use of

the military instrument. US Army Command and General Staff College, 1994, p. 6.

17. War Department, General of the Army, Annual Report of the Secretary of War (1880).

18. Elmer R. Burkey, "The Thornburgh Battle With the Utes on Milk River," The Colorado Magazine 13 (May 1936): 93.

19. Santala, Russel Dale. The Ute campaign of 1879: a study in the use of the military instrument. US Army Command and General Staff College, 1994, p. 52.

20. Santala, Russel Dale. The Ute campaign of 1879: a study in the use of the military instrument. US Army Command and General Staff College, 1994, p. 52.

21. Athearn, Frederic J. An Isolated Empire: A History of Northwestern Colorado. 3rd ed. Colorado Bureau of Land Management, Cultural Resource Series No. 2, 1982, p. 53.

22. Santala, Russel Dale. The Ute campaign of 1879: a study in the use of the military instrument. US Army Command and General Staff College, 1994, p. 6.

23. https://www.aspendailynews.com/news/plight-of-the-utes-part-iii-removal-policy-comes-to-a-head-in-the-1887/article_e5cf88f8-1e38-11ee-aa3e-bf5a44584d46.html (accessed online December 7, 2022).

24. https://aspenjournalism.org/ute-removal-policy-comes-to-a-head-in-the-1887-colorow-war/ (accessed online June 30, 2024).

25. https://www.aspendailynews.com/news/plight-of-the-utes-part-iii-removal-policy-comes-to-a-head-in-the-1887/article_e5cf88f8-1e38-11ee-aa3e-bf5a44584d46.html (accessed online December 7, 2022).

26. Baker, James Hutchins, and LeRoy Reuben Hafen, eds. History of Colorado. Vol. 2. Linderman Company, Incorporated, 1927, p. 459.

27. Santala, Russel Dale. The Ute campaign of 1879: a study in the use of the military instrument. US Army Command and General Staff College, 1994, p. 70.

28. https://www.aspendailynews.com/news/plight-of-the-utes-part-iii-removal-policy-comes-to-a-head-in-the-1887/article_e5cf88f8-1e38-11ee-aa3e-bf5a44584d46.html (accessed online December 7, 2022).

29. https://aspenjournalism.org/ute-removal-policy-comes-to-a-head-in-the-1887-colorow-war/ (accessed online June 30, 2024).

30. Early History of Plateau Valley, Colorado, and Pioneer Life ..., Colorado Department of Education. https://spl.cde.state.co.us/artemis/umcserials/umc319internet/umc319v15n42000internet.pdf (accessed online July 20, 2024).

31. Report of the Governor of Utah to the Secretary of the Interior. Utah. Governor, U.S. Government Printing Office, 1890, p. 13.

32. Report of the Commissioner of Indian Affairs to the Secretary of the Interior, United States. Office of Indian Affairs, 1890, p. XLIV. Letter from the Secretary of the Interior, transmitting a communication from Attorney-General and report of Commissioner of General Land Office, also report of Commissioner of Indian Affairs, in response to Senate resolution of January 10, 1882, calling for information touching the opening for settlement under the pre-emption laws of the United States of part of the Ute Reservation in Colorado. 130 S. Exec. Doc. No. 108, 47th Cong., 1st Sess. (1882).

11

Mining and Cattle Industries

Mining Geology

The mining geology program began in earnest in 1879 with studies of the geology and technology of three great mining districts--Leadville in Colorado and the Comstock and Eureka in Nevada. Mineral data was to be collected and analyzed in all of the western States so that the probability of development could be assessed. ... [1]

Essentials for Mineral Development

Low wages, populous settlements, agriculture, and a favorable attitude of the authorities toward mining all made for a successful mining environment. Obstacles included a lack of transportation, Indian conflicts and in the arid west, the scarcity of water.

> These elements are evidenced in Commissioner of Indian Affairs E. A. Hayt's report to the Secretary of the Interior in 1877 that all Indians in Colorado and Arizona should be removed to the Indian Territory in what is now Oklahoma. Then, miners, in search of gold and silver, could claim lands without regard to Indian reservations established by the federal government by treaty or legislative authority. He further stated that all of the arable land was required by white settlers and feeding them was of paramount importance. Certainly, this evidences, without a doubt, the government's favorable attitude toward mining and the need for agriculture to feed the influx of miners and their suppliers of goods.[2]

James W. Taylor, a renowned mineral statistician, alerted Congress in 1867 to his prerequisites for successful mining: "There are two indispensable requisites to the development of the western mines: *security from Indian hostilities*, and the establishment of railway communication to the Pacific coast." (Emphasis added).[3]

Colorado Moguls: Mining and Real Estate

One of Colorado's mining moguls was Spencer Penrose. He came west and as a businessman, miner, mill owner, and investor who worked primarily in the Pike's Peak region, he built up the city of Colorado Springs. He had assets in Colorado, Utah, Arizona, and Kansas, including mines and real estate properties. He is most notable for owning the Cash On Delivery mine in Cripple Creek, building the Broadmoor Hotel and for his philanthropy.[4]

In 1902, with the Cripple Creek gold rush slowing down, Spencer Penrose and Charles L. Tutt, Sr., along with the Guggenheims, invested in the speculative technology for extracting copper from low-grade ore proposed by Daniel Jackling, a mineralogist. The Bingham Canyon Mine in Utah started with underground mining and switched to open-pit mining, using steam shovels, with railway access to transport the ore for processing. It produced about 30 percent of all the copper used by the Allied Forces for weapons, equipment, tools, and communication wires. One of the largest man-made excavations on earth, it is visible from outer space. In 2013, it reached a width of 2.5 miles and a depth of 3,900 feet. Still in operation, it has produced more copper than any other mine in the world.

Metal Processing Enterprises

Nathaniel Peter Hill (1832-1900) was a mining entrepreneur and U.S. senator from Colorado. In the 1860s, Hill, an accomplished chemist and metallurgist, bought mining interests in Black Hawk and developed the first successful smelter in Colorado. In the decade before Hill's smelter opened, miners in Gilpin County had extracted a total of $9.4 million in gold. In the decade after Hill's smelter opened, Gilpin County miners more than doubled their gold production to $20.2 million. Hill's company ruled Colorado's smelting industry in those years.

After his move to Denver, Hill expanded his business interests. He acquired real estate and helped develop property around the growing city. In 1887 he helped form the Denargo Land Company and served as its president. He also served as president of the United Oil Company and purchased a local newspaper, the Denver Republican. In his later years, he sat on the board of trustees of the Colorado School of Mines, where he also taught classes.[5]

With the usual social congregation of the wealthy, his neighbors included the Evanses, Iliffs and the Byers. This led to financial and political leverage, along with the consolidation and integration of common industrial interests. Byers owned the Rocky Mountain News and fifteen years after the Sand Creek Massacre still believed that Sand Creek had "saved Colorado and taught the Indians the most salutary lesson they ever learned."[6]

Meyer Guggenheim made his fortune (one of the largest of the 19th century) through business ventures in mining and smelting, mostly in the U.S. After investing in silver mines in the Leadville mining district of Colorado, he expanded into ore smelting in Colorado. Later, he expanded into copper (Utah's Bingham Canyon, Canada and Chile) and lead—needed in telephone and electrical systems.[7]

Colorado Metals Production History

The total Colorado production of the precious and allied metals from 1859 to 1870, inclusive, was: Gold $27,213,081; silver $330,000; copper $40,000; total, $27,583,081. The annual gold output of the state increased from $4,150,000 in 1890 to $28,702,036 in 1900.

The total gross value of the gold, silver, copper, lead and zinc was $1,531,000,000 to the end of 1923, very close to the assessed valuation of the State of Colorado for 1923, $1,550,000,000.[8]

Cattle Enterprises

Once the Utes were moved to Utah in 1881, the open range cattle industry expanded. As the U.S. forced the Cheyenne and Arapaho off their Colorado land, cattle could graze for free on thousands of acres. For a scant $10,000 investment, John Wesley Iliff soon became the largest landowner in northeast Colorado, with approximately 15,500 acres. Feeding his herds on the open range created an opportunity for large profits. While grazing on the range was free, buying land and appropriating water rights secured Iliff water along the South Platte River. He sold cattle to Indian reservations, army posts like Fort Laramie, the city of Cheyenne, and Union Pacific railroad construction crews in Nebraska, Wyoming and Utah. With refrigerated cattle cars, he could ship cattle and dressed beef to Chicago's Union Stockyards.[9]

Notes:

1. Rabbitt, Mary C. The United States Geological Survey: 1879–1989, U.S. Geological Survey Circular 1050, p. 7.

2. Report of the Commissioner of Indian Affairs to the Secretary of the Interior, United States. Office of Indian Affairs, 1877, p. 6.

3. Report of James W. Taylor, special commissioner for the collection of statistics upon gold and silver mining east of the Rocky mountains. February 15, 1867. 39th Congress, 2d Session. House of Representatives. Ex. Doc. No. 92, p. 28.

4. Philip F. Anschutz with William J. Convery and Thomas J. Noel, Out Where the West Begins: Profiles, Visions and Strategies of Early Western Business Leaders (Denver: Cloud Camp Press, 2015).

5. Philip F. Anschutz with William J. Convery and Thomas J. Noel, Out Where the West Begins: Profiles, Visions and Strategies of Early Western Business Leaders (Denver: Cloud Camp Press, 2015), p. 236.

6. Flowers, Kaylyn Mercuri. "William N. Byers." Colorado Encyclopedia. https://coloradoencyclopedia.org/article/william-n-byers (accessed online December 15, 2022).

7. Philip F. Anschutz with William J. Convery and Thomas J. Noel, Out Where the West Begins: Profiles, Visions and Strategies of Early Western Business Leaders (Denver: Cloud Camp Press, 2015).

8. MINING IN COLORADO A HISTORY OF DISCOVERY, DEVELOPMENT AND PRODUCTION BY CHARLES W. HENDERSON, DEPARTMENT OF THE INTERIOR, Hubert Work,

Secretary U.S. GEOLOGICAL SURVEY, George Otis Smith, Director, Professional Paper 138, Washington Government Printing Office, 1926, p. 249.

9. Athearn, Frederic J. An Isolated Empire: A History of Northwestern Colorado. 3rd ed. Colorado Bureau of Land Management, Cultural Resource Series No. 2, 1982, p. 4.

12

Further Federal Actions Impacting Tribal Autonomy

American Indian Wars

The numerous wars fought by Indians to protect their lands unquestionably documents their belief in ownership of their lands. They were under-armed and under-populated, at times, yet they willingly put their lives and liberty at risk.

> The U.S. Army used the methods outlined by Prussian General and military theorist Carl von Clausewitz: The *first* of these is invasion, that is the seizure of enemy territory; not with the object of retaining it but in order to exact financial contributions, or even to lay it waste. The immediate object here is neither to conquer the enemy country nor to destroy its army, but simply to cause general damage. The *second* method is to give priority to operations that will increase the enemy's suffering. The *third*, and by far the most important method, judging from the frequency of its use, is to wear down the enemy. ... Wearing down the enemy in a conflict means using the duration of the war to bring about a gradual exhaustion of his physical and moral resistance.[1]

As Navajo leader Manuelito said of the Navajo-American War of 1860-1868:

> We fought for [our] country because we did not want to lose it. We lost nearly everything. The American nation is too powerful for us to fight. When we had to fight for a few days we felt fresh, but in a short time we were worn out and the soldiers starved us out.[2]

On September 1, 1866, six years after the Navajo-American War's start, Manuelito surrendered with 23 warriors:

> *They were all in rags, their bodies emaciated. They still wore leather bands on their wrists for protection from the slaps of the bowstrings but they had no bows or arrows. One of Manuelito's arms hung useless at his side from a wound. Now there were no more war chiefs.* (Emphasis added).[3]

In his vision of Manifest Destiny, Brigadier General Carleton, the commander of the U.S. Army's Department of New Mexico, who led the U.S. forces during the Navajo-American War, reported on the "insatiable progress of our race," from the Navajo Prisoner of War Camp at Fort Sumner, New Mexico:

> The exodus of this whole people from the land of their fathers is not only an interesting but a touching sight. They have fought us gallantly for years on years; they have defended their mountains and their stupendous canyons with a heroism which any people might be proud to emulate; but when, at length, they found it was their destiny, too, as it had been that of their brethren, tribe after tribe, away back toward the rising of the sun, to give way to the insatiable progress of our race, they threw down their arms, and, are brave men entitled to our admiration and respect, have come to us with confidence in our magnanimity, and feeling that we are too powerful and too just a people to repay that confidence with meanness and neglect, feeling that having sacrificed to us their beautiful country, their homes, the associations of their lives, the scenes rendered classic in their traditions, we will not dole out to them a miser's pittance in return for what they know to be and what we know to be a princely realm.[4]

Two of the Navajo's four sacred mountains representing the original boundaries of the Navajo's land are in southern Colorado: Mt. Hesperus (Northern boundary) and Mt. Blanca (Eastern boundary).

1861: Treaty of Fort Wise, Confine Cheyenne and Arapaho on Reservation, 1/13 Size of Fort Laramie Treaty Lands

Under the 1851 Treaty of Fort Laramie, there was no authority for settlers to settle or mine for gold on any of the Indians lands. The fifty thousand miners and traders who came to Colorado in 1859 alone squatted on the legal homelands of the Cheyenne and Arapaho. The influential lobby of the miners and mercantilists that settled in Denver pressured the U.S. to renegotiate the 1851 Treaty and redefine Cheyenne and Arapaho lands to allow for continued settlement of the gold-rich Rocky Mountains, without fear of violence.

To this end, the U.S. sent Commissioner Greenwood to Bent's New Fort in the fall of 1860 to negotiate a treaty. It was planned to cordon the Cheyenne and Arapaho onto a subdivided, roughly triangular reservation of 4 million acres in the area near Sand Creek. However, only ten chiefs signed the treaty: six Cheyennes, including Black Kettle (Motevato), and four Arapahos. Cheyenne chief Black Kettle protested since under Cheyenne political doctrine all tribal and military leaders (most of whom were not in attendance) had to be consulted before the treaty could be consummated. Many would later say they did not understand the terms and had not intended to cede the lands granted them under the 1851 Fort Laramie Treaty, which encompassed over 44 million acres. The majority of the Cheyenne and Arapaho did not move to the Reservation which was one-thirteenth the size of their former territory. The Indian Office considered the Treaty of Fort Wise to be applicable only to those bands whose leaders had agreed to it. Historian Frank Hall in his 1895 History of Colorado concurred with the Indians that it was secured by "presents and mystification." (Emphasis added).[5]

1863: Commissioner Dole to Governor/Superintendent Evans - Get Cheyenne and Arapaho that Have Not Signed Treaty of Fort Wise to Do So

Commissioner Dole wanted Governor Evans to get all of the Cheyenne and Arapaho that had not signed the Treaty of Fort Wise to do so. On July 16, 1863, Commissioner Dole wrote to Governor/Superintendent Evans: "I hope you will find it possible to arrange with the Cheyennes and Arapahos that have not signed the Treaty to do so and put them together, or make some other arrangement that will be just to them, and satisfactory to the whites."[6]

1871: Indian Appropriations Act Ends Treaty-Making with American Indian Nations

The 1871 Indian Appropriations Act ended treaty making with Indian nations.

1887: General Allotment Act

The General Allotment Act divided Indian tribal land into individual allotments, forcing Indians into private property ownership. Up until this time the reservations had been held communally by all members of the tribe(s) living on the reservation. The alleged rationale for the GAA was that it would assimilate Indians into the mainstream of U.S. society by encouraging farming and agriculture. Also, a transition to farming would lessen the amount of land needed by Indians such that it would justify reducing their land base. Alternatively, there was no need for a separate land base for Indians assimilated into the general society.

To that end, individual Indians were given a certain number of acres, generally in 40-, 80- and 160-acre parcels, to be held in trust by the U.S. for the individual for 25 years and then patented in fee.[7] Allotment was not new; certain treaties provided for it prior to the GAA, but the GAA enshrined it into law.

After the twenty-five years that the allotment was held in trust by the U.S., it was expected that the Indian owner would be "civilized" and "competent enough" to manage his own affairs and the government would issue a fee patent for his allotment. (General Allotment Act § 5). The patent-in-fee vested fee simple ownership in an allottee.

Reservation lands not allotted or reserved for tribal or other use were considered surplus to Indian needs and opened to purchase and settlement by non-Indians. While the GAA marked the destruction of a tribe's land base, the Burke Act of 1906 triggered the rapid loss of lands from individual Indian ownership. The Burke Act amended the GAA by authorizing the Secretary to issue a patent in fee on allotments before the expiration of the twenty-five-year trust period "whenever he shall be satisfied that any Indian allottee is competent and capable of managing his or her affairs".[8]

Once an individual was certified competent, the Burke Act authorized the issuance of a fee patent to the allottee, immediately subjecting his/her lands to state property taxes and the option of sale to Indians or non-Indians.[9]

Commissioner, Edward P. Smith, supported allotment prior to the enactment of the GAA. In 1874, he stated:

> A fundamental difference between barbarians and a civilized people is the difference between a herd and an individual. ... Where everything is held in common, thrift and enterprise have no stimulus of reward and thus individual progress is rendered very improbable, if not impossible. The starting point of individualism for an Indian is the personal possession of his portion of the reservation. Give him a house within a tract of land, whose corner-stakes are plainly recognized by himself and his neighbors, and let whatever can be produced out of this landed estate be considered property in his own name, and the first principle of industry and thrift is recognized. In order to reach this first step, the survey and allotment in severalty of the lands belonging to the Indians must be provided for by congressional legislation.[10]

Colorado Senator Henry Teller tried, unsuccessfully, to change the Republican Party policy on Indian Affairs. In 1881, when allotment was being studied, he said that the policy would "despoil the Indians of their lands and make them vagabonds on the face of the earth."

> The Minority Report of the House Indian Affairs Committee stated: that the real aim [of allotment] was to get at the Indian lands and open them up to settlement. The provisions for the apparent benefit of the Indians are but the pretext to get at his [the Indians'] lands and occupy them... If this were done in the name of greed it would be bad enough; but to do it in the name of Humanity, and under the cloak of an ardent desire to promote the Indian's welfare by making him like ourselves, whether he will or not, is infinitely worse.[11]

Commissioner of Indian Affairs Atkins would expound from the bully pulpit in 1885:

> The advantages to the Indians of taking their lands in severalty are so important and far-reaching in their effects that I fear to dwell upon them in this report ...Every step taken, every move made, every

suggestion offered, everything done with reference to the Indians should be with a view of impressing upon them that this is the policy which has been permanently decided upon by the Government in reference to their management. They must abandon tribal relations; they must give up their superstitions; they must forsake their savage habits and learn the arts of civilization; they must learn to labor, and must learn to rear their families as white people do, and to know more of their obligations to the Government and to society. In a word, they must learn to work for a living, and they must understand that it is in their interest and duty to send their children to school.[12]

Southern Utes' Land Allotted; Weenuche Band Refuses Allotment

Under acts passed by Congress in 1880 and 1895, the remaining Reservation lands in southwestern Colorado were the subject of Indian allotment. Under the authority of the Acts of 1880 and 1895, a Presidential proclamation issued in 1899 opened the lands remaining after allotment to entry under the public land disposal laws. Over the next 35-year period, agricultural entrymen entered upon the opened Reservation lands and acquired homestead patents pursuant to various public land laws.

The Muache and Capote bands accepted allotment,[13] while the Weenuche (Ute Mountain Ute) resisted the Dawes Act.[14]

Social and Economic Effects of Allotment

The BIA contribution to the Land Planning Report on the social and economic effects of allotment is tragic.

The physical liquidation of the Indian landed estate is only one side of the devastation wrought by the allotment system. The effects upon the social and economic condition of the tribe were equally unhappy. Here are some of the outstanding results of the GAA:

1. Allotment broke up the community organization of the tribes as it was frankly intended to do. Tribalism was held in abhorrence by the advocates of allotment. The partition of land in severalty, it was hoped, would dissolve the tribal association and substitute

therefor individual status. But the allotment system thus weakened or destroyed the cohesion of the one unit to which the Indians were culturally attuned—the tribe. In weakening this native means of organization, the allotment theorists assailed the only sound foundation upon which a transformed Indian society could have been built.

2. Allotment shattered family interests and worked as a divisive factor in the lives of all allotted Indians. It did this because allotments were made to the individual and not to the family.

3. *The allotment system, in the manner of its application, attempted to force Indians to become commercial farmers, especially upon the irrigated units.* Many Indians who had been accustomed to sustenance farming were thus forced to attempt commercial farming for which they had little training, knowledge or technology. Thus, whole Indian populations that were known for farming ended up with none of them farming at all.

4. The inheritance of allotments reduced Indian lands to uneconomic units by progressive subdivision. *It transformed Indians into petty landholders and the Office of Indian Affairs into a huge banking and realtor enterprise.*

5. Due to the trust character of Indian allotments, the owners could not pledge their lands for credit, without which it was impossible for them properly to develop their land.

6. Allotment, because of the subdivision produced in heirship status and because of the lack of adequate credit, forced the system of leasing to whites upon the Indians, making of them idlers dependent upon pittances of rental.

7. Allotment led to the creation of a system of probate in the Indian Office which was excessively tardy and unaccountable to the courts.

8. Allotment led directly to making a hundred thousand Indians landless through alienation of land following issuance of fee patents and *failure to provide enough land for future generations*. (Emphasis added).[15]

Allotment's Effects on Grazing and Forest Land

The BIA's contribution to the Land Planning Report on allotment's effect on grazing and forest land is devastating.

The effects of checkerboarding on potential Indian use of land are especially acute in the case of grazing and forest lands, which constitute 92 percent of all Indian land. *An average Indian allotment of 160 acres of grazing land is much too small to maintain even a subsistence herd of cattle or sheep.* Moreover, for the best utilization and management of grazing lands, it is essential to have large contiguous areas used in common. On such areas, a minimum of fencing and water development is required, and systematic programs of rotation grazing, range revegetation, erosion control, seasonal grazing, and proper distribution of livestock on the range can be carried out. When a potential Indian grazing range is fragmented into small allotments and minute heirship parcels and further checkerboarded and shared by numerous alienations, the tangle becomes almost hopeless so far as promoting use by Indians is concerned. (Emphasis added).[16]

In the case of Indian forests the problem is even more acute. *Permanent sustained-yield forestry can be practiced in general only on large contiguous areas in one ownership, thus permitting logging and reforestation to progress systematically over natural logging units related to topography and logical transport lines; and ultimately to return, after 50 or 100 years, to renew the cycle at the first point of beginning on the new crop of timber.* Much of the Indian timberland is fragmented by allotment and alienation. Alienated lands, if sufficiently numerous, are an absolute block to sustained yield management; allotted lands are a partial and expensive block. (Emphasis added).[17]

Plenary Power of Congress over American Indian Affairs

Plenary authority refers to the complete or absolute power that is wide-ranging, broadly construed, and often limitless regarding a specific issue.

While the General Allotment Act established a mandate for allotting Indian lands, separate legislation was required to actually allot the lands of a particular Indian nation. Usually, government officials would negotiate with a tribe's leaders to secure their cooperation in the allotment process. In addition to the grant of individual lands and monetary compensation to the tribe, other incentives were given to induce Indians to relinquish their tribal lands. Often, however, these incentives failed to have their desired effect.

Then the government proceeded to allot the reservations anyway, even when doing so violated prior treaties with the affected Indian nation. Kiowa leader Lone Wolf sued Secretary of the Interior Ethan Allen Hitchcock to halt the allotment of the Kiowa, Comanche, and Apache Reservation. *The U.S. Supreme Court's opinion upheld the forced allotment of their lands, based on the supremacy of federal plenary power over tribes.* Though it violated and abrogated the terms of the Medicine Lodge Treaty of 1867, the Court approved the dispossession of the Kiowa, Comanche, and Apache Reservation by opening non-allotted surplus lands to non-Indian settlers after the forced allotment.[18] Indian nations do not have recourse to the federal courts to remedy violations of treaties by the federal government.

It wasn't until 1977, in *Delaware Tribal Business Committee v. Weeks*, 430 U.S. 73 (1977), that the Court put limitations on Congress' power. Justice William J. Brennan, Jr., held that "The power of Congress over Indian affairs may be of a plenary nature; but it is not absolute." Federal legislation must be rationally related to furtherance of the federal trust responsibility to Indians. However, *rational basis scrutiny is not a strong standard for review of Congressional action.*

Bureau of Indian Affairs ("BIA") American Indian Citizenship Ceremony

Individuals deemed "competent" by the BIA were encouraged to take up U.S. citizenship. The term "competent" denoted an Indian's ability to manage his/her own affairs, hold fee simple title to trust land, and be released from government control. Fee simple title is the most basic form of ownership in which the owner holds the title and total control over the property, including the right to sell, mortgage or lease.

The BIA devised a Citizenship Ceremony.[19] At the ceremonial setting, a tipi was set up. The citizen-to-be was directed to enter the tipi, take off his regalia, and put on clothes a white man would wear. He was then given a white man's name, to the applause of those attending. With the Indian man properly dressed and named, the BIA representative then conducted the Ceremony:

> I hand you a bow and an arrow. Take this bow and shoot the arrow. (He shoots.) You have shot your last arrow. That means that you are

no longer to live the life of an Indian. You are from this day forward to live the life of the white man. But you may keep that arrow, it will be to you a symbol of your noble race and of the pride you feel that you come from the first of all Americans.

[The white name given him is now used.] Take in your hand this plow. (He takes the handles of the plow.) This act means that you have chosen to live the life of the white man—and the white man lives by work.

There was also a BIA Citizenship Ceremony for Indian women.

The text of the full Ceremony is attached in Appendix 3.

The photo above was taken on the Standing Rock reservation during a citizenship ceremony. One man poses with a drawn bow and arrow, others hold their "last arrows." The plow and the flag are displayed as symbols of U.S. citizenship.

1924: Indian Citizenship Act - Double Edged Sword

The Indian Citizenship Act of 1924 (43 Stat. 253) made all non citizen Indians born within the territorial limits of the United States citizens of the United States, without impairing or otherwise affecting the right of any Indian to tribal or other property. Citizenship did not impose suffrage rights and this matter was litigated in many states. Native Americans living on tribal lands in Colorado did not have guaranteed voting rights until as late as 1970.[20]

> *"The Snyder Act was a double-edged sword,"* Southern Ute Chairman Melvin J. Baker said. *"It offered citizenship on paper, but also sought to dismantle our identity. We were expected to abandon our traditions and languages to fit a mold. True citizenship, however, is about respect, not assimilation. It's about honoring our shared history and upholding our right to self-determination. This fight for genuine citizenship and recognition continues to this day."* (Emphasis added).[21]

1934: Indian Reorganization Act

The 1934 Indian Reorganization Act (IRA) ended the policy of allotment, banned the further sale of Indian land and decreed that any unallotted land not yet sold should be returned to tribal control. Land was restored to the SUIT and UMUT. It also granted Indian communities a measure of governmental and judicial autonomy by authorizing tribes to organize governments.[22]

1946: Indian Claims Commission– Pre-Cursor to Termination of Indian Tribes

The first step towards terminating the reservations came in 1946 when Congress, in part to reward Native Americans for their contribution to the war effort, set up the Indian Claims Commission to hear Indian claims for any lands stolen from them from 1776 forward. The Commission would provide only financial compensation and not return any land. *The federal government regarded the Commission as the first step to 'getting out of the Indian business.'*

President Truman stated:

> I hope that this bill will mark the beginning of a new era for our Indian citizens. They have valiantly served on every battle front. ... With the final settlement of all outstanding claims which this measure ensures, Indians can take their place without special handicaps or

> special advantages in the economic life of our nation and share fully in its progress.²³

The original intention was for the Commission to sit for five years, but there were so many claims that it remained in existence until 1978.

1950–1967: Termination of Tribes' Federal Status

> Termination may be defined simply as the cessation of the federal-tribal relationship, whether that relationship was established through treaty or otherwise. The thrust was to eliminate the reservations and to turn Indian affairs over to the states. Indians would become subject to state control without any federal support or restrictions. Indian land would no longer be held in trust and would be fully taxable and alienable, just like non-Indian land in the states. Special federal health, education, and general assistance programs for Indians would end.²⁴

Starting in 1950, over 100 tribes had their federal trust relationship terminated, meaning their lands and governments were lost; tribal governments dismantled; reservation lands divided and sold to individual developers, then subjected to local property taxes; and federal Indian programs dissolved. Thousands of American Indians were also moved off reservations to cities as a means of forced assimilation. It mostly meant exchanging rural poverty for urban poverty.

Dillon Myer, former director of the detention camp program for Japanese-Americans during World War II, became BIA Commissioner in 1950. He advocated for and enforced a withdrawal of federal services "as rapidly as circumstances" permitted, and he actively encouraged young Native Americans to relocate to urban centers where he believed federal responsibility ended.

The U.S. approved House Concurrent Resolution 108 establishing the congressional goal of subjecting American Indians "to the same laws and entitled to the same privileges and responsibilities" as other Americans, i.e., termination of their Indian tribes.²⁵

The BIA specified how their withdrawal of services would occur:

Federal responsibility for administering the affairs of individual Indian tribes ... should be terminated as rapidly as the circumstances of each tribe will permit. This should be accomplished by arrangements with the proper public bodies of the political subdivisions [i.e., states] to assume responsibility for the services customarily enjoyed by the non-Indian residents of such political subdivisions and by [the federal government's] distribution of tribal assets to the tribes as a unit or by division of the tribal assets among the individual members, whichever may appear to be the better plan in each case. In addition, responsibility for trust properties should be transferred to the Indians themselves, either as groups or individuals as soon as feasible.[26]

Com'r Glenn Emmons, Myer's successor, refined the termination process, emphasizing consultation with, but not the consent of, tribal nations.[27]

Senator Arthur Watkins of Utah, the principal Congressional advocate of termination, claimed in a 1957 article that it could be compared to the abolition of slavery: 'Following in the footsteps of the Emancipation Proclamation of 94 years ago, I see the following words emblazoned in letters of fire above the heads of the Indians—THESE PEOPLE SHALL BE FREE!'[28]

There were 109 tribes and bands whose federal recognition was terminated. Although the Nixon administration repudiated termination in 1970 and shifted federal Indian policy toward self-determination, the effect of termination was nevertheless devastating for many tribes.[29]

Nearly twenty years after the first termination legislation, Menominee leader Ada Deer and an organization called Determination of Rights and Unity for Menominee Shareholders (DRUMS) lobbied Congress for the restoration of their tribal status. On December 22, 1973, President Richard M. Nixon signed the Menominee Restoration Act. Four years later, twenty-eight bills were introduced in Congress to restore tribal status to other tribes, with more to come.

1968: Indian Civil Rights Act

Indian nations, whose political systems predate the United States and the passage of the Constitution, never agreed to any of the terms in the

Constitution, including the Bill of Rights. Concerns with individual Indian civil rights violations by federal, state and tribal authorities led to the enactment of the Indian Civil Rights Act in 1968 ("ICRA"). (25 U.S.C. §§ 1301-1304). It contained provisions similar to those found in the Bill of Rights, excluding the equivalent of the establishment clause, right to appointed counsel, grand jury indictment requirement, and civil jury trial. It is commonly known as the Indian Bill of Rights. Recognizing the role of religion in the structuring of tribal life, culture, and sometimes government, the ICRA guarantees free exercise of religion but does not prohibit its establishment. Cognizant of tribal economic constraints, the Act does not require tribes to provide free counsel for criminally accused or a jury trial for civil cases.

In *Santa Clara Pueblo v. Martinez*, 439 U.S. 49 (1978), the U.S. Supreme Court interpreted ICRA as not giving the federal court any power to review any complaints of ICRA violations by a tribal government, except those arising as writ of habeas corpus actions—complaints of unlawful detention raised by individuals being held in tribal custody. The decision held that violations of all the other rights guaranteed under the ICRA, including equal protection rights, fell under tribal jurisdiction, and thus could only be brought in tribal court. The Supreme Court concluded that providing a federal forum for ICRA litigation would constitute an interference with tribal autonomy and self-government.

Notes:

1. Clausewitz, Carl. "Carl von Clausewitz: On war." (2007). https://www.usmcu.edu/Portals/218/EWS%20On%20War%20Reading%20Book%201%20Ch%201%20Ch%202.pdf (accessed online January 20, 2024).

2. Brown, Dee. Bury my heart at Wounded Knee: an Indian history of the American West. Macmillan, 2007.

3. Brown, Dee. Bury my heart at Wounded Knee: an Indian history of the American West. Macmillan, 2007.

4. Brown, Dee. Bury my heart at Wounded Knee: an Indian history of the American West. Macmillan, 2007.

5. Hall, Frank. History of the State of Colorado from 1858 to 1890. Vol. 4, Blakely Printing Company, 1895.

6. Letter of William P. Dole to John Evans, 07-16-1863, Governor's Papers, Transcript of original Letter Press Book Record. Governor John Evans. Colorado State Archives, History Colorado. MSS Evans 226.

7. General Allotment Act, 24 Stat. 388, 389 (1887).

8. Burke Act, 34 Stat. 182, 183 (1906).

9. Nash, Douglas R. and Burke, Cecelia E. (2006). "The Changing Landscape of Indian Estate Planning and Probate: The American Indian Probate Reform Act (AIPRA)," Seattle Journal for Social Justice: Vol. 5: Iss. 1, Article 15, p. 126. https://digitalcommons.law.seattleu.edu/sjsj/vol5/iss1/15 (accessed online March 15, 2024).

10. Report of the Commissioner of Indian Affairs to the Secretary of the Interior, U.S. Government Printing Office, 1874, p. 4.

11. H. Rept. No. 1576, vol. V (H. R. 5038), May 28, 1880, p. 1155. Minority report on lands in severalty to Indians.

12. Report of the Commissioner of Indian Affairs to the Secretary of the Interior. United States. Office of Indian Affairs. U.S. Government Printing Office, 1885, p. V.

13. The Tribe and the Southern Ute Indian Reservation Are an Important Part of the History of Our Area. https://www.southernute-nsn.gov/natural-resources/lands/assignments/living-in-la-plata-county/ (accessed online January 13, 2024).

14. UTE MOUNTAIN UTE TRIBE CULTURAL RESOURCES MANAGEMENT PLAN 1.3 Ute Mountain Ute Culture and History. https://www.utemountainutetribe.com/images/THPO%20information/UMTU%20CRMP.pdf (accessed online January 13, 2024).

15. INDIAN LAND TENURE, ECONOMIC STATUS, AND POPULATION TRENDS, PART X OF THE REPORT ON LAND PLANNING, Office of Indian Affairs, United States Printing Office, 1935, p. 10.

16. Ibid., 9.

17. Id.

18. See *Lone Wolf v. Hitchcock*, 187 U.S. 553 (1903).

19. See https://www.ndstudies.gov/curriculum/high-school/standing-rock-oyate/documents-standing-rock (accessed online April 9, 2023).

20. https://www.sos.state.co.us/pubs/newsRoom/pressReleases/2022/PR20221103TribalVoting.html (accessed online June 20, 2024).

21. https://www.sudrum.com/news/2024/06/14/strands-of-strength-the-indian-citizenship-act-100th-anniversary/ (accessed online June 22, 2024).

22. 48 Stat. 984.

23. https://www.trumanlibrary.gov/library/public-papers/204/statement-president-upon-signing-bill-creating-indian-claims-commission (accessed online June 22, 2024).

24. Charles F. Wilkinson & Eric R. Biggs, The Evolution of the Termination Policy, 5 Am. Indian L. Rev. 139, 140 (1977).

25. Indians, HCR 108, 67 Stat. B132 (August 1, 1953).

26. Report of the Commissioner of Indian Affairs to the Secretary of the Interior, United States. Office of Indian Affairs, 1953, p. 23.

27. Report of the Commissioner of Indian Affairs to the Secretary of the Interior, United States. Office of Indian Affairs, 1955, p. 237.

28. Congressional Record: Proceedings and Debates of the ... Congress, Volume 115, Part 28, U.S. Government Printing Office, 1969, p. 38238.

29. https://www.archives.gov/research/native-americans/bia/termination (accessed online March 21, 2024).

13

INDIAN CHILD WELFARE ACT—A CIVICS MODEL IN ROLE OF JUDICIARY AND PUBLIC INTEREST GROUPS

Congress enacted ICWA in 1978 to address the Federal, State, and private agency policies and practices that resulted in the "wholesale separation of Indian children from their families." Congress found "that an alarmingly high percentage of Indian families are broken up by the removal, often unwarranted, of their children from them by nontribal public and private agencies and that an alarmingly high percentage of such children are placed in non-Indian foster and adoptive homes and institutions. ..." Although the crisis flowed from multiple causes, Congress found that non-Tribal public and private agencies had played a significant role, and that State agencies and courts had often failed to recognize the essential Tribal relations of Indian people and the cultural and social standards prevailing in Indian communities and families. To address this failure, ICWA establishes minimum Federal standards for the removal of Indian children from their families and the placement of these children in foster or adoptive homes, and confirms Tribal jurisdiction over child-custody proceedings involving Indian children.[1]

Appendix 4: American Indian Child Welfare Act Case Study is included in this book given the importance of this topic to American Indian Tribal Nations. It is composed of six Parts providing more information on specific topics discussed in this Chapter 13.

> Part 1: *Haaland v. Brackeen*, 599 U.S. 255, 268-270 (2023), provides information on the subject matter of the case brought to overturn ICWA as unconstitutional.

Part 2: Significant Parties Opposing ICWA provides information on the parties who filed Amicus Curiae briefs opposing ICWA.

Part 3: Significant Parties Supporting ICWA provides information on the parties who filed Amicus Curiae briefs in support of ICWA.

Part 4: Colorado - Pioneering State for Adoption Intervention Cases: 2,500 Cases Filed by 2022—Primary Attorney's Firm Used Discredited Child Adoption Expert.

THIS PART IS EXTREMELY IMPORTANT. It discusses the trend in foster care using it as a road to adoption given the scarcity of adoptable children. The plan is for the foster parent to refuse to relinquish the foster child and instead bring litigation to adopt the child. ProPublica found that the child adoption expert used across Colorado and the western states [Diane Baird] used a method she admitted was unscientific, unstandardized and unpublished. Indian Child Welfare Act cases should be reviewed to determine if Baird was an expert in the cases.

Part 5: Federal and Colorado Adoption Legislation, Restricting Intervention. Given the prevalence of foster parents abusing the system, federal and Colorado state legislation was enacted to *give preference to adult relatives and kin and restrict litigation intervention tactics.* The National Coalition for Child Protection Reform cited data that Colorado used kinship care at a rate 30% below the national average. In 2020, 10% of Dependency and Neglect cases in Colorado had intervenors. When foster parents intervene, the chance of reunification decreases from 62% to 22% for the birth parents.

Part 6: American Indian/Alaska Native (AI/AN) Families Attachment and Bonding Research. This research focuses on the tribal community and kin as a resource for adoption of American Indian children.

"Adoption Cliff"

In a phenomenon that has been described as the "adoption cliff," international adoptions to the United States have fallen and domestic infant adoptions began dropping exponentially due to (1) increased access to reproductive healthcare; (2) abortion; (3) declining pregnancies and births among teenagers; and (4) increased acceptance of single motherhood.

The falling number of children available for adoption has not coincided with a drop in the number of prospective U.S. adoptive parents. In fact, that number seems only to have grown, due in part to the phenomenal rise of the Christian adoption movement.[2]

Christian Adoption Movement: Ultimate Purpose of Adoption by Christians *"Is to Place Them [Children] in a Christian Home That They Might Be Positioned to Receive the Gospel"*

In [his book] Reclaiming Adoption, Dan Cruver bluntly declares, "The ultimate purpose of human adoption by Christians, therefore, is not to give orphans parents, as important as that is. *It is to place them in a Christian home that they might be positioned to receive the gospel.*" (Emphasis added).[3] Numerous other writers profess this same evangelical adoption tenet.[4]

The Brackeens have said they attend an evangelical Church of Christ church twice a week and cited their Christian faith as part of their motivation to adopt...[5]

Southern Baptist Convention's Resolution No. 2 on Adoption and Orphan Care

The intensity of this adoption zeal is encapsulated in the excerpt below of the Southern Baptist Convention's adoption of RESOLUTION NO. 2 ON ADOPTION AND ORPHAN CARE:

WHEREAS, Churches defined by the Great Commission must be concerned for the evangelism of children—including those who have no parents;

RESOLVED, That we call on each Southern Baptist family to pray for guidance as to whether God is calling them to adopt or foster a child or children; and be it further

RESOLVED, That we pray what God is doing in creating an adoption culture in so many churches and families can point us to a gospel oneness that is determined not by "the flesh," or race, or economics, or cultural sameness, but by the Spirit, unity, and peace in Christ Jesus; ... (Emphasis added).[6]

Academy of Adoption and Assisted Reproduction Attorneys; Eager to Support a "Hot Commodity"

Adoption is an incredibly lucrative business, with average adoption fees ranging from $15,000—$40,000 per child.

> With the supply of adoptable babies dropping, *foster children were becoming a "hot commodity,"* Dale Dove, who co-chairs the Academy of Adoption & Assisted Reproduction Attorneys' foster-care committee said (Emphasis added).

> Fostering to adopt became an option, but it, too, can be a long process, because the law requires that nearly all birth parents be given a chance before their rights are terminated. *Intervening in family court cases has emerged as a way for aspiring adopters to move things along and have more of a say in whether the birth family should be reunified.* (Emphasis added).[7]

Attorneys stood to make money in capturing this niche of representing foster parents who exploited the foster care system as a way to adopt children, arguing that the foster child had become attached to the foster parent and would be irreparably injured if separated from them.

Increasing Number of American Indian Children in Adoption and Foster Pool

Factor into the equation the increasing number of American Indian children in the adoption and foster pools. Their presence though is complicated by the Indian Child Welfare Act ("ICWA") . It affords rights to American Indian children, parents, and tribes designed to protect American Indian families, regulating proceedings for termination of parental rights, adoptions, and foster care placement involving American Indian children.[8]

Litigation Seeking to Declare ICWA Unconstitutional

Haaland v. Brackeen, 599 U.S. 255 (2023), is a case in which the plaintiffs sought to adopt American Indian children but ran into the bar of ICWA. They challenged ICWA as being unconstitutional on multiple grounds, claiming that it constitutes racial discrimination and violates the Equal Protection Clause. See Appendix 4, Part 1: *Haaland v. Brackeen*, 599 U.S. 255, 268-270 (2023). See Appendix 4, Part 2: Significant Parties Opposing ICWA.

The U.S. government and tribes argued American Indian identity is inherently political, and not racial. Tribes are governmental and political entities, not racial groups. This is a principle which was explicitly recognized by the Supreme Court in *Morton v. Mancari* in 1974. *Mancari* established that federally recognized Indian tribes and their tribal members represent a "political classification," not a racial class.

> As such, Congress may enact legislation, and executive branch agencies may implement policy, that is unique to Indian peoples without violating the requirement of equal protection of the law, when such legislation or policies are reasonable and rationally designed to further tribal self-government. *Morton v. Mancari*, 417 U.S. at 555 (1974).

The duty of the U.S. government to carry out the mandates of federal law with respect to American Indians is axiomatic, developed from treaties, congressional laws, executive orders and court decisions.

More than three-quarters of the 574 federally recognized tribes in the country and nearly two dozen state attorneys general across the political spectrum supported upholding ICWA.[9] Eighty-seven members of Congress submitted an amicus brief defending ICWA. In addition, medical organizations, law professors, public interest groups and others aligned themselves with the tribes. See Appendix 4, Part 3: Significant Parties Supporting ICWA.

Political Machine Seeking to Dismantle ICWA

Stanford Law Professor Greg Ablavsky in his analysis of what was the heart of this case cited two objectives of the group opposing ICWA: (1) an anti-tribal sovereignty movement seeking to attack tribal sovereignty; and (2) opposition to racial classifications.

> There are so many things that are at the heart of the case. Let's start with the politics. I think the case reflects both a very longstanding attack and critique of tribal sovereignty, what some scholars have called the anti-sovereignty movement, coupled with the culmination of a certain kind of conservative colorblindness that views anything that they deem to be a racial classification as anathema. The confluence of those two things in this case has been striking.[10]

Anti-Tribal Sovereignty Movement

For example, one of the ICWA opponents in the corner of the anti-sovereignty movement is the Citizen Equal Rights Foundation ("CERF"), established by the Citizens Equal Rights Alliance ("CERA"). According to an article in The Nation, Darrel Smith, Vice President, Board of Directors of the Citizens for Equal Rights Foundation, supports doing away with federal Indian policy:

> "Maybe we should get serious about the 14th Amendment and equality and do away with federal Indian policy and say, 'You're an American like everybody else is an American,'" said Darrel Smith, who serves on the board of directors of the Citizens for Equal Rights Foundation, a national organization that has long fought to diminish the power of tribes.[11]

This is in accord with his two articles on CERA's website.

> Federal Indian policy, modern tribal governments and the concept of tribal sovereignty violate the most basic principles of the American Revolution and also the vast majority of early Indian traditions.[12]

> Federal Indian policy is blatant official racism.[13]

Opposition to Racial Classifications

> Dismantling ICWA on the basis of race has been a years-long effort

by broader special interest groups as well. They include the Goldwater Institute, a conservative Arizona-based think tank that has argued against ICWA in court more than a dozen times, and Gibson Dunn & Crutcher, a corporate law firm that has fought tribes over land, water and gaming rights.[14]

Another ICWA opponent is the Pacific Legal Foundation ("PLF"), a California nonprofit, formed for the purpose of engaging in litigation in matters affecting the public interest. ... *PLF has extensive litigation experience in the areas of racial discrimination, racial preferences, and civil rights.* It has served as lead counsel in lawsuits challenging race-based laws ... and participated as amicus curiae in nearly every major United States Supreme Court case involving racial classifications in the past four decades. (Emphasis added).[15]

Conservative 'Go-to-Judge' - Federal Judge Reed O'Connor, United States District Court for the Northern District of Texas, Fort Worth

In addition, ICWA opponents found a favorable judge and forum:

Between 2015 and 2018, nearly half of the lawsuits that [Texas Attorney General] Paxton filed to overturn federal laws were heard by Judge O'Connor. In October 2018, Judge O'Connor ruled that ICWA violates the Fifth Amendment's equal protection guarantee, paving the way for the appeal to the Supreme Court.[16]

Law Firm in Multi-Billion Dollar Machine Opposing ICWA: Gibson, Dunn & Crutcher LLP, Law Firm

Gibson Dunn & Crutcher, a corporate law firm, represented the Brackeens pro bono. Journalist Rebecca Nagle, a Cherokee Nation citizen, investigated the *Brackeen* case and reported her findings in the podcast: This Land. Rebecca Nagle. Podcast.[17] In an interview with National Public Radio, she stated the following about Gibson, Dunn:

They represent a lot of casino companies. And so the fear is that this case is really kind of like the first domino in a row of dominoes, and that it's not really about the kids. It's not really about ICWA. It's not even really about these foster parents. It's more about this broader attack on tribal sovereignty. And if they can get ICWA to fall, then they can get all these other dominoes to fall. And so there was speculation about that. And then I think when they filed this lawsuit on behalf of this casino company in Washington called Maverick Gaming, it was kind of like the other shoe dropped. You know, the gloves were taken off, and it became pretty transparent.[18]

Gibson Dunn is [also] known for representing Chevron in the decade-long lawsuit brought by indigenous communities in Ecuador, as well as the corporation behind the Dakota Access Pipeline.[19]

Gibson, Dunn Counsel for Maverick Gaming, Casino Company in Washington, Argues Tribes Agreement with State Discriminates Based on Race and Ancestry

A Washington federal judge on Tuesday axed gambling company Maverick Gaming LLC's lawsuit challenging an agreement that gives the state's Native American tribes exclusive rights to sports betting in a ruling that Maverick plans to appeal to the Ninth Circuit.[20]

Maverick alleges in its lawsuit that the *tribal monopoly on sports wagering also "violates the [U.S.] constitution's guarantee of equal protection of the laws by irrationally and impermissibly discriminating on the basis of race and ancestry.*" (Emphasis added).[21]

SCOTUS Decision in Brackeen ICWA Challenge

On June 15, 2023, the U.S. Supreme Court released its decision in *Haaland v. Brackeen* and, in a 7–2 opinion, affirmed the constitutionality of the Indian Child Welfare Act (ICWA). The opinion was seen as a victory in Indian Country—a victory for Tribal sovereignty, Native children and families, and the future of tribes and Native people in the United States.[22]

In his concurrence in *Haaland v. Brackeen*, Justice Neil Gorsuch declared:

In adopting the Indian Child Welfare Act, Congress exercised that lawful authority to secure the right of Indian parents to raise their families as they please; the right of Indian children to grow in their culture; and the right of Indian communities to resist fading into the twilight of history. *Haaland v. Brackeen,* 143 S.Ct. 1609, 1661 (2023).

President's Pronouncement on ICWA Case Victory for Tribal Nations

I stand alongside Tribal Nations as they celebrate today's Supreme Court decision. This lawsuit sought to undermine the Indian Child Welfare Act—a vital law I was proud to support. The Indian Child Welfare Act was passed to protect the future of Tribal Nations and promote the best interests of Native children, and it does just that. The touchstone law respects tribal sovereignty and protects Native children by helping Native families stay together and, whenever possible, keeping children with their extended families or community who already know them, love them, and can help them understand who they are as Native people and citizens of their Tribal Nations. The Indian Child Welfare Act safeguards that which is most precious to us all—our children. Today's decision from the Supreme Court keeps in place a vital protection for tribal sovereignty and Native children.

Our Nation's painful history looms large over today's decision. In the not-so-distant past, Native children were stolen from the arms of the people who loved them. They were sent to boarding schools or to be raised by non-Indian families—all with the aim of erasing who they are as Native people and tribal citizens. These were acts of unspeakable cruelty that affected generations of Native children and threatened the very survival of Tribal Nations. The Indian Child Welfare Act was our Nation's promise: never again.[23]

Tribes' Hope Political Attacks on Tribal Sovereignty Cease

"We hope this decision will lay to rest the political attacks aimed at diminishing tribal sovereignty and creating instability throughout Indian law that have persisted for too long," said a joint statement from Cherokee Nation Principal Chief Chuck Hoskin, Jr., Morongo Band of Mission Indians Chairman Charles Martin, Oneida Nation Chairman Tehassi Hill and Quinault Indian Nation President Guy Capoeman.[24]

"ICWA Lives to Die Another Day"

Tribes have to be even more vigilant because the flood gates are open to challenge ICWA. The opponents of ICWA will continue to challenge it on grounds they see opened by *Haaland v. Brackeen*:

> One of the plaintiffs' attorneys, Mark Fiddler, told The Imprint that "the inequalities created by ICWA were not examined or considered by the Court," adding, "rest assured, more challenges to ICWA under equal protection grounds are guaranteed." In a tweet earlier in the day, he declared, "*ICWA lives to die another day!*" (Emphasis added).[25]

> The Goldwater Institute stated the high court's rejection of the legal challenges was "based largely on legal technicalities," and that, "while it's shameful that the Court would turn a deaf ear to the cries of our country's most at-risk children, it is at least gratifying that *the Court left open the door to future lawsuits challenging the race-based injustices caused by ICWA.*" (Emphasis added).[26]

> Lana Marcussen, counsel for Citizens Equal Rights Foundation and the Citizens Equal Rights Alliance, said, "Today's decision allows persons who are affected by potentially overreaching federal laws like ICWA to now challenge their constitutionality directly in the forum that is applying the law to them."[27]

The Cato Institute promised more cases where the children and parents have never lived in tribal relations or in Indian country:

> In *Haaland v. Brackeen*, the Supreme Court addressed important structural issues of Indian law, including the wide power of Congress and correspondingly narrow power of state governments. It did not reach potential problems for individual rights and equal protection created by the Indian Child Welfare Act of 1978, and *these remain to be resolved another day*. (Emphasis added).[28]

> *Future cases* may frame more sharply than this one did such questions as whether children and parents who have never lived in tribal relations or in Indian country may nonetheless be subjected to tribal

sovereignty and special custody presumptions because of blood descent alone. (Emphasis added).[29]

Op-Ed Written by Legal Counsel for Pacific Legal Org., *Adi Dynar*, Implies American Indian Societies Are Uncivilized

> *Civilized societies place a very high, if not the highest, value on protecting children.* The child's best interest animates every facet of family law: taking a child into government custody, foster placement, parent and caregiver conduct regulation, efforts to rehabilitate parents and caregivers, terminating parental rights, adoption, divorce, visitation rights, child support and so on. In all of these decisions, the individual child's best interest is and should be unquestionably paramount.
>
> *But ICWA fails that standard. It creates a separate and inferior child-welfare system for "Indian children," based entirely on their race or descent from a family member* with even a distant relationship to an Indian child. If a child is determined to be Indian, that child's best interest—if it is considered at all—is at best a secondary, tertiary or throwaway factor in matters of custody. Instead, the child becomes a pawn in a most sordid chess match, too often with tragic consequences. (Emphasis added).[30]

ICWA Kills—Another Op-Ed Written by Legal Counsel for Pacific Legal Org., Adi Dynar, Proclaims ICWA Is Merely to Protect Tribal Governments' Bruised Egos

> The Indian Child Welfare Act (ICWA) has been called "the most unconstitutional law in America," and for good reason. The 1978 law hasn't aged well. ICWA is a complicated law, but in essence, it creates a separate and inferior child-welfare system for "Indian children." Last week, the Supreme Court issued a decision in Brackeen v. Haaland — a case challenging the constitutionality of ICWA — that leaves this national embarrassment untouched and on the books. Congress must act....
>
> Enough is enough. We don't need any more dead children to prove that ICWA kills. It is time to treat Indian children, their parents, and extended family, as individuals. The child-welfare law in each state

already carefully protects parental rights and the child's rights. *ICWA disregards both to protect some tribal government's bruised ego.*

Congress must amend the Indian Child Welfare Act and excise these offensive, unconstitutional, and all too often deadly provisions. (Emphasis added).[31]

Federal and Colorado Adoption Legislation Enacted Giving Preference to Family and Kin and Restricting Intervention

Given the prevalence of foster parents abusing the system, federal and Colorado state legislation was enacted to *give preference to adult relatives and kin and restrict litigation intervention tactics.*

See Appendix 4, Part 4: Colorado - Pioneering State for Adoption Intervention Cases: 2,500 Cases Filed by 2022—Primary Attorney's Firm Used Discredited Child Adoption Expert.

See Appendix 4, Part 5: Federal and Colorado Adoption Legislation, Restricting Intervention.

See Appendix 4, Part 6: American Indian/Alaska Native (AI/AN) Families Attachment and Bonding Research.

Notes:

1. https://www.bia.gov/sites/default/files/dup/assets/bia/ois/pdf/idc2-056831.pdf (accessed online July 10, 2024).

2. Kathryn Joyce, "The Adoption Crunch, the Christian Right, and the Challenge to Indian Sovereignty," The Public Eye, no. 78 (Winter 2014). https://www.politicalresearch.org/2014/02/23/the-adoption-crunch-the-christian-right-and-the-challenge-to-indian-sovereignty/ (accessed online July 10, 2024).

3. Cruver, Dan, ed. Reclaiming adoption: Missional living through the rediscovery of Abba Father. Cruciform Press, 2010. https://www.thenation.com/article/archive/evangelical-adoption-

crusade/#:~:text=In%20Reclaiming%20Adoption%2C%20Cruver%20bluntly,positioned%20to%20receive%20the%20gospel.%E2%80%9D (accessed online July 8, 2024). Meske, John J. The Spirit of Adoption: Writers on Religion, Adoption, Faith, and More. Wipf and Stock Publishers, 2014. Evangelical adoption movement faces criticism, David Crary, Associated Press, October 28, 2013. https://www.csmonitor.com/The-Culture/Family/2013/1028/Evangelical-adoption-movement-faces-criticism / (accessed online July 8, 2024).

4. Mason, Corinne Wohlford, "Putting Government in its Place: Cultural Racism, Sentiment, and Neoliberalism in Contemporary United States Responses to Natural Disasters Abroad" (2015). All Theses, Dissertations, and Capstone Projects, pp. 105-106. https://griffinshare.fontbonne.edu/all-etds/161/ (accessed online July 8, 2024). Other writers: Moore's Adopted for Life: The Priority of Adoption for Christian Families and Churches (2009). Tony Merida and Rick Morton's Orphanology (2011). Daniel J. Bennett's A Passion for the Fatherless: Developing a God-Centered Ministry to Orphans (2011). Lawrence E. Bergeron's Journey to the Fatherless: Preparing for the Journey of Adoption, Orphan Care, Foster Care and Humanitarian Relief for Vulnerable Children (2012). Johnny Carr's Orphan Justice: How to Care for Orphans Beyond Adopting (2013). Jedd Medefind's Becoming Home: Adoption, Foster Care, and Mentoring—Living Out God's Heart for Orphans (2013). Morton's Know Orphans: Mobilizing the Church for Global Orphanology (2014).

5. Religion Plays a Role in Native American Adoption Case Before Supreme Court, Emily McFarlan Miller. November 10, 2022. https://churchleaders.com/news/438343-indian-child-welfare-act-religion-native-american-adoption-case-supreme-court-rns.html/2 (accessed online July 9, 2024).

6. On Adoption And Orphan Care. https://www.sbc.net/resource-library/resolutions/on-adoption-and-orphan-care/ (accessed online July 8, 2024).

7. When Foster Parents Don't Want to Give Back the Baby. The New Yorker. https://www.newyorker.com›magazine›2023/10/23 (accessed online July 1, 2024).

8. The Christian Groups Fighting Against the Indian Child Welfare Act, Kiera Butler. https://www.motherjones.com/politics/2023/02/the-christian-groups-fighting-against-the-indian-child-welfare-act/ (accessed online July 16, 2024).
Kathryn Joyce, "The Adoption Crunch, the Christian Right, and the Challenge to Indian Sovereignty," The Public Eye, no. 78 (Winter 2014). https://www.politicalresearch.org/2014/02/23/the-adoption-crunch-the-christian-right-and-the-challenge-to-indian-sovereignty/ (accessed online July 10, 2024).
Peter Smith, "Adoption Growing among Evangelical Christians," Orphan Care Alliance, excerpt from the Louisville Courier Journal. https://orphancarealliance.org/adoption-growing-among-evangelical-christians/ (accessed online July 10, 2024).

9. BRIEF OF 180 INDIAN TRIBES AND 35 TRIBAL ORGANIZATIONS AS AMICI CURIAE IN SUPPORT OF CHEROKEE NATION, ET AL. https://sct.narf.org/documents/cherokee_v_brackeen/cert_amicus_180.pdf (accessed online July 1, 2024).

10. Stanford's Greg Ablavsky on the Brackeen Indian Child Welfare Act Decision, June 30, 2023. https://law.stanford.edu/2023/06/30/stanfords-greg-ablavsky-on-the-brackeen-indian-child-welfare-act-decision/ (accessed online July 10, 2024). Rebecca Clarren, "A Right-Wing Think Tank is Trying to Bring Down the Indian Child Welfare Act. Why?" The Nation, April, 6, 2017. https://www.thenation.com/article/a-right-wing-think-tank-is-trying-to-bring-down-the-indian-child-welfare-act-why/ (accessed online July 10, 2024).

11. Rebecca Clarren, "A Right-Wing Think Tank is Trying to Bring Down the Indian Child Welfare Act. Why?" The Nation, April, 6, 2017. https://www.thenation.com/article/archive/a-right-wing-think-tank-is-trying-to-bring-down-the-indian-child-welfare-act-why/ (accessed online July 10, 2024).

12. The Tragedy of Tribal Sovereignty, Darrel Smith. https://citizensalliance.org/links-articles-4.html (accessed online July 16, 2024).

13. Blatant Racism. Darrel Smith. https://citizensalliance.org/major-concerns-12.html (accessed online July 16, 2024).

14. Rebecca Clarren, "A Right-Wing Think Tank is Trying to Bring Down the Indian Child Welfare Act. Why?" The Nation, April, 6, 2017. https://www.thenation.com/article/a-right-wing-think-tank-is-trying-to-bring-down-the-indian-child-welfare-act-why/ (accessed online July 10, 2024).

15. Amicus Curiae Brief of Foster Parents & Pacific Legal Foundation in Support of Chad Everett Brackeen, et al., Haaland v. Brackeen, Nos. 21-376, 21-377, 21-378 & 21-380 (U.S. June 1, 2022). https://www.supremecourt.gov/DocketPDF/21/21-376/226812/20220601155110941_PLF%20Amicus%20Brief%20-%20BRACKEEN%20-%202022.06.01%20-%20FINAL.pdf (accessed online July 15, 2024).

16. https://www.motherjones.com/politics/2023/02/brackeen-haaland-scotus-indian-child-welfare-act-icwa/ (accessed online July 1, 2024).

17. See This Land, CROOKED Media (2021). https://crooked.com/podcast-series/this-land [https://perma.cc/7SAZ-K3RE] (accessed online July 10, 2024). Patrice, Joe (November 8, 2022). "Most Firms Don't Advocate Cultural Genocide Pro Bono, But This Biglaw Firm Will! - Above the Law". Firm with deep anti-Native rights practice brings assault on Indian Child Welfare Act to SCOTUS free of charge. https://abovethelaw.com/2022/11/supreme-court-indian-child-welfare-act-gibson-dunn/ (accessed online July 1, 2024).

18. Id.

19. https://www.motherjones.com/politics/2022/11/supreme-court-indian-child-welfare-act-native-sovereignty-icwa-tribes/ (accessed online July 1, 2024).

20. https://www.law360.com/cases/627995dd5d4ae302f6ae96db/articles (accessed online July 16, 2024).

21. Heavy-Hitters Hired To Challenge Washington Tribes' Sports-Betting Exclusivity.

January 12, 2022. https://www.vixio.com/insights/gc-maverick-gaming-challenges-washington-tribes-sports-betting-exclusivity (accessed online July 16, 2024).

22. *Haaland v. Brackeen* Affirms the Constitutionality of ICWA, Grace Carson, January 22, 2024. https://www.americanbar.org/groups/crsj/publications/human_rights_magazine_home/native-american-issues/haaland-v-brackeen/#:~:text=Brackeen%20and%2C%20in%20a%207,people%20in%20the (accessed online July 16, 2024).

23. https://www.whitehouse.gov/briefing-room/statements-releases/2023/06/15/statement-from-president-joe-biden-on-supreme-court-decision-in-haaland-v-brackeen/ (accessed online July 16, 2024).

24. Indian Child Welfare Act Stands, Native Families Empowered 7-2 ruling hailed by Indigenous leaders as a victory for tribal sovereignty. Nancy Marie Spears. https://imprintnews.org/icwa/indian-child-welfare-act-stands-native-families-empowered/242263 (accessed online July 16, 2024).

25. What Does the ICWA Ruling Mean for Native American Kids, Timothy Sandefur. https://www.goldwaterinstitute.org/what-does-the-icwa-ruling-mean-for-native-american-kids/ (accessed online July 10, 2024).

26. Supreme Court Decision Is Latest Injustice Inflicted on Native Americans. https://www.goldwaterinstitute.org/supreme-court-decision-is-latest-injustice-inflicted-on-native-americans/ (accessed online July 10, 2024).

27. Indian Child Welfare Act Stands, Native Families Empowered 7-2 ruling hailed by Indigenous leaders as a victory for tribal sovereignty. Nancy Marie Spears. https://imprintnews.org/icwa/indian-child-welfare-act-stands-native-families-empowered/242263 (accessed online July 16, 2024).

28. https://www.cato.org/sites/cato.org/files/2021-10/41455-pdf-Schlott.pdf (accessed online July 10, 2024).

29. https://www.cato.org/blog/supreme-courts-icwa-ruling-doesnt-reach-individual-rights-claims (accessed online July 10, 2024).

30. How Congress Should Fix ICWA, Op-Ed Originally Published at Discourse Magazine, Adi Dynar, August 1, 2023. https://pacificlegal.org/discourse-magazine-fixing-the-indian-child-welfare-act/ (accessed online July 1, 2024). https://pacificlegal.org/staff/adi-dynar/ (accessed online July 4, 2024).

31. The Hill: Now more than ever, Congress must amend the Indian Child Welfare Act, Adi Dynar, Opinion Contributor, June 22, 2023. https://thehill.com/opinion/congress-blog/4061152-now-more-than-ever-congress-must-amend-the-indian-child-welfare-act/ (accessed online July 4, 2024).

14

OKLAHOMA CASES REGARDING TRIBAL CRIMINAL LAW JURISDICTION

2020: *McGirt v. Oklahoma* Case

In *McGirt v. Oklahoma*, 140 S. Ct. 2452 (2020), the U.S. Supreme Court held that Congress had never disestablished the Muscogee (Creek) Nation reservation in eastern Oklahoma; therefore, the State of Oklahoma lacked jurisdiction to prosecute crimes committed by or against Indians within the reservation.[1] Large areas of Oklahoma, including much of the City of Tulsa, are thus on reservation land.

2022: *Oklahoma v. Castro-Huerta* Case

The *Oklahoma v. Castro-Huerta* case (597 U.S. 629 (2022)) was a continuation of the state of Oklahoma's efforts to overturn the 2020 *McGirt* decision, which reaffirmed the Muscogee (Creek) Nation's Reservation had not been disestablished and, in effect, reaffirmed that much of Oklahoma remains Indian Country to this day for legal purposes. In the *Castro-Huerta* case, the U.S. Supreme Court fundamentally altered the long-established understanding of how criminal jurisdiction over non-Indians functions with respect to the federal government, state governments, and Tribal Nation governments. The Supreme Court held that the General Crimes Act (18 U.S.C. § 1152) does not preempt or otherwise limit state criminal jurisdiction to prosecute non-Indian defendants who commit crimes against Indian victims in Indian country. Thus, the federal government and the state have concurrent jurisdiction to prosecute crimes committed by non-Indians against Indians in Indian country.[2]

> In his dissent, Justice Gorsuch stated: "Where this Court once stood firm, today it wilts. After the Cherokee's exile to what became Oklahoma, the federal government promised the Tribe that it would remain forever free from interference by state authorities. Only the Tribe or the federal government could punish crimes by or against tribal members on tribal lands. At various points in its history, Oklahoma has chafed at this limitation....Where our predecessors refused to participate in one State's unlawful power grab at the expense of the Cherokee, today's Court accedes to another's." (Emphasis added).

NARF/NCAI Joint Statement on U.S. Supreme Court Ruling in *Oklahoma v. Castro-Huerta*, July 7, 2022

> "The Supreme Court's decision today is an attack on tribal sovereignty and the hard-fought progress of our ancestors to exercise our inherent sovereignty over our own territories," said National Congress of American Indians (NCAI) President Fawn Sharp.
>
> John Echohawk, Executive Director of the Native American Rights Fund (NARF) agreed. "Unauthorized and unconsented intrusions on tribal sovereignty are antithetical to tribal sovereignty and tribal treaty rights."[3]

SUIT's Statement on Sovereignty after Adverse Supreme Court Ruling in *Oklahoma v. Castro-Huerta*

Chairman Baker announced the SUIT's Statement on Sovereignty, on July 26, 2022, after the U.S. Supreme Court ruling in *Oklahoma v. Castro-Huerta*:

> The Supreme Court ruling on Oklahoma v. Castro-Huerta undermines the true definition of sovereignty, and restrains tribes' ability to govern themselves and ultimately protect tribal members and resources. "The [SUIT] statement on sovereignty reasserts the foundation for which the tribe operates and governs itself," said Chairman Melvin J. Baker. "The tribe will continue to fight to protect its inherent sovereignty which our past Ute leaders fought to

preserve through treaties and declared by federal law in exchange for the land stolen and the attempted eradication of our Ute culture and language." (Emphasis added).

The Southern Ute Indian Tribe is a sovereign and will remain a sovereign. The Mouache and Kaputa bands have retained their sovereignty through European settlement, the formation of the United States, the establishment of the Reservation, and the creation of the State of Colorado. The tribe's sovereign authority was not conferred on it by the federal government; rather, its authority is inherent, having always existed and having never been extinguished. The tribe exercises its sovereignty daily by operating the tribal government; exercising jurisdiction within the exterior boundaries of the Southern Ute Indian Reservation; overseeing its current territory; regulating and providing for the tribal membership; and acting on a government-to-government basis with other sovereigns, including the United States, the State of Colorado, and other tribal nations. (Emphasis added).[4]

Jurisdictional Quagmire Post-2022 U.S. Supreme Court *Oklahoma v. Castro-Huerta* Decision

Arvo Q. Mikkanen, Assistant U.S. Attorney & Tribal Liaison, U.S. Attorney's Office, Western District of Oklahoma, created a Criminal Law jurisdiction chart post *Oklahoma v. Castro-Huerta*, No. 21-429 (U.S. Supr. Ct., 2022), set forth in Appendix 5, detailing the confusion in this area of the law.

Notes:

1. https://www.bia.gov/sites/default/files/dup/tcinfo/castro-huerta_tribal_comment_summary_report_11.29.22_sgs_edits_508.pdf (accessed online July 1, 2024).

2. https://www.bia.gov/sites/default/files/dup/tcinfo/castro-huerta_tribal_comment_summary_report_11.29.22_sgs_edits_508.pdf (accessed online July 1, 2024).

3. https://narf.org/castro-huerta-v-oklahoma-scotus-ruling/#:~:text=With%20today's%20decision%2C%20Oklahoma%20has,governments%2C%20and%20Tribal%20Nation%20governments (accessed online April 23, 2023).

4. https://www.indiangaming.com/southern-ute-tribal-council-reaffirms-significance-of-tribal-sovereignty/ (accessed online April 21, 2023).

15

U.S. Congressional Committees on Indian Affairs

U.S. Senate Committee on Indian Affairs

The Senate Committee has jurisdiction to study the unique problems of American Indian, Native Hawaiian, and Alaska Native peoples and to propose legislation to alleviate these difficulties. These issues include, but are not limited to, Indian education, economic development, land management, trust responsibilities, health care, and claims against the United States. Additionally, all legislation proposed by members of the Senate that specifically pertains to American Indians, Native Hawaiians, or Alaska Natives is under the jurisdiction of the Committee. Tribes communicate directly with the Senate Committee, individually and through oversight hearings.

U.S. Senate Committee on Indian Affairs Oversight Hearing on Water as a Trust Resource: Examining Access in Native Communities

WASHINGTON, DC—U.S. Senator Brian Schatz (D-HI), Chairman of the Senate Committee on Indian Affairs, and U.S. Senator Lisa Murkowski (R-AK), Vice Chairman of the Committee, led an oversight hearing titled, "Water as a Trust Resource: Examining Access in Native Communities."

> "For too many Native communities, the total lack of access to clean and safe drinking water and sanitation facilities is an everyday reality," said Chairman Senator Schatz. "Ensuring water access is not just the right thing to do, it's the federal government's trust and treaty responsibility. It's our legal obligation—not just to reserve water

rights—but to live up to our promises and take affirmative steps to secure this access to the best of our ability."[1]

U.S. House Natural Resources Subcommittee on Indian and Insular Affairs

The Subcommittee on Indian and Insular Affairs oversees the relations between the federal government and Native Americans and U.S. Territories. The House Subcommittee also conducts oversight hearings. An example of the kinds of hearings they conduct is that of the high rates of missing and murdered indigenous women across the country.[2]

Major Congressional Statutes regarding American Indian Affairs

See Appendix 6.

Notes:

1. https://www.murkowski.senate.gov/press/release/schatz-murkowski-lead-oversight-hearing-on-water-access-in-native-communities (accessed online January 13, 2024).

2. https://www.c-span.org/video/?458789-1/missing-murdered-indigenous-women (accessed online January 13, 2024).

16

NEW ERA OF INDIAN SELF-DETERMINATION

1968: President Lyndon B. Johnson, Indian Self-Determination

Lyndon B. Johnson, "Special Message to Congress on the Problems of the American Indian: The Forgotten American," March 6, 1968:

I propose a new goal for our Indian programs: *A goal that ends the old debate about 'termination' of Indian programs and stresses self-determination*... The greatest hope for Indian progress lies in the emergence of Indian leadership and initiative in solving Indian problems. *Indians must have a voice in making the plans and decisions in programs which are important to their daily life.* ... (Emphasis added).

1970: President Richard M. Nixon, Indian Self-Determination

In a Special Message to Congress on Indian Affairs, President Richard Nixon denounced the Eisenhower-era policy of terminating Indian nations and announced a policy under which "the Indian future is determined by Indian acts and Indian decisions."

Richard M. Nixon, Special Message to Congress, July 1970:

> It is long past time that the Indian policies of the Federal government began to recognize and build upon the capacities and insights of the Indian people. ... The time has come to break decisively with the past and to create the conditions for a new era in which the Indian future is determined by Indian acts and Indian decisions....

Federal termination errs in one direction, Federal paternalism errs in the other. Only by clearly rejecting both of these extremes can we achieve a policy which truly serves the best interests of the Indian people. *Self-determination among the Indian people can and must be encouraged without the threat of eventual termination. In my view, in fact, that is the only way that self-determination can effectively be fostered.* ... (Emphasis added).

1975: Indian Self-Determination and Education Assistance Act

The Indian Self Determination Act of 1975 implemented the Indian self-determination policy that tribes had advocated for, allowing the growth of modern tribal governments where tribal institutions have stepped up and began overseeing federal programs in place of the BIA (e.g., education, health). The Self Determination Act facilitated that by providing the funds that usually went to the BIA to tribes so they could manage these programs.

Successive Presidential Administrations Confirm Tribal Sovereignty

Successive presidential administrations have affirmed this policy of protecting the integrity of tribal governments through the maintenance of federal-tribal government-to-government relationships.

> Ronald Reagan, Indian Policy Statement, January 24, 1983
> William Clinton, "Government-to-Government Relations with Native American Tribal Governments: Memorandum for the Heads of Executive Departments and Agencies," April 29, 1994
> George W. Bush, Memorandum for the Heads of Executive Departments and Agencies, "Government-to-Government Relationship With Tribal Governments," September 2004
> Barack Obama, Tribal Nations Conference, U.S. Department of Interior, Washington, DC, November 5, 2009
> Joseph Biden, Executive Order 14112 on Reforming Federal Funding and Support for Tribal Nations to Better Embrace Our Trust Responsibilities and Promote the Next Era of Tribal Self-Determination, December 6, 2023.

President Biden's November 22, 2022, Memorandum regarding Tribal Consultation

President Biden's 2022 Memorandum ordering Tribal Consultation expresses the unique, legally affirmed Nation-to-Nation relationship with American Indian and Alaska Native Tribal Nations and affirms the principles of Tribal Sovereignty, Self-Determination and Self-Governance.

Uniform Standards for U.S. and Tribal Government-to-Government Consultation

November 30, 2022, Memorandum on Uniform Standards for Tribal Consultation for the Heads of Executive Departments and Agencies

> *By the authority vested in me as President by the Constitution and the laws of the United States of America, it is hereby ordered as follows*:

The United States has a unique, legally affirmed Nation-to-Nation relationship with American Indian and Alaska Native Tribal Nations, which is recognized under the Constitution of the United States, treaties, statutes, Executive Orders, and court decisions. The United States recognizes the right of Tribal governments to self-govern and supports Tribal sovereignty and self-determination. The United States also has a unique trust relationship with and responsibility to protect and support Tribal Nations. In recognition of this unique legal relationship, and to strengthen the government-to-government relationship, Executive Order 13175 of November 6, 2000 (Consultation and Coordination With Indian Tribal Governments), charges all executive departments and agencies with engaging in regular, meaningful, and robust consultation with Tribal officials in the development of Federal policies that have Tribal implications.

17

WHITE HOUSE TRIBAL NATIONS SUMMIT DECEMBER 6, 2023

At the third White House Tribal Nations Summit December 6, 2023, President Biden declared a new era of collaboration with Native American tribes. *He issued a historic Executive Order on Reforming Federal Funding and Support for Tribal Nations to Better Embrace Our Trust Responsibilities and Promote the Next Era of Tribal Self Determination.*[1]

December 6, 2023: President Biden's Historical Contribution of Funding to Tribes for Improvement of Quality of Life

The Executive Order affirms that Tribal self-governance is about the fundamental right of a people to determine their own destiny and to prosper and flourish on their own terms. *It also affirms that Tribal governments must be treated as permanent, equal, and vital parts of America's overlapping system of government.* It ensures that Tribal Nations have greater autonomy over how they invest federal funding.[2]

U.S. Government Accountability Office's (GAO) Tribal Advisory Council

> Gene L. Dodaro, Comptroller General of the United States and head of the U.S. Government Accountability Office (GAO), announced the first appointments to GAO's newly established Tribal Advisory Council. *Christopher Adam Red, Auditor, Internal Audit Department, Southern Ute Indian Tribe, is a member of GAO's Tribal Advisory Council.* (Emphasis added).[3]

The Federal Initiative on Access to Capital in Indian Country—a multi-agency strategy to improve awareness of, access to, and utilization of federal funding resources for Tribal governments, Tribal enterprises, Native entrepreneurs, and CDFIs [will be under the jurisdiction of the *GAO's Tribal Advisory Council.*] (Emphasis added).[4]

Direct Funding to Tribes Critical

The direct funding to tribes ensures that Indian tribes will get the monies and have greater autonomy over how they invest it. *In the past states received monies with a federal expectation that a portion of the federal funding received would be earmarked for tribes. Certain states did not have a formula to allocate funds to tribes and they simply were not delivered to tribes or entities providing services to tribal members, such as urban Indian health organizations.*

Notes:
1. https://www.whitehouse.gov/briefing-room/presidential-actions/2023/12/06/executive-order-on-reforming-federal-funding-and-support-for-tribal-nations-to-better-embrace-our-trust-responsibilities-and-promote-the-next-era-of-tribal-self-determination/ (accessed online January 23, 2024).

2. https://www.whitehouse.gov/briefing-room/presidential-actions/2023/12/06/executive-order-on-reforming-federal-funding-and-support-for-tribal-nations-to-better-embrace-our-trust-responsibilities-and-promote-the-next-era-of-tribal-self-determination/ (accessed online January 23, 2024).

3. https://www.gao.gov/press-release/gao-makes-first-appointments-newly-created-tribal-advisory-council (accessed online January 13, 2024).

4. https://www.bia.gov/sites/default/files/dup/inline-files/access_to_capital_in_indian_country.pdf (accessed online June 13, 2024).

18

Sovereignty of Indian Nations

Tribes predate the Constitution, and Federal recognition and regulation of them does not make them part of the Federal Government. Tribal powers are inherent and not derived from the Federal Government.

Sovereignty

> Tribes were not granted sovereignty--the right to govern themselves; they have always possessed it. They have retained all of the authority of a sovereign government, unless diminished by treaty or statute.

The Supreme Court summarized this in *United States v. Wheeler* as follows:

> [O]ur cases recognize that Indian tribes have not given up their full sovereignty. ... The sovereignty that the Indian tribes retain is of a unique and limited character. It exists only at the sufferance of Congress and is subject to complete defeasance. But until Congress acts, the tribes retain their existing sovereign powers. In sum, Indian tribes still possess those aspects of sovereignty not withdrawn by treaty or statute, or by implication as a necessary result of their dependent status. 435 U.S. 313 (1978).

Certain of Indian Nations' Sovereign Powers:

Power to establish a form of government.
Power to protect their lands.
Power to determine membership.
Power to legislate or otherwise adopt substantive civil and criminal laws.
Power to levy taxes.

Power to license and regulate property and activities within their jurisdiction.
Power to zone.
Power to enforce environmental controls.
Power to regulate hunting and fishing.
Power to impose health requirements (e.g., COVID regulations).
Power to administer justice.
Power to exclude persons from territory or reservation.
Power to charter business organizations.
Power of sovereign immunity.[1]

Sovereign Immunity from Suit

Tribes, like states, possess sovereign immunity from suit. Congress, or a tribe itself, may waive a tribe's immunity from suit. Tribal sovereign immunity does not prevent suit by the United States. A federal statute may also abrogate tribal immunity such as the Indian Gaming Regulatory Act—only for suits brought by states to enjoin a Class III gaming activity conducted in violation of a tribal-state compact between the tribe and the state pursuant to the Act.

Collaborating with Other Tribes to Seek Social, Economic, and Educational Opportunities

National Congress of American Indians

> Founded in 1944, the National Congress of American Indians ("NCAI") is the oldest, largest, and most representative American Indian and Alaska Native organization serving broad interests of tribal governments and communities.[2]

NCAI Founding Principles

> To secure and preserve American Indian and Alaska Native sovereign rights under treaties and agreements with United States, as well as under federal statutes, case law, and administration decisions and rulings.
> To protect American Indian and Alaska Native traditional, cultural, and religious rights.

To seek appropriate, equitable, and beneficial services and programs for American Indian and Alaska Native governments and people.
To promote common welfare and enhance quality of life of American Indian and Alaska Native people.
To educate general public regarding American Indian and Alaska Native governments, people, and rights.[3]

Notes:

1. Section 1: The Governmental Relationship. p. 35. https://www.fs.usda.gov/people/tribal/trib-1.pdf (accessed online June 22, 2024).

2. https://www.ncai.org/ (accessed online June 21, 2024).

3. https://www.ncai.org/about-ncai/ncai-history#ncai-founding-principles (accessed online June 21, 2024).

19

DEVELOPING AND MAINTAINING ACTIVE RELATIONS WITH FEDERAL EXECUTIVE BRANCH, DEPARTMENTS AND AGENCIES

Tribal Communication with Federal Executive Branch

There are numerous examples of tribal communication with the executive branch, including those with the SUIT and the UMUT. SUIT member Diane Millich joined other Native women and tribal leaders on March 7, 2013, to celebrate with President Obama the reauthorization of the Violence Against Women Act. Millich opened the event and introduced then Vice President Joe Biden.[1]

In July of 2015, leaders from the Hopi Tribe, Navajo Nation, Ute Mountain Ute Indian Tribe, Pueblo of Zuni, and Ute Indian Tribe founded the Bears Ears Inter-Tribal Coalition. The Coalition represents a historic consortium to work collaboratively to protect and promote sacred, spiritual, historical, natural, scientific and cultural resources on lands within the Bears Ears landscape. ... Importantly, they've done all this with an intentional focus on healing and incorporating Traditional Knowledge into public land management. President Biden restored protections for Bears Ears monument, 4 years after Trump downsized it.[2]

Federal Executive Agencies with Tribal Trust Responsibilities

As of 1970, by law, the U.S.' federal departments and agencies are required to work in partnership with Indian tribes on a government-to-government basis and engage in "regular, meaningful, and robust consultation with Tribal officials in the development of Federal policies that have Tribal implications."

There are incredibly numerous executive agency-tribal relationships. A chart summarizing some of those relationships is set forth in Appendix 7.

Department of Interior

Mission: The U.S. Department of the Interior ("DOI") protects and manages the Nation's natural resources and cultural heritage; provides scientific and other information about those resources; and honors its trust responsibilities or special commitments to American Indians, Alaska Natives, Native Hawaiians, and affiliated Island Communities.[3] The head of the DOI is the Secretary of the Interior. The DOI has a staff of 70,000 employees.

Secretary of Interior Deb Haaland

Secretary Deb Haaland made history when she became the first Native American to serve as a cabinet secretary. She is a member of the Pueblo of Laguna in New Mexico.[4]

U.S. Military

Native Americans (American Indian and Alaskan Natives) have served in the military with great honor, dedication and distinction, building a legacy of courage, professionalism and selfless service that will inspire generations to come. Historically, American Indians have the highest record of military service per capita when compared to other ethnic groups. Today more than 9,000 Native Americans serve in the Total Force.[5]

Procurement Technical Assistance Center ("PTAC")

> The National Center's PTAC has provided American Indian owned businesses and tribal enterprises assistance with securing prime contract and subcontract opportunities with the Department of Defense, other federal, state, and local government agencies, and prime contractors. The DOI Assistant Secretary-Indian Affairs

Office of Indian Energy and Economic Development is also assisting tribes in this crucial area to help more Native businesses on and off reservations to secure jobs in the defense and related industries, thereby decreasing unemployment and increasing the economies of the reservations serviced. This is a huge financial engine for tribal businesses. The DOI's Office has prepared a whole online series on business primers on taking advantage of government and private procurement opportunities; building the legal infrastructure necessary for economic growth; and most importantly, the ability to obtain from a disinterested third party an analysis of each potential tribal business opportunity to ensure that scarce resources are prudently invested.[6]

Environmental Protection Agency ("EPA") Programs

In 1987, Congress amended the Clean Water Act ("CWA") to provide a mechanism for tribes to be treated as states for the purposes of administering certain CWA programs on their reservations. Interested tribes apply to EPA for approval to run specific water quality programs. A tribe's application must demonstrate that the tribe is federally recognized; that it has a government that carries out substantial duties and powers over a defined area; that it has authority to regulate surface water quality; and that it is capable of administering an effective water quality standards program. within their borders. If a tribe's application is approved by EPA, the tribe develops water quality standards ("WQS") based on identifying appropriate uses for reservation waters and then developing criteria to protect the designated uses of the water. *It is in the development of designated uses for reservation waters that a tribe can act to protect culturally significant uses of water, such as subsistence-related and ceremonial uses.*

The SUIT is authorized to be treated as a state under the Clean Water Act and is eligible to receive and compete for funding. Also, the U.S. Environmental Protection Agency Region 8 ("EPA") announced its approval of the SUIT's water quality standards under the federal Clean Water Act. This milestone approval culminates a 20-year effort by the Tribe's Environmental Programs Division. With EPA's action, the SUIT becomes only the 47th federally recognized tribe, out of

574 nationally, to have tribal water quality standards approved by EPA under the Clean Water Act. The approval allows the Tribe to protect the water quality of the lakes and rivers on its lands. With the approval of the SUIT's water quality standards, combined with the prior and separate EPA approval of the UMUT's water quality standards, all federally recognized American Indian tribes with reservation lands in Colorado now have EPA-approved water quality standards.[7]

The SUIT received the 2016 EPA Clean Air Excellence Award in Washington, DC[8]

Indian Health Service

Founded in 1955, the Indian Health Service, an agency within the Department of Health and Human Services, is tasked with providing health care services to American Indian and Alaska Natives, providing a wide range of culturally competent clinical health care and community services for about 2.8 million American Indians and Alaskan Natives through a system of federally and tribally operated facilities. The agency currently operates 24 hospitals, 51 health centers, and an additional 42 facilities across 37 states. The Indian Health Service also partners with tribal governments and urban Indian organizations (UIOs) to operate tribal and UIO-managed health facilities. Denver has one of these UIOs.[9]

Denver Indian Health and Family Services, Inc.

Denver Indian Health and Family Services, Inc. ("DIHFS") is an Urban Indian Health Program providing services to the American Indian/Alaska Native ("AI/AN") community in the Denver area since 1978. Although Denver is centrally located within "Indian Country", it is isolated from tribal health and Indian Health Service ("IHS") facilities. Over the years, DIHFS service area has grown to include the Denver-Aurora-Lakewood metropolitan area.[10]

U.S. Department of Health and Human Services' Office of Minority Health Investing in Food Sovereignty, April 2023

The U.S. Department of Health and Human Services' Office of Minority

Health has allocated $50M to develop and expand Indigenous food sovereignty initiatives. The Indigenous Animals Grant (IAG) supports traditional harvesting methods, and community animal protein processing operations. Eligible activities will demonstrate the ability to improve harvesting, processing, and packaging to create more resilient, diverse, and secure indigenous food systems.[11]

This is critical because:

> *To stave off starvation and malnutrition that would have resulted from disrupted food systems, during the nineteenth century the US government distributed food rations* on many Indian reservations, as stipulated in many treaties to make up for the loss of hunting, fishing, and agricultural lands. *These rations consisted of foods that were foreign to Indian people: beef, bacon, flour, coffee, salt, and sugar.* (Emphasis added).[12]

> *The disruption of traditional food system led to a number of health and social problems in Indigenous communities.* (Emphasis added).[13]

U.S. Department of Agriculture's Secretary Tom Vilsack at the White House Tribal Nations Summit, fulfilled long-standing tribal requests to strengthen food sovereignty and also to expand indigenous roles in forest management.[14]

September 2024: 'Gross Negligence': Shortages in USDA Food Aid for Native Americans Blasted in Congress

Agriculture Secretary Vilsack apologized to tribes for (1) delays and missed shipments and (2) delivery of expired food over the past four months. "Missed and delayed deliveries, empty shelves and bare warehouses have become commonplace," said House Appropriations Chairman Tom Cole, who is a member of the Chickasaw Nation of Oklahoma. "This is a dire issue that's evoked a genuine bipartisan and bicameral concern in Congress," said Cole in a rare joint Agriculture and Appropriations Congressional Committees Hearing. House Appropriations ranking member Rosa DeLauro, a Connecticut Democrat, said the food shortage was unacceptable. "It must be among our government's highest priorities that the most vulnerable communities among us do not suffer from hunger," she said. Further congressional hearings will be held to be assured the "crisis is resolved quickly." [Jennifer Shutt, South Dakota Searchlight. https://southdakotasearchrlight.com/2024/09/13/gross-negligence-shortages-in-usda-food-aid-for-native-americans-blasted-in-congress/ (accessed online September 20, 2024)].

Notes:

1. https://obamawhitehouse.archives.gov/the-press-office/2013/03/07/remarks-president-and-vice-president-signing-violence-against-women-act (accessed online June 21, 2024).

2. https://alnoba.org/our-work-worldwide/strategic-partners/bears-ears-coalition/ (accessed online June 21, 2024).

3. https://www.doi.gov/about (accessed online January 13, 2024).

4. https://www.doi.gov/secretary-deb-haaland (accessed online June 21, 2024).

5. https://www.usar.army.mil/NativeAmericanHeritage/#:~:text=Historically%2C%20American%20Indians%20have%20the,National%20American%20Indian%20Heritage%20Month (accessed online January 27, 2024).

6. https://www.bia.gov/as-ia/ied/online-primers-economic-development-glance (accessed online January 27, 2024).

7. https://www.epa.gov/newsreleases/epa-approves-southern-ute-indian-tribes-water-quality-standards (accessed online April 20, 2023).

8. https://www.sudrum.com/top-stories/2016/07/07/tribe-receives-epa-clean-air-excellence-award/ (accessed online June 21, 2024).

9. https://www.ihs.gov/aboutihs/ (accessed online January 13, 2024).

10. https://www.dihfs.org/our-story.html (accessed online April 20, 2023).

11. https://www.usda.gov/iag (accessed online January 13, 2024).

12. Mihesuah, Devon A., and Elizabeth Hoover. Indigenous food sovereignty in the United States. 2019, p. 6.

13. Lois Ellen Frank, How Native American Diets Shifted After European Colonization, Jul 12, 2023. https://www.history.com/news/native-american-food-shifts) (accessed online June 21, 2024). Rachel M. Gurney, Beth Schaefer Caniglia, Tamara L. Mix, and Kristen A. Baum, "Native American Food Security and Traditional Foods: A Review of the Literature," Sociology Compass 9, no. 8 (2015): 681-93.

14. https://www.usda.gov/media/press-releases/2023/12/06/white-house-tribal-nations-summit-usda-fulfills-long-standing (accessed online January 13, 2024).

20

Developing and Maintaining Active Relations with State and Counties

Colorado Commission of Indian Affairs

In 1976, the Colorado General Assembly created the Colorado Commission of Indian Affairs (CCIA) within the Office of the Lieutenant Governor. The Commission was designed to be the official liaison between the Southern Ute Indian Tribe, the Ute Mountain Ute Indian Tribe, and the State of Colorado. The Commission is fully committed to work on a government-to-government basis with each of the two Tribal governments and to maintain direct contact with the Tribes and American Indian/Alaska Native communities statewide. Specific duties of CCIA are outlined in the Mandated Responsibilities: CCIA Enabling Statute, C.R.S. 24-44-101. Statutory duties are set forth at C.R.S. 24-44-103.

The Commission is committed to facilitating communication between the Southern Ute Indian Tribe, Ute Mountain Ute Indian Tribe, the other 46 Historic Tribes of Colorado, American Indian/Alaska Native (AI/AN) organizations, state agencies, and affiliated groups. Their ongoing goal is to positively impact the lives of Colorado's American Indians and communities statewide.[1]

The breadth of issues impacting the sovereign relationship of the SUIT and UMUT and the state of Colorado is reflected in the extent of the high-level official membership of the CCIA and the numerous member state departments. Regional high-level federal U.S. officials from the U.S.

Dept. of Health & Human Services Region VIII and the Department of Justice are non-voting members of the Commission, but their presence on the CCIA demonstrates the government-to-government relationship of the SUIT and UMUT at the federal, state, county and local levels. Delegates from the two counties near the SUIT and UMUT Indian Country—La Plata County and Montezuma—and the Montezuma-Cortez and Ignacio School Districts ensure local input. Native community representation is also a part of the CCIA.

> Executive Director, Colorado. Dept. of Human Services
> Executive Director, Colorado. Dept. of Natural Resources
> Executive Director, Colorado. Dept. of Local Affairs
> Tribal Liaison, Colorado. Dept. of Public Health &, Environment
> Region 5 Director, Colorado. Dept. of Transportation
> Commissioner of Education, Colorado. Dept. of Education
> Executive Director, Colorado. Dept. of Health Care Policy & Financing [Oversee and operate Health First Colorado (Colorado's Medicaid program), Child Health Plan Plus (CHP+), and other public health care programs for Coloradans who qualify.]
> Executive Director, Colorado. Dept. of Corrections
> Staff Attorney, Native American Rights Fund
> Director, Office of Archaeology and Preservation, History Colorado
> Acting U.S. Attorney, Colorado U.S. Attorney
> Acting Regional Director & Executive Officer, U.S. Dept. of Health &, Human Services Region VIII
> Executive Director, Colorado. Dept. of Regulatory Agencies
> County Commissioner, La Plata County
> Superintendent, Montezuma-Cortez School District
> Superintendent, Ignacio School District
> County Extension Director, Montezuma County
> Director of Division of Community Engagement, Attorney General's Office.

The Colorado Commission of Indian Affairs acts as the convener and liaison for all issues related to American Indian issues in the State of Colorado. As such, we work in a variety of fields, including but certainly not limited to human services, natural resources, public health and environment, local affairs, transportation, education, health care and policy, corrections, public safety, Colorado history, Native American Graves Protection and Repatriation Act (NAGPRA), data collection, economic development, and State legislation affecting Native Americans. CCIA has an active Health and Wellness Committee.[2]

State Office of Liaison for Missing and Murdered Indigenous Relatives

The Office of the Liaison for Missing and Murdered Indigenous Relatives (OMMIR) is a newly created office established in 2022 through Senate Bill 22-150. The office shall serve as a liaison on behalf of the indigenous community on issues related to missing or murdered indigenous relatives, support the advisory board created in subsection (4) of this section, and carry out any duties assigned by the executive director. In carrying out its duties, the office shall collaborate with any relevant entities, including the Colorado Commission of Indian Affairs, federally recognized tribes, indigenous-led organizations, tribal and local law enforcement agencies, the Colorado Bureau of Investigation, and the Colorado State Patrol.[3]

Colorado State Legislation to Protect Colorado Tribal Lands from Annexation without Tribal Consent

Vice Chairman Lorelei Cloud testified in support of Senate Bill 24-193: Protect Tribal Lands from Unauthorized Annexation. The City of Durango planned to annex lands within the exterior boundaries of the Southern Ute Indian Reservation without the SUIT's consent.

> *This critical legislation is in response to the City of Durango's attempt to seize Reservation land from the Southern Ute Indian Tribe for the economic benefit of the City.* ... The Southern Ute Indian Tribe, a strong neighbor, proven business partner, and significant investor in the local economy, *will fiercely defend its land status, sovereignty, self-determination, and cultural heritage.*[4]
>
> "This is a momentous day for Colorado," Southern Ute Chairman Melvin J. Baker said. "The Southern Ute Indian Tribe is incredibly grateful to the sponsors of this bill for their unwavering support. ... *Their commitment echoes the deep respect Coloradans have for tribal sovereignty and the sanctity of reservation lands.*" ...

The bill ensures that any future annexation efforts within the Reservation boundaries must involve the Tribe's meaningful participation and consent. (Emphasis added).[5]

Colorado Tribal-State Compacts

Taxation Compacts

Tribal-state tax compacts regulate tax collection and distribution, providing income tax credits within Indian Country. The Taxation Compact between the Southern Ute Indian Tribe, La Plata County and the State of Colorado, CRS §24-61-102, is primarily concerned with allocating severance taxes on oil and gas production and property taxes. In 1992, the Ute Mountain Ute Indian Tribe and the State of Colorado also entered into a taxation compact.[6]

Gaming Compacts

The State of Colorado has gaming compacts with the Southern Ute and the Ute Mountain Ute Indian Tribes. Colorado CRS §12-47.2-101 through 103 - Tribal-State Gaming Compact.

No Internet Betting for Colorado Indian Tribes

When [Colorado] voters legalized sports betting in Colorado through Proposition DD in 2019, they also approved a state tax on sports betting, with most of the revenue dedicated to water conservation and other water-related projects.

Tribes do not pay state taxes on gambling revenue, however, and federal law requires they use gambling proceeds for Tribal services. In-person sports betting is allowed at the Tribes' casinos—the Sky Ute Casino Resort in Ignacio and the Ute Mountain Casino Hotel in Towaoc—but they have not been able to implement online sports betting. They have been blocked from working with the state's authorized sports betting operators because of the Tribes' different tax structure and dedicated uses for gambling proceeds.

"Enough is enough. We are tired of broken promises," Baker said.

"When I addressed this body last year, I made one request that the state resolve this issue. We met with the governor. He assured us that under the new director, one of the policy priorities would be to visit the Tribe and to resolve this issue."

[The governor's office said it has engaged with the Tribes about sports betting, but the parties have not yet been able to find a solution.]

Baker said the lack of progress drove the Tribes to turn to the legislature to solve the problem. They are working on a bill with Senate Majority Leader Robert Rodriguez to close the sports betting equity gaps. Rodriguez said the bill is in its early stages and may not be introduced before the end of this legislative session in early May.[7]

Southern Ute Indian Tribe Takes Legal Action against Colorado

The Southern Ute Indian Tribe announced that the Tribe has filed a lawsuit against the State of Colorado to ensure fair access to economic opportunities voted into law by Colorado voters in 2019. ... The Southern Ute Indian Tribe and the Ute Mountain Ute Tribe have been unfairly blocked by the Colorado Department of Revenue from engaging in online sports betting, despite longstanding State-Tribal Compacts explicitly allowing them to do so. After years of attempts to negotiate a fair agreement, the Tribe is asking the federal court for a preliminary injunction so they may compete in an economic market that, effectively, only non-Indian private entities have had primary access to in Colorado since 2020.[8]

Tribal Ordinances for Hunting and Fishing

Fishing and Hunting Memorandum of Understanding with State of Colorado

The SUIT has a Memorandum of Understanding (September 15, 2008) with Colorado regarding year-round hunting and fishing by tribal members in southwestern Colorado which is in accord with the 1874 Brunot Agreement signed by President Ulysses Grant, reserving the Tribe's right to "hunt upon said lands so long as the game lasts and the Indians are at peace with the white people".[9]

UMUT's Members Gain Access to Brunot Area for Hunting and Fishing

Hunting and Fishing was also opened up for UMUT members in 2013.[10]

Colorado's General Assembly, 2023, SUIT and UMUT

In an inaugural address to the Colorado General Assembly, Chairman Heart of the UMUT and Melvin J. Baker, Chairman of the SUIT, focused on gaming, water and education issues in separate speeches to nearly 100 Colorado lawmakers gathered for a joint session of the state Legislature. They were the first addresses delivered under Senate Bill 22-105 which invites tribal representatives to give an annual address modeled on the governor's State of the State speech. The Chairmen received a standing ovation.

Colorado's General Assembly, 2024, SUIT and UMUT

Chairman Heart of the UMUT and Melvin J. Baker, Chairman of the SUIT, addressed a joint session of the legislature and called on the state to follow through on its commitments to the Tribes. "Enough is enough. We are tired of broken promises," Baker said.

> "Colorado, like many states, has a turbulent history with tribal governments, which includes broken promises, and ignored treaties. The Southern Ute Indian Tribe and the Ute Mountain Indian Tribe have worked hard over the past decades to overcome that difficult history," Southern Ute Tribal Chairman Melvin J. Baker said in his address. "But I am here today to tell you that we are in danger (of) damaging that relationship because of the actions of a few individuals who would rather dishonor our longstanding commitments for the short term gain."

Baker and Ute Mountain Ute Chairman Manuel Heart repeated many of the same concerns they expressed last year, including state gambling laws that prevent Tribal participation in sports betting and a need for increased state support for health care infrastructure, education, and Tribal water rights.

> "We as a Ute people lost a majority of our aboriginal lands, which started with our first treaty in 1849 moving us to reservations. We did not become citizens until 1924. The Native Americans were the first in this country and the last to receive citizenship, and that history should be taught."

> "The Colorado Department of Gaming has prevented my tribe and our sister tribe from engaging in sports betting, refusing to honor the compact," stated Baker. "Today, not a single Native casino or Native-owned business is operating sports betting in the state of Colorado. There has been a four-year delay in the tribes entering this market."

> Both tribes entered into agreements with the state in 1995 allowing them to operate "any or all Class III gaming that is permitted within the State for any purpose by any person, organization or entity, now or hereafter.

> Health care, education and water

> Ute Mountain Ute Chairman Heart said investments in Indian Country continue to be insufficient, especially when it comes to health care, education and water access.[11]

SUIT and UMUT Assume State Historic Preservation Officers' (SHPO) Roles

> To "preserve and promote the cultural heritage of the Ute people," both the SUIT and UMUT have taken over the role of the State Historical Preservation office as it applies to their ancestral lands.[12] Governor Hickenlooper recognized and awarded Terry Knight (UMUT THPO Officer) and Lynn W. Hartman, Contract Administration, for their work on Historic Preservation.[13]

Civil Jurisdiction of State Governments Outside Indian Country

> Indian tribes and their members when outside of Indian country are subject to nondiscriminatory state law unless federal law provides otherwise. State courts have jurisdiction over suits against individual

Indians arising outside Indian country. Limits imposed by treaty, such as for off-reservation hunting, fishing and gathering rights, and statutes such as the Indian Child Welfare Act must be considered.

Colorado Counties

All of today's 64 Colorado counties have a history of Indian occupation. Forty-eight contemporary tribes are historically tied to the lands that make up the State of Colorado.

Notes:

1. https://ccia.colorado.gov/home/about-us (accessed online January 28, 2024).

2. https://ccia.colorado.gov/initiatives (accessed online June 23, 2024).

3. https://ccia.colorado.gov/resources/community-resources (accessed online June 23, 2024).
https://www.sudrum.com/news/2024/06/14/tribe-celebrates-state-bill-protecting-self-determination/(accessed online June 23, 2024).

4. SUDrum-20240517.pdf (accessed online June 23, 2024).

5. https://www.sudrum.com/news/2024/06/14/tribe-celebrates-state-bill-protecting-self-determination/ (accessed online June 23, 2024).

6. https://www.bia.gov/sites/default/files/dup/assets/as-ia/oig/oig/pdf/idc-038257.pdf (accessed online January 13, 2024).

7. 'Tired of broken promises': Ute leaders call on state to follow through on Tribal commitments, KUNC, Lucas Brady Woods, March 19, 2024 (accessed online July 2, 2024). Https://Www.Ksjd.Org/2024-03-24/Tired-Of-Broken-Promises-Ute-Leaders-Call-On-State-To-Follow-Through-On-Tribal-Commitments (accessed online July 2, 2024).

8. Southern Ute Indian Tribe takes legal action against Colorado, July 12, 2024. https://www.sudrum.com/news/2024/07/12/southern-ute-indian-

tribe-takes-legal-action-against-colorado/ (accessed online July 16, 2024).

9. https://www.southernute-nsn.gov/wp-content/uploads/sites/15/2019/08/2019-20_Brunot-Proc.pdf (accessed online April 20, 2023).

10. Carol Berry, Sep 13, 2018, January 17, 2013. https://ictnews.org/archive/ute-mountain-ute-hunters-and-anglers-gain-access-to-brunot-area (accessed online January 13, 2024).

11. 'Tired of broken promises': Ute leaders call on state to follow through on Tribal commitments, KUNC, Lucas Brady Woods, March 19, 2024 (accessed online July 2, 2024). Https://Www.Ksjd.Org/2024-03-24/Tired-Of-Broken-Promises-Ute-Leaders-Call-On-State-To-Follow-Through-On-Tribal-Commitments (accessed online July 2, 2024).

12. https://www.utemountainutetribe.com/cultural%20preservation%20THPO.html (accessed online January 13, 2024). https://www.linkedin.com/in/ute-mountain-ute-tribal-historic-preservation-office-b8bb81178 (accessed online January 13, 2024).

13. https://www.historycolorado.org/2017-stephen-h-hart-awards-historic-preservation (accessed online January 13, 2024).

21

PUBLIC SERVANTS

Serving in Federal and State Legislatures

Hon. U.S. Senator Ben Nighthorse Campbell, Northern Cheyenne

Hon. U.S. Senator Campbell served 12 years in the United States Senate. Prior to his service in the Senate, Campbell served three terms in the U.S. House of Representatives, preceded by two terms in the Colorado Legislature. After 22 years in Congress, he retired with accolades from so many. His years in Congress witnessed many victories for Native Americans. These included grants to individual tribes to establish and run schools and a law that required museums and the federal government to return all human remains and sacred objects that were taken from tribes without their consent. In 1993, the passage of the Religious Freedom Restoration Act guaranteed the right of Native Americans to practice traditional religions without state interference. He also worked to prevent fetal alcohol syndrome, a disease that affects the babies of mothers who drink alcohol during pregnancy. He sponsored legislation creating the Sand Creek Massacre National Historic Site and advocated for Ute water rights.[1]

Colorado State Legislature: Hon. State Senator Suzanne Williams, Comanche

From 1997-2012, State Senator Suzanne Williams (D-Aurora), Comanche, was the only legislator in the state of Colorado who was a registered member of an American Indian tribe. After serving 16 years with the Colorado General Assembly (under four Governors), she was prevented by term limits from running for reelection. Williams introduced numerous bills and resolutions that directly affected the American Indian community in the state of Colorado. In an interview with Reporter Simon Moya, Senator Williams was asked about what achievements she was most proud of from her 16 years in the Colorado state legislature. Here is her response:

> The first year in the House of Representatives I proposed a law that required Colorado public schools to teach American Indian history as part of the state history curriculum. Governor Roy Romer signed HB1186 into law on April 17, 1998. That was a good start—and it was a highlight, really, of my whole 16 years.
>
> Next, I presented a bill to ensure Colorado compliance with the Indian Child Welfare Act (ICWA), enacted by the state legislature in 2002, that required Colorado to follow the national ICWA law. See CRS §19-1-126 - Compliance with the Federal Indian Child Welfare Act of 1978.
>
> I presented a bill in 2004 for the issuance of the American Indian Scholars' license plate. The initial reason for the American Indian scholars' license plate was to provide some extra income for college expenses so Native students could fulfill their dreams and get a college degree. See CRS §42-3-217. It took two years to get that license plate bill passed. Administered by the Rocky Mountain Indian Chamber of Commerce ("RMICC"), it has been a huge success. In the first two years hundreds of dollars were given to Native students and after growing over the past decade, five $2,000 scholarships were awarded in 2010–2011 twelve years ago. As of November 12, 2022, through memberships and corporate sponsors, RMICC has awarded more than $330,000 in scholarships to help further the college education of Native students.[2]
>
> I introduced and Governor John Hickenlooper signed Senate Bill 12-057, A Bill for an Act Concerning Indigenous Language Instruction, on April 16, 2012. SB 12-057 allows Native American languages and culture courses to be taught in public schools. It allows an individual to apply to the District Board of Education for approval of a Native American language and culture instruction authorization, if the

individual has demonstrated expertise in a Native American language of a federally recognized tribe, even if not certified as a teacher. Senator Williams stated: "In the past children have been discouraged from speaking their native tongue in classrooms, and now we know that we should be allowing children to embrace their heritage. Allowing tribal elders to share their immense knowledge and experiences with children will enrich their educational experience and encourage them to connect with their roots." See CRS §22-60.5-111.

2010: Colorado State Senator Williams Introduces Indian Mascot Bill

The Indian mascot bill, introduced on January 20, 2010, SB 10-107, would have established a process to educate schools and communities about the Indians who used to live in their vicinity. After years of addressing this issue of inappropriate Indian mascots, in 2022 a bill was signed by Governor Jared Polis which set penalties for inappropriate naming of teams and schools in Colorado. Seeds often take many years to sprout.[3]

2012: Colorado State Senator Williams Introduces Genocide Resolution, SJR12-0466

The Colorado legislature passed resolutions condemning the genocide of Jewish, Armenian and Sudanese people. But after a marathon session tossing around numerous terms, the legislators failed to apply 'genocide' to America's treatment of its Native people; on April 20, 2012, they picked 'atrocity' instead. State Senator Suzanne Williams, who pushed a resolution on Native genocide, told Indian Country Today: "Every year the Senate and House legislators acknowledge the holocaust and genocide of Jewish people and we also acknowledge the genocide of Armenian people. But it's important to acknowledge the first genocide on our own land—the genocide of American Indians."[4]

2020: Colorado's Official Recognition of Columbus Day Terminated

In 2020, based, in part, on Senator Williams' negotiation, Colorado lawmakers established Frances Xavier Cabrini Day ("Mother Cabrini"), to replace Columbus Day. Mother Cabrini founded an order of religious women and 67 schools, hospitals, camps and orphanages.[5]

Federal Judiciary Appointments

Hon. Diane J. Humetewa, Judge, U.S. District Court, District of Arizona, May 2014

Judge Humetewa is the first female Native American Federal Judge. She spent much of her childhood on the Hopi and Hualapai Indian Reservations in Northern Arizona. Her parents raised her with Hopi traditions, culture, and language.

During law school at Arizona State University, she interned for Sen. John McCain, R-Ariz, in Washington, DC. After graduating from law school, she served as deputy counsel for the Senate Committee on Indian Affairs, of which Sen. McCain was the chairman.

She says that "Senator McCain would remind his Senate colleagues that the United States must adhere to the solemn vows it made when entering into Treaties with Indian tribes." She adds that Sen. McCain "truly believed that our Government, and those who worked in it had a moral obligation to uphold the promises made, and to avoid the past mistakes of the laws and policies that led to tribal population and government diminishment." Judge Humetewa notes that "Senator McCain's, along with my parents' view of public work as being noble work, all directly influenced my desire to be a public servant."

Chief Judge Snow of the District of Arizona adds that Judge Humetewa "has been invaluable in giving her extra time to educate judges on tribal life and cultures, in clarifying issues of access to justice and services, and in tirelessly serving as a leader and role model." Judge Humetewa enjoys running long-distance races throughout the country, in homage to her Hopi roots.[6]

Hon. Sara Hill, U.S. District Court for Northern District of Oklahoma, December 2023

The U.S. Senate confirmed Oklahoma's Sara Hill as a federal judge, overcoming GOP opposition.[7] She previously served as a special assistant U.S. attorney in the Northern District from 2014 to 2015 while simultaneously serving as the Cherokee Nation deputy attorney general.

She also served as the Cherokee Nation's secretary of natural resources from 2015 to 2019 and was assistant attorney general from 2004 to 2014.

"Sara Hill exemplifies Native excellence and legal leadership through her success as a litigator, policy advocate, and senior tribal government official for the Cherokee Nation," said National Native American Bar Association President Makalika Naholowaa.[8]

Notes:

1. https://bennighthorseconsultants.com/bennighthorseconsultants.com/About_Ben.html (accessed online April 23, 2023).

2. American Indian Scholars License Plate Introduced by Colorado State Senator Williams. https://ccia.colorado.gov/initiatives/education#:~:text=American%20Indian%20Scholars%20License%20Plate&text=Colorado%20residents%20may%20secure%20one,call%20303%2D629%2D0102 (accessed online April 20, 2023).

3. Mascot Bill Introduced by Colorado State Senator Williams. https://nahmus.org/indianmascotbill1.pdf (accessed online April 20, 2023).

4. https://nahmus.org/cogenocidelegislation.pdf (accessed online April 20, 2023).

5. https://www.cpr.org/2020/10/03/monday-is-colorados-1st-mother-cabrini-day-heres-why-the-state-chose-her-to-replace-columbus-day/ (accessed online April 20, 2023).

6. https://www.fedbar.org/wp-content/uploads/2021/04/JudicialProfile_Humetewa_TFL_MarApr.pdf (accessed online June 21, 2024).

7. https://idahocapitalsun.com/2023/12/19/us-senate-confirms-oklahomas-sara-hill-as-a-federal-judge-overcoming-gop-opposition/#:~:text=Sara%20Hill%2C%20the%20Nation's%20former,judicial%20positions%20in%20U.S.%20history (accessed online June 21, 2024).

8. https://narf.org/sara-hill-nomination/ (accessed online June 21, 2024).

22

SOVEREIGN SOUTHERN UTE INDIAN TRIBE

(1) Power to Establish a Form of Government

The purpose of their government is to exercise their inherent rights of self-government, to administer tribal affairs and to preserve and increase tribal resources.

SUIT's Constitution

> The Constitution of the Southern Ute Indian Tribe, which was initially approved on November 4, 1936 and subsequently amended on October 1, 1975 and August 27, 1991, authorizes and defines the Tribe's governing body as the Southern Ute Indian Tribal Council. The council is composed of seven (7) members (chairman and six (6) councilmen) all of whom shall be elected on an at-large basis for three (3) year staggered terms or until their successors are duly elected and installed.
>
> Subject to approval by the Secretary or the Interior, or his authorized representative, the tribal council may enact ordinances and codes to protect the peace, safety, property, health and general welfare of the members of the Southern Ute Indian Tribe and to govern the administration of justice through the tribal courts, prescribe the powers, rules and procedures of the tribal courts in the adjudication or cases involving criminal offenses, domestic relations, civil actions and the inheritance and probate of trust, real and personal property of tribal members within the reservation.[1]

SUIT's Council's Mission Statement

> We are a sovereign tribe, managing resources and protecting our culture as we serve our people now and into the future.
> We strengthen sovereignty by exercising self-determination and self-sufficiency.
> We act as guardian of Tribal natural, fiscal, human, and cultural resources through sound business practices demonstrating accountability, responsibility, and efficiency.
> We provide a foundation for our people to prosper, while sustaining Ute identity and quality of life.
> We foster quality relationships with respect and dignity.
> We communicate with our Tribal Members ensuring they are aware of important issues and building trust.[2]

The SUIT is actively involved in providing housing and loan programs for tribal members.

SUIT's Boards and Committees

Election Board

> The Election Board is responsible for conducting and certifying tribal elections.[3]

Wildlife Advisory Board

> The purpose of the Wildlife Advisory Board is to work in an advisory capacity to the Tribal government on the development of wildlife regulations, including, but not limited to, the establishment of all hunting and fishing seasons, bag limits, species restrictions, guiding and outfitting rules, and other regulations related to the harvest of game animals under the jurisdiction of the Tribe.[4]

Powwow Committee

> The Powwow Committee is responsible for the Bear Dance and Tribal Fair Powwow.[5]

Royalty Committee

The Southern Ute Indian Tribe's Royalty are to nurture and promote the positive image of the Tribe.[6]

Boys and Girls Club

The Boys and Girls Club Board of Directors creates the club's vision, plans programs, develops funding, and more.[7]

Boys and Girls Club of the Southern Ute Indian Tribe CEO, Bruce LeClaire, received a "Recognition of Exemplary Service" national award from the Boys & Girls Clubs of America on June 14, 2024.[8]

The Sunshine Cloud Smith Youth Advisory Council is a group of young Southern Ute Tribal members that engage in community service and leadership activities and are an influential voice for their community.[9]

Southern Ute Indian Tribe's Statement on Sovereignty after Adverse U.S. Supreme Court Ruling in *Oklahoma v. Castro-Huerta*

Chairman Baker announced the Southern Ute Indian Tribe's Statement on Sovereignty, on July 26, 2022, after the U.S. Supreme Court ruling in *Oklahoma v. Castro-Huerta*, 142 S. Ct. 2486 (2022):

> The Supreme Court ruling on Oklahoma v. Castro-Huerta undermines the true definition of sovereignty, and restrains tribes' ability to govern themselves and ultimately protect tribal members and resources. "The [Southern Ute Indian Tribe] statement on sovereignty reasserts the foundation for which the tribe operates and governs itself," said Chairman Melvin J. Baker. "The tribe will continue to fight to protect its inherent sovereignty which our past Ute leaders fought to preserve through treaties and declared by federal law in exchange for the land stolen and the attempted eradication of our Ute culture and language."
>
> The Southern Ute Indian Tribe is a sovereign and will remain a sovereign. The Mouache and Kaputa bands have retained their

sovereignty through European settlement, the formation of the United States, the establishment of the Reservation, and the creation of the State of Colorado. The tribe's sovereign authority was not conferred on it by the federal government; rather, its authority is inherent, having always existed and having never been extinguished. The tribe exercises its sovereignty daily by operating the tribal government; exercising jurisdiction within the exterior boundaries of the Southern Ute Indian Reservation; overseeing its current territory; regulating and providing for the tribal membership; and acting on a government-to-government basis with other sovereigns, including the United States, the State of Colorado, and other tribal nations.[10]

(2) Power to Legislate

The SUIT has exercised its Power to Legislate or Otherwise Adopt Substantive Civil and Criminal Laws by enacting the Tribe's Code promulgating civil, criminal and other laws. It includes laws applicable to: Civil Procedure; Criminal Procedure; Election Code; Gaming; Tax Code; Tribal Employment Rights; Membership; Range, Wildlife; Traffic; and Exclusion and Removal.[11]

(3) Power to Administer Justice

Its Power to Administer Justice is exercised by its Tribal Department of Justice and Regulatory Administration:

Mission: The Southern Ute Indian Tribal Department of Justice and Regulatory Administration is responsible for ensuring fair and consistent application of laws and regulations by the divisions within the Department in order to protect the resources, membership, sovereignty, culture, and traditions of the Southern Ute Indian Tribe.[12]

SUIT's Court

Mission: The Tribal Court exercises and protects the sovereignty and jurisdiction of the Southern Ute Indian Tribe, providing a forum for the enforcement of Tribal law and the administration of justice, while honoring its culture.[13]

SUIT's Legal Department

> Mission: The mission of the Legal Department is to provide timely, quality, and effective legal advice and support to the Southern Ute Indian Tribal Council and Tribal entities in furtherance and protection of the Tribe's sovereignty, constitution, and laws.[14]

SUIT's Police Department

> Mission: To ensure that professional, effective, and efficient law enforcement services are provided utilizing accepted law enforcement techniques and practices to uphold the constitutional sovereignty and the customs of the Southern Ute Indian Tribe. SUPD's services shall provide for protection of lives and property for all persons visiting, residing, or traveling within the exterior boundaries of the Southern Ute Indian Tribe.[15]

> The Southern Ute Police Department (SUPD) patrols 677,622 acres of Southwestern Colorado covering parts of La Plata, Archuleta, and Montezuma counties. It collaborates with the Ignacio Police Department that has jurisdiction over the Town of Ignacio, which is located within the boundaries of the reservation.

(4) Power to Protect Reservation Land

City of Durango's Unilateral Secret Plan to Annex Southern Ute Indian Reservation Land

Chairman of the SUIT, Melvin J. Baker, informed the public of the City of Durango's attempt to annex Reservation land and the Tribe's response:

> "The Tribe will stand firm in protecting its lands and sovereignty. We will protect the health, safety, and welfare of our tribal members and future generations."

Also,

> It was over 140 years ago that Felix Brunot, Chairman of the Board

of Indian Commissioners, made promises and assurances to the Utes about protecting tribal interests while secretly hiding his intentions to turn over 3.7 million acres of land reserved to the Utes in the Treaty of 1868 to mining interests. Despite evidence of his wrongdoing, Congress approved the agreement he reached in 1874, resulting in the loss of Ute land to state jurisdiction.

... this year the Tribe experienced another attack with the actions of the City of Durango (City) in attempting to annex Reservation land, which Tribal Council swiftly addressed.

We believe it is important for everyone to know exactly what City employees were doing to secretly annex Reservation lands since they have chosen not to honestly disclose it themselves.

Therefore, Tribal Council requested a meeting, which was held in March of 2023. Barbara Noseworthy, the City's Mayor at the time, acknowledged the lack of communication with the Tribe on these and other material issues and apologized to the Tribal Council for that shortcoming. She assured the Tribe that Scott Shine, the City's Community Development Director, would provide monthly updates regarding the La Posta project.

What the Tribe actually received from the City of Durango was largely silence....

Therefore, on March 26, Chairman Baker wrote then City Mayor Melissa Youssef, insisting that the City not move forward with its plans to annex Reservation lands. As Chairman Baker expressed in that letter:

"On behalf of the Tribal Council, this letter is to make clear to the City of Durango that the Southern Ute Indian Tribe intends to oppose any efforts by the City to annex lands within the exterior boundaries of the Southern Ute Indian Reservation without our explicit consent. The City's effort to take tribal lands is part of a shameful legacy that should have no place in our current time. We will no longer tolerate broken treaties and promises...

> Efforts to take Reservation land should be an artifact of history. It is troubling that today, we have to fight such efforts by the City. To be clear: we will continue to protect what remains of our homeland from annexation without our consent. We will not tolerate any violation of our Treaty rights. We ask that you respect the Tribe's sovereignty as we respect yours. We ask that any further plans for annexation of Reservation lands immediately cease."

Mayor Youssef chose not to respond to the Chairman. Instead, she sent a letter to various government officials, insisting that the City had no plans for annexation and had prepared no petitions for annexation. Instead, it was simply performing due diligence in case there was an annexation request from a landowner.

Not only were City employees actively engaging in the annexation of Reservation lands, but they were also questioning the Tribe's treaties and longstanding legal principles establishing the Tribe's sovereignty and right of self-government within the Reservation boundaries.

Tribal Council offered to discuss the matter with the City Council, which was refused. This left the Tribal Council with a number of options. As the first option, the Tribe authorized legislation, Senate Bill 24-193, with bipartisan support in the Colorado legislature, ensuring there could be no annexation of Reservation lands without the Tribe's consent. ... SB 24-193 passed unanimously in the Committee and the full Senate.[16]

City of Durango's Illegal Unilateral Secret Plan to Tap into Water at Lake Nighthorse Campbell

> Chairman Baker also stated it would oppose the City's plans to place a pipeline to Lake Nighthorse where the water interests are principally those of the Southern Ute and the Ute Mountain Ute Tribes and the City's interests are minimal.[17]

(5) Power to Protect Its Children

Indian Child Welfare Act ("ICWA")

The SUIT is strongly committed to upholding ICWA. Chairman Baker attended the signing by Gov. Polis (D-Colorado) on May 4, 2023, of Senate Bill 23-211, ensuring Colorado's compliance with ICWA.[18]

(6) Power to Manage Its Resources

SUIT's Department of Natural Resources

> Mission: The Department of Natural Resources is empowered by the Southern Ute Indian Tribal Council with the mission to develop, administer, and manage the natural resources of the Southern Ute Indian Reservation for the benefit of the Tribe and Tribal Members. The Department is entrusted with promoting the beneficial use, protection, conservation, preservation, and developmental enhancement of the Tribe's natural resource by using sound administrative, ecological, cultural, socioeconomic, and educational methods for the benefit of present and future generations.[19]

SUIT's Environmental Programs Department

> Mission: The mission of the Environmental Programs Department is to make available the resources needed to protect the health, welfare, and environment of the Tribal membership and the Reservation.[20]

SUIT's Utilities Management

The Southern Ute Utilities Division is the Tribe's utility company.[21]

(7) Power to Establish Tribal and Individual Tribal Member Enterprises on Indian Lands, Communities, or Reservations

SUIT's Businesses

> Southern Ute Indian Tribal business activity generates millions of dollars each year for La Plata and Archuleta Counties. The Tribe is aggressively creating and operating new businesses both on and off Reservation in the areas of oil and gas production, natural gas gathering, real estate development, housing construction, and gaming. The Tribe is currently the largest employer in La Plata

County and supports many area non-profit organizations.

Sky Ute Casino Resort

The Sky Ute Casino Resort is owned and operated by the Southern Ute Indian Tribe. There is a hotel, conference center, entertainment, dining, other family activities (bowling, swimming, mini-golf), and outdoor adventures in southwest Colorado. The Southern Ute Cultural Center and Museum, the Durango & Silverton Narrow Gauge Railroad, Mesa Verde National Park, Purgatory Resort, Chimney Rock Archaeological Heritage Site, and Navajo Lake are all in close proximity, and the opportunities for skiing, camping, hiking, fishing, and white water rafting abound.[22]

Southern Ute Indian Tribe Growth Fund

The Southern Ute Indian Tribe Growth Fund operates and manages the Southern Ute Indian Tribe's businesses and business investments. In this role, the Growth Fund oversees a significant portfolio of companies and investments in energy, real estate, construction, and private equity. The Growth Fund's headquarters are located in the heart of the Southern Ute Indian Reservation in Ignacio, Colorado. Since the Tribe created the Growth Fund in 2000, it has committed substantial capital to a broadening range of businesses and investments. The value of the Growth Fund's holdings has grown substantially. Operations and assets are spread out over fourteen states and the Gulf of Mexico.[23]

Red Willow Production Company

Red Willow Production Company is a private oil and gas exploration and production company owned by the Southern Ute Indian Tribe. Founded in 1992, it holds an interest in over 1,800 operated and non-operated wells with net production in excess of 70 billion cubic feet of gas equivalent per year. Although Red Willow has expanded operations significantly off the reservation, the San Juan Basin remains the backbone of the company's operations. The company also has a significant interest in a number of projects in the Deepwater Gulf of Mexico and is actively developing assets in the Delaware basin in West Texas and other onshore regions.[24]

Red Cedar Gathering Company

Red Cedar Gathering is a natural gas gathering and treating company located in La Plata County, Colorado. Operations occur primarily on the Southern Ute Indian Reservation. Gas is produced from conventional and coal seam sources in the Mesa Verde group of the San Juan Basin geologic province. Pipeline quality gas is delivered at several locations on the edge of the gathering system for Intrastate and Interstate transport to market.[25]

GF Properties Group

GF Properties Group, LLC is a wholly owned subsidiary of the Southern Ute Growth Fund engaged in real estate investment, development and management activities through direct ownership and nationally recognized partnerships.[26]

GF Private Equity Group, LLC

GF Private Equity Group, LLC is one of several component companies of the Southern Ute Growth Fund—a diversified investment and business management organization owned by the Southern Ute Indian Tribe. The Tribe has achieved extraordinary financial and business success, having earned a triple-A rating from the Fitch and Standard & Poor's rating agencies and amassing a considerable investment base. The Southern Ute Growth Fund is the business investment arm of the Tribe.[27]

GF Ventures, LLC

The Southern Ute Indian Tribe has a long history of progressive business building and agile capital. In 2019, the Southern Ute Growth Fund created GF Ventures, LLC to manage the Tribe's direct investment in new industries and markets. GF Ventures is dedicated to discovering and managing new business development opportunities resulting from direct investment, business acquisition and strategic partnerships.[28]

SUIT's Cultural Museum

Artwork, artifacts and photographs are exhibited at the Museum. It is an excellent source for information about the Tribe.[29]

(8) Power to Manage Health Care

SUIT's Health Department

> Mission: Strengthening the circle of wellness by providing progressive, traditionally balanced, compassionate, comprehensive healthcare to members of the Southern Ute Indian Tribe and other American Indian and Alaska Natives.
>
> Our Goal: The goal of the Tribal Health Department is to be the first choice for primary and preventive health care for its beneficiaries; to be their medical home by providing all necessary healthcare services and assisting with navigation for all their healthcare needs.[30]

(9) Power to Manage Education

Department of Education

> Mission: The Department of Education's goal is to encourage, provide resources, and assist Tribal Members seeking an education at all levels. The department works to provide opportunities for the membership, other American Indians, and employees to enhance their education and employment. The director and staff will communicate and collaborate with students to help them progress, remain consistent with program policies, as well as remain compliant with public and private educational institutes.[31]

Southern Ute Indian Montessori Academy

> Mission Statement: The Southern Ute Indian Montessori Academy will provide a strong educational foundation to preserve and share the Southern Ute Indian culture and language within a Montessori environment.
> Vision Statement: To provide an environment that creates future tribal and world leaders who appreciate and support their culture, language, family, and lifelong learning.[32]

American Indian Boarding School Trauma Still Present

The SUIT doesn't want its children to go through the brutal assimilation processes of the U.S. Indian boarding schools.

> "When children returned to their communities, they were unable to communicate with their loved ones and were sometimes ostracized by their own communities," said Chairman Baker in a statement. "This traumatic experience produced intergenerational trauma that continues to manifest itself in numerous ways throughout Indian country, such as abuse, such as substance abuse, as well as psychological and emotional disorders, which result in lower graduation rates, poverty and lower life expectancy."... "In order to heal from the generational trauma, we must confront the past and shed light on the hidden cruelty," Baker said.[33]

Chairman Baker also supported the Colorado legislation for Native American students' right to wear tribal regalia at graduation.

> "Schools asking Native American students to remove or throw away items is like a school asking a student to get rid of a Jewish or Christian symbol," said Melvin Baker in his legislative testimony. He added that the U.S. has a history of trying to erase Native American culture, and the bill would ensure students get to honor their identity and their achievement. "Tribal regalia plays a unique role for graduating Native students," Baker said. "These items are often gifted to students by parents or tribal elders in recognition of this achievement."[34]

On May 4, 2023, Chairman Baker attended Governor Polis' (D-Colorado) signing of Senate Bill 23-202, Wearing Of Native American Traditional Regalia, which allows Native American graduates to wear traditional regalia at graduation ceremonies. It applies to both Colorado's public schools and universities.

Bison

> Herds of bison were seen on the eastern plains of Colorado up to 1871, but all have since disappeared, due to the commercial

huntsmen and hide gatherers. The wholesale decimation began in great force and for a distinct purpose—that of collecting hides—in 1869-70. The railways afforded transportation for the hides ($1-2 apiece), heads, and the edible parts of the carcasses. Then came a cloud of bone gatherers, who collected the whitened remnants of skeletons and sold them at five dollars a ton, to be converted into buttons, knife handles, combs and fertilizers. At nearly all the railway stations vast heaps of these bones were stacked up, awaiting shipment to markets east of the Missouri. The Kansas Pacific and Atchison, Topeka & Santa Fe took away hundreds of carloads.

Leavenworth became a trading center for buffalo hides, and tanneries found even more uses for the material, such as making drive belts for industrial machines and grinding buffalo bones into fertilizer. In some places, buffalo tongues became a delicacy in fine restaurants. Soon, the demand for buffalo had increased to such a degree that year-round work was available for buffalo hunters.... Armed with powerful, long-range rifles, individual hunters could kill as many as 250 buffalo a day. Tanneries paid as much as $3.00 per hide and 25¢ for each tongue, which made a nice living for hundreds of men, including Wyatt Earp, Bat Masterson, Pat Garrett, Wild Bill Hickok, and William F. Cody, just to name a few. ... By the 1880s, over 5,000 hunters and skinners were involved in the trade.[35]

General Phil Sheridan stated: "These men have done more in the last two years, and will do more in the next year, to settle the vexed Indian question, than the entire regular army has done in the last forty years. They are destroying the Indians' commissary. And it is a well known fact that an army losing its base of supplies is placed at a great disadvantage. Send them powder and lead, if you will; but for a lasting peace, let them kill, skin and sell until the buffaloes are exterminated. Then your prairies can be covered with speckled cattle."[36]

SUIT's Bison Herd

Given the tragic history of the decimation of bison herds across the U.S., it is encouraging to see the resurgence of tribal buffalo herds. SUIT's bison herd, though, is at maximum capacity due to environmental restrictions.[37]

Notes:

1. https://www.southernute-nsn.gov/government/ (accessed online January 13, 2024).

2. https://www.southernute-nsn.gov/government/southern-ute-tribal-council/ (accessed online June 21, 2024).

3. https://www.southernute-nsn.gov/election-board/ (accessed online January 13, 2024).

4. https://www.southernute-nsn.gov/wildlife-advisory-board/ (accessed online January 13, 2024).

5. https://www.southernute-nsn.gov/powwow-committee/ (accessed online January 13, 2024).

6. https://www.southernute-nsn.gov/royalty-committee/ (accessed online January 13, 2024).

7. https://www.bgcsu.org/board-of-directors/ (accessed online January 13, 2024).

8. https://www.sudrum.com/news-main-article/2024/06/14/leclaire-earns-recognition-at-bgc-national-conference-in-atlanta/ (accessed online June 23, 2024).

9. https://www.southernute-nsn.gov/education/ (accessed online January 13, 2024).

10. https://www.indiangaming.com/southern-ute-tribal-council-reaffirms-significance-of-tribal-sovereignty/ (accessed online April 21, 2023).

11. https://www.southernute-nsn.gov/government/tribal-code/ (accessed online January 13, 2024).

12. https://www.southernute-nsn.gov/justice-and-regulatory/ (accessed online January 13, 2024).

13. https://www.southernute-nsn.gov/tribal-court/ (accessed online January 13, 2024).

14. https://www.southernute-nsn.gov/legal/ (accessed online January 13, 2024).

15. https://www.southernute-nsn.gov/justice-and-regulatory/supd/ (accessed online January 13, 2024).

16. Durango's Secret Efforts to Annex Reservation Lands, May 17, 2024, Southern Ute Indian Tribe. https://www.sudrum.com/top-stories/2024/05/17/durangos-secret-efforts-to-annex-reservation-lands/ (accessed online July 2, 2024).

17. Durango's Secret Efforts to Annex Reservation Lands, May 17, 2024, Southern Ute Indian Tribe. https://www.sudrum.com/top-stories/2024/05/17/durangos-secret-efforts-to-annex-reservation-lands/ (accessed online July 2, 2024).

18. https://news.kgnu.org/2023/05/colorado-creates-state-law-to-protect-indian-child-welfare-act/ (accessed online May 9, 2023).

19. https://www.southernute-nsn.gov/natural-resources/ (accessed online January 13, 2024).

20. https://www.epa.gov/newsreleases/epa-approves-southern-ute-indian-tribes-water-quality-standards (accessed online April 20, 2023).

21. https://www.suitutil.com/ (accessed online April 20, 2023).

22. https://www. skyutecasino.com/ (accessed online April 21, 2023).

23. https://www.sugf.com/ (accessed online April 21, 2023).

24. https://www.rwpc.us/ (accessed online April 21, 2023).

25. https://www. redcedargathering.com/ (accessed online April 21, 2023).

26. https:// www.gfpropertiesgroup.com/ (accessed online April 21, 2023).

27. https://www.gfprivateequity.com/ (accessed online April 21, 2023).

28. https://www.sugf.com/gf-ventures-llc/ (accessed online April 21, 2023).

29. https://www.southernutemuseum.org/ (accessed online April 20, 2023).

30. https://www.southernute-nsn.gov/tribal-health/ (accessed online January 13, 2024).

31. https://www.southernute-nsn.gov/education/ (accessed online June 21, 2024).

32. https://www.suima.org/ (accessed online June 21, 2024).

33. https://apnews.com/article/science-health-denver-e5cdf892b4a2b1081aa425f9d78eb4e4 (accessed online April 23, 2023); https://www.cpr.org/2021/08/02/indigenous-boarding-schools-colorado-unmarked-graves-generational-scars/ (accessed online April 20, 2023).

34. https://www.rmpbs.org/blogs/news/native-american-graduation-regalia-colorado/ (accessed online April 23, 2023).

35. Hall, Frank. History of the State of Colorado from 1858 to 1890. Vol. 4. Blakely Printing Company, 1895, p. 355.

36. Gilbert King, Where the Buffalo No Longer Roamed, July 17, 2012, Smithsonian Magazine. https://www.smithsonianmag.com/history/where-the-buffalo-no-longer-roamed-3067904/ (accessed online January 13, 2024).

37. Amanda Horvath September 4, 2023. https://www.rmpbs.org/blogs/rocky-mountain-pbs/southern-ute-tribe-bison-herd-environment/ (accessed online January 13, 2024).
https://www.kunc.org/news/2023-09-10/southern-ute-tribes-bison-herd-at-maximum-capacity-due-to-environmental-restrictions (accessed online January 13, 2024).

23

SOVEREIGN UTE MOUNTAIN UTE INDIAN TRIBE

(1) Power to Establish a Form of Government

UMUT's Government

>The UMUT is a sovereign Nation. Six years after the Indian Reorganization Act of 1934, the Weenuche Band at Ute Mountain Ute Reservation organized a tribal government and enacted a tribal constitution (UMUT, 1985). The Weenuche Band became the UMUT. The governing body of the UMUT is the Tribal Council consisting of seven members. The Council is elected by popular vote of Tribal membership. The Chairman of the Tribal council is selected through popular vote for a three year term. The Council governs the Reservation and manages a tribal government.[1]

Constitution of Ute Mountain Tribe, Preamble

>CONSTITUTION AND BYLAWS OF THE UTE MOUNTAIN TRIBE OF THE UTE MOUNTAIN RESERVATION IN COLORADO, NEW MEXICO, UTAH

>PREAMBLE We, the people of the Ute Mountain Tribe of the Ute Mountain Reservation, in Colorado, New Mexico and Utah, under the jurisdiction of the Consolidated Ute Agency, Ignacio, Colorado, in order to exercise the rights of self-government, to administer our tribal affairs, to preserve, develop and increase our tribal resources, do ordain and establish this Constitution.[2]

Roberta Carol Harvey   239

(2) Power to Legislate

> The tribe determines its own course of action in all matters of importance to development and progress. Subject to the Constitution and By-Laws of the Ute Mountain Ute Tribe, the Council has the right and powers to: (1) manage tribal real and personal property; (2) negotiate and perform contracts and agreements; (3) engage in business enterprise; (4) negotiate and assign tribal security for loans; and (5) enact and enforce ordinances to promote public peace, safety, and welfare.[3]

1988 UMUT's Law and Order Code

The UMUT has promulgated civil, criminal and other laws including: a law and order code; a homesite land ordinance; resolutions and ordinances; personnel policies and procedures; the Ute mountain tribal hunting code for the Brunot agreement area; and a children's code.[4]

Power to Determine Membership; Power to Exclude Persons from Reservation

Article II of the UMUT's Constitution governs Membership and also the ability to exclude or remove persons from the Ute Mountain Ute Reservation.

(3) Power to Administer Justice

> The Department of Justice of the UMUT advises the Tribal Council on all legal issues affecting the Tribe, its resources, departments, employees, and members, ensures that the legal rights and responsibilities of the Tribe are appropriately addressed, and continually endeavors to improve and strengthen the sovereign status of the Tribe and the legal status of its members.[5]

UMUT's Court

> The CFR Court of the UMUT provides a fair and impartial outcome to matters requiring the services of the Court and its staff. It will uphold the law, as prescribed in the Law and Order Code of the

UMUT to ensure that justice has been obtained within the Ute Mountain Ute Indian Reservation, not only to the members of the Tribe but to all others living and passing through our reservation.[6]

UMUT's Legal Department

The UMUT's attorneys work on a daily basis with the Tribal Council to identify, analyze, and resolve legal issues.

UMUT's Police Department

This department is under the BIA-Law Enforcement program which manages the Chief Ignacio detention center and the local BIA police.[7]

(4) Power to Protect Its Children

UMUT Is Indian Child Welfare Act ("ICWA") Advocate

The UMUT is strongly committed to upholding ICWA.[8]

(5) Power to Manage Its Resources

The EPA approved the UMUT's water quality standards in 2011.

UMUT's Solar Project

The UMUT invested over one million dollars in the solar project (funds from Animas-La Plata Water Rights Settlement). The U.S. Department of Energy Office of Indian Energy matched their investment with a grant.[9]

2019 Office of Indian Energy Program, Indian Energy Champion Award, Bernadette Cuthair, UMUT

Ms. Cuthair was recognized for her role in the UMUT's 1-megawatt community solar project and her renewable energy vision for the future. "I am an advocate for renewable energy and am passionate about helping the Tribe build a sustainable community for the future and for our children."[10]

UMUT's Climate Action Plan

The climate in this region has warmed 2 degrees Fahrenheit (°F) in the last century. By the middle of this century, the region is expected to warm an additional 3 to 8°F. In response to the growing concerns about extreme drought events from Núchíú (UMU Tribe) Elders, natural resources managers, Tribal leadership, and community members, the Tribe initiated the climate change adaptation planning process.

UMU people depend on natural resources to maintain our cultural practices, identity, and sovereignty as a people. These warmer temperatures have caused reduced precipitation, changes in seasonality, and exacerbated health concerns such as asthma and cardiovascular disease, among other things. UMU leadership is taking efforts towards energy independence. This year a 1-megawatt community solar project was launched. The Tribe is considering other renewable energy proposals. These projects will help create jobs for our people and contribute to the world-wide effort to cool our planet. Climate change is a challenge that will be with us for many generations. It is important that we care for the land, plants, water, air, and animals that keep us connected to our culture. Our Elders and community members worked together to create this plan with the foresight to help us prepare for the effects of climate change.

The UMU Tribe is already actively engaged in efforts that directly and indirectly contribute to building resilience to climate change. The Tribe has managed its water resources for several decades and has secured reliable drinking water for the community. These efforts have increased economic development opportunities, including managing a casino resort and a 7,000-acre agricultural facility. The Tribe is exploring renewable energy projects to meet the increased energy demands in the Four Corners region while decreasing their own dependence on carbon-based energy sources that create climate-warming greenhouse gases. In addition, current climate-smart actions include solar installations, comprehensive water management planning, micro-scale hydroelectric development, energy efficiency upgrades to tribal agricultural enterprises, and diesel emissions reduction. Tribal leadership is supportive of these efforts.[11]

(6) Power to Establish Tribal and Individual Tribal Member Enterprises on Indian Lands, Communities, or Reservations

UMUT's Casino

The UMUT Casino celebrated its 30th anniversary in September 2022, with an honorary blessing and traditional dancing and music.[12]

> Gaming is successful because it stimulates the economy, increases tourism to reservations, provides opportunities for employment, raises incomes, and increases tribal independence. Once a reservation has established a strong economic foundation, it can open businesses that are unrelated to gaming. For instance, tribes, such as the UMUT, often open facilities that draw visitors such as hotels, conference centers, entertainment venues, travel centers and RV parks.[13]

The Indian Gaming Regulatory Act of 1988 ("IGRA") requires that gaming revenues go toward tribal government operations, promotion of the welfare of the tribe and its citizens, economic development, support of charitable organizations, and compensation to local non-Native governments for support of services provided by those governments.

Farming, Ranching and Construction

The state-of-the-art UMUT Farm & Ranch Enterprise, with its sought-after Bow & Arrow brand of non-GMO cornmeal, is an important income source. In normal times, the Enterprise employs several dozen tribal members and distributes more than $1 million in paychecks annually. But these are not normal times. The present drought has hit the farm hard. Today, it scrapes by on just 10 percent of the water normally flowing along a clay canal from the McPhee Reservoir. As a result, corn harvests have been cut by 75 percent, and half of the 50-person workforce, mostly tribal members, were laid off.

Weeminuche Construction Authority Received National Minority Enterprise Development Award as Minority Construction Firm of Year

In the past, the Weeminuche Construction Authority (WCA) received the

National Minority Enterprise Development (MED) award as Minority Construction Firm of the Year. WCA has extensive experience in heavy construction, including site preparation and clearing, earthwork and grading, plus drainage and utilities. WCA is a U.S. Small Business 8(a) and HUBZone business.[14]

UMUT's Tribal Park

> Selected by National Geographic Traveler as one of "80 World Destinations for Travel in the 21st Century," one of only nine places in U.S. to receive this special designation, the Park encompasses approximately 125,000 acres around a 25-mile stretch of the Mancos River, and is located in the Mesa Verde/Mancos Canyon area. Tribal members interpret tribal culture, pictographs, cliff dwellings, surface ruins, and artifacts.[15]

(7) Power to Manage Health Care

Towaoc Health Center

> The UMUT's Health Center, located on the Ute Mountain Ute Reservation in Towaoc, Colorado, is a comprehensive healthcare facility offering a wide range of services to the community. Services provided include primary care, behavioral health, dental care, radiology, pharmacy, and specialized care for women, children, and individuals with chronic conditions.
>
> With a focus on improving the health and well-being of patients, the Center also offers nutrition counseling, tobacco cessation programs, and assistance with enrolling in private insurance plans. The dedicated team of healthcare professionals at the Ute Mountain Ute Health Center is committed to providing quality care to individuals of all ages and backgrounds. Healthcare is often limited by access to care due to lack of insurance, or mistrust due to racism experienced in non-Indian health care settings. This is why tribal health care facilities are so important.[16]

Chairman Heart of the UMUT and Melvin J. Baker, Chairman of the SUIT, addressed a joint session of the legislature in March 2024 and called on the state to follow through on its commitments to the Tribes. Chairman Heart stressed the need for better health services.

> Heart said the understaffing, long distances and transportation challenges lead to infrequent check-ups, which in turn can cause long-term health issues, especially for patients with diabetes. When left unchecked, diabetes can advance to the point that a patient requires dialysis or amputations. Heart called on the state to create a program that employs full-time health care professionals to conduct in-person visits on the reservation.

> "We need prevention and education for these clients, our Tribal members, before they go into a stage of amputation of their limbs," Heart said in his address to lawmakers on Friday. "When a client gets to a point of amputation, then they lose hope from the lack of mobility. A majority of them eventually give up due to their challenges and their new limited conditions in their life."[17]

2022: Colorado Health Foundation's Dr. Virgilio Licona Community Health Leadership Award, Bernadette Cuthair, UMUT

> The Dr. Virgilio Licona Community Health Leadership Award honors on-the-ground changemakers tackling significant community health barriers and advancing health equity on both community and systems levels. Ms. Bernadette Cuthair, UMUT, received the award in 2022.[18]

(8) Power to Manage Education

Kwiyagat Community Academy

The Tribe started a charter school focused on imparting Ute language, tradition and culture as part of its studies to counter the lack of these areas in the public school system. It's called the Kwiyagat ('bear') Academy. Presently, it has kindergarten and first grade classes.[19]

> There is a generation gap based on the past when the federal government tried to assimilate children, who would be our grandparents today, to start learning the English language and getting away from the

tradition and culture. So we said, 'Well, maybe we should rethink this. And maybe we should build a school on the reservation.' That way we can have more of our tribal elders involved and others that know the different traditions and cultures...[20]

The Academy is named after the bear which is sacred to Ute people. The Bear Dance songs show respect for the animal and give the people strength. The bear's awakening signals the end of winter and the beginning of spring.

Part of Chairman Heart's dream is that eventually the UMUT would have its own educational system from K-12, as well as a tribal community college. Chairman Heart included this in his 2024 address to the Colorado General Assembly.

UMUT's Adult Education Family Learning Center

> To provide vocational training resources and support to members of the Ute Mountain Ute Tribe and other Native American tribes to increase employability, career satisfaction, and overall quality of life. [It provides] workforce training through its HPOG (Health Professionals Opportunity Grant) and SEEDS (Sustainable Employment and Economic Development Strategies) programs.[21]

UMUT Actively Engaged in Restoring Language and Culture

One UMUT project for a Ute Mountain Ute dictionary was funded with a Living Languages Grant from the BIA.[22]

Notes:

1. https://www.utemountainutetribe.com/ (accessed online January 21, 2024).

2. https://utemountainutetribe.com/images/legal/Constituational_Bylaws_091500.pdf (accessed online January 13, 2024).

3. https://www.utemountainutetribe.com/tribal%20government_MAIN.html (accessed online January 13, 2024).

4. https://narf.org/nill/codes/utemtnutecode/index.html (accessed online January 13, 2024).

5. https://www.utemountainutetribe.com/justice.html (accessed online January 13, 2024).

6. https://www.utemountainutetribe.com/CFR%20courts.html (accessed online January 13, 2024).

7. https://www.utemountainutetribe.com/other%20fed%20gov%20services.html (accessed online January 13, 2024).

8. https://www.kuer.org/politics-government/2023-02-01/indigenous-leaders-urge-utah-to-pass-a-state-indian-child-welfare-act (accessed online January 13, 2024).

9. https://www.hcn.org/articles/tribal-affairs-the-ute-mountain-ute-tribe-goes-solar/@@gallery_only?gallery_num= (accessed online January 13, 2024).

10. https://www.energy.gov/indianenergy/articles/indian-energy-champion-bernadette-cuthair (accessed online February 28, 2024).

11. https://www.utemountainuteenvironmental.org/sites/umep/assets/PDF/UteMountainUteClimateActionPlan2020%202.pdf (accessed online January 21, 2024).

12. https://utemountaincasino.com (accessed online January 21, 2024).

13. Colorado River Basin Tribes Address a Historic Drought—and Their Water Rights—Head-On, Tim Vanderpool, November 14, 2022. https://www.nrdc.org/stories/colorado-river-basin-tribes-address- historic-drought-and-their-water-rights-head (accessed online April 21, 2023). As Drought in the West Worsens, the Ute Mountain Ute Tribe Faces a Dwindling Water Supply, Sarah Tory, July 19, 2021. https:// collective.coloradotrust.org/stories/as-drought-in-the-west-worsens- the-ute-mountain-ute-tribe-faces-a-dwindling-water-supply/ (accessed online April 21, 2023).

14. https://archive.mbda.gov/news/blog/2015/11/weeminuche-construction-authority-recognized-minority-construction-firm-year.html (accessed online January 27, 2024).

15. https://www.sudrum.com/culture/2018/10/12/ute-mountain-ute-tribal-park/ (accessed online January 13, 2024).

16. https://www.utemountainutetribe.com/health%20services%20departments.html (accessed online January 13, 2024).

17. 'Tired of broken promises': Ute leaders call on state to follow through on Tribal commitments, KUNC, Lucas Brady Woods, March 19, 2024 (accessed online July 2, 2024). Https://Www.Ksjd.Org/2024-03-24/Tired-Of-Broken-Promises-Ute-Leaders-Call-On-State-To-Follow-Through-On-Tribal-Commitments (accessed online July 2, 2024).

18. https://coloradohealth.org/2022-dr-virgilio-licona-community-health-leadership-award-recipient (accessed online February 28, 2024). https://www.rmpbs.org/blogs/rocky-mountain-pbs/bernadette-cuthair-community-health-leadership-award/ (accessed online February 28, 2024).

19. https://utekca.org/ (accessed online February 28, 2024).

20. https://www.ksut.org/news/2021-03-30/ute-mountain-ute-chairman-manuel-heart-discusses-vaccines-reopening-education (accessed online February 28, 2024).

21. https://www.utemountainutetribe.com/Adult%20Education.html (accessed online January 13, 2024).

22. honored-by-tribal-council-in-towaoc/ (accessed online January 13, 2024).

24

AMERICAN INDIAN WATER RIGHTS

"Whiskey Is for Drinking, Water Is for Fighting"

Mark Twain's adage, 'Whiskey's for drinking, water's for fighting,' would be played out in the arid west. In western mining, agriculture and ranching, whoever controlled the water supply, controlled production. Indian nations are aware of the need to be vigilant in protecting their limited water resources.

Colorado Ute Indian Water Rights Settlement Act of 1988 (Southern Ute and Ute Mountain Ute Indian Tribes)

The 1986 Settlement Agreement, signed on December 10, 1986 ... quantified the Southern Ute and Ute Mountain Ute Tribes' water rights on several rivers and projects. Due to a lack of infrastructure, the Tribe is limited in how it can currently utilize its Animas-La Plata (Lake Nighthorse) storage allocation, but efforts are being made to address this issue.[1]

New Water Delivery Infrastructure Needed

Probably the greatest challenge the SUIT faces in trying to access and utilize its reserved water rights relates to the costs of maintaining existing and developing new water delivery infrastructure for both agricultural and municipal purposes.[2]

1922: Colorado River Compact

In 1922, representatives of the seven U.S. states in the Basin negotiated and entered into the Colorado River Compact, on how to "equitably" divide up the river to speed up development across the west. The execution of this Congressionally sanctioned deal paved the way for massive federal investment in water infrastructure. Federally funded dams were built to create Lakes Powell and Mead. *Tribes were not parties to this Compact* and had no direct say in how the water they had relied on for millennia was allocated. The apportioning of the River was also based on the overly optimistic premise that nearly 20 million acre-feet of water would flow through it each year.[3]

2019: Colorado River Drought Contingency Plan

Tribes were left out of the 2019 guidelines drought negotiations, even though according to a study by the Bureau of Reclamation tribes have rights to about 20% of all water in the Colorado River watershed.[4]

2026: Colorado River Basin Managing Guidelines

The Basin's managing guidelines expire in 2026. State leaders, water agencies, farm groups, environmentalists and recreational interests are deciding who will participate in formulating the new guidelines.

> Certainly, the stakes could not be higher for the troubled Colorado River Basin. The Colorado River is drying up from climate change and there is growing demand on a river system that was over-allocated from the start. The 246,000-square-mile watershed typically provides water for more than 40 million people across seven western states and supports a $15 billion agriculture industry.[5]

Ten Tribes Partnership Push for Role in 2026 Colorado River Basin Guidelines Negotiations

> The Southern Ute Indian Tribe is a member of the Ten Tribes Partnership ("Partnership"), led by Ute Mountain Ute Indian Tribal Chairman Manuel Heart, which includes tribes in the Basin. It was organized to ensure participation in the 2026 Colorado River

Basin guidelines negotiations. The Partnership and the Bureau of Reclamation conducted a Basin Study, which "documents how Partnership Tribes currently use their water, projects how future water development could occur and describes the potential effects of future tribal water development on the Colorado River System. The study also identifies challenges related to the use of tribal water and explores opportunities that provide a wide range of benefits to both Partnership Tribes and other water users."[6]

Colorado River Basin Tribal Coalition Seeks DOI's Use of Political Influence on Its Behalf

The SUIT is also a member of the Colorado River Basin Tribal Coalition ("Coalition"). In a critically important article, "Community in the Colorado River Basin," the authors set forth the general themes in response to the question of "what do tribes want?" out of negotiations over the new Basin management framework. The article "is dedicated to the brilliant, passionate leaders of the 30 Colorado River Basin tribes who have joined together in the recently established Tribal Leaders Forum. Your inspiring voices will shape the basin's future, and we admire you and your work."[7]

> First, as made abundantly clear by basin leaders, tribes want to have a formative role in the framework's development. They want to be treated as sovereigns alongside their counterparts: the federal government and basin states. Relationship building is key here. Basin tribes want the federal government to engage in more meaningful, more impactful government-to-government consultation in fulfillment of its trustee role.
>
> Second, big surprise: basin tribes want to use their water rights. And they need funding for construction and management of infrastructure.
>
> Third, another general theme growing out of the question of "what do tribes want?" from negotiations over the new management framework concerns self-determination. Tribes want to exercise that promise as it has framed federal Indian policy for the past half century. Along with empowering tribes to promote economic development, to build governmental infrastructure, to manage natural and cultural resources, to meet health care and educational needs, and to perform other

essential functions, the principle of self-determination should be extended unequivocally to tribal water rights. In short, basin tribes should have autonomy. They should determine whether they wish to use their water rights for social, economic, cultural, or environmental purposes on their reservations, as well as whether they wish to transfer, market, or otherwise share their water rights off those reservations.

Recently, the Coalition sent a letter to U.S. Secretary of the Interior Haaland seeking to ensure that the tribes are included in developing and carrying out the policies and rules that govern how the Colorado River is managed, including tribal access to clean water. "Our perspective, which is undoubtedly shared by others in the basin, is that we should all be working together as soon as possible..."[8]

May 3, 2024, Memorandum of Understanding between States and Tribes on Colorado River Management

In a move hailed as a significant development for the Colorado River, the Upper Basin Tribes and Upper Basin States signed a historic memorandum of understanding (MOU) on Monday, April 22, in Chama, N.M. This agreement marks a new era of cooperation and inclusion in managing this critical waterway. The MOU includes the Jicarilla Apache Nation, Navajo Nation, Ute Mountain Ute Tribe, Southern Ute Indian Tribe, Ute Indian Tribe, and the Paiute Indian Tribe of Utah. Representing the Upper Basin States through the Upper Colorado River Commission (UCRC) are Colorado, New Mexico, Utah, and Wyoming. This agreement emphasizes information sharing, identifying common interests, and working together to achieve shared goals for the Colorado River. It follows nearly two years of close collaboration between Tribal leaders and representatives from the Upper Basin States' Governors' offices.[9]

Ultimately Lorelei Cloud [the vice chairman of the Southern Ute Indian Tribal Council and the first tribal member of the Colorado Water Conservation Board] would like to see each of the Upper Basin tribes have a formal position on the Upper Colorado River Commission, though that would take congressional approval.[10]

UMUT's Water Rights

Due to state allocation of water to private users, and in some cases over-allocation, Indian tribes have to litigate or negotiate settlements to determine their water rights. The UMUT is currently litigating its federal Indian reserved water rights associated with the portion of its Reservation located in New Mexico. The Tribe has not yet litigated or settled its federal reserved water rights for the portion of its Reservation in Utah. At this time, the Tribe's estimated 9,000 acre-feet in the San Juan River are not being utilized by it. It goes into Lake Powell.

The UMUT is confronted with a number of challenges in developing its water resources on Reservation lands that span three states and on noncontiguous off-Reservation ranch lands. Securing a delivery system from Lake Nighthorse over to the Ute Mountain Ute Reservation is the Tribe's No. 1 priority.

Notes:

1. https://www.usbr.gov/lc/region/programs/crbstudy/tws/finalreport.html (accessed online April 21, 2023).

2. https://tentribespartnership.org/wp-content/uploads/2020/01/Ch.-5.2-Southern Ute Indian Tribe-Current-Future-Water-Use-12-13-2018.pdf (accessed online April 21, 2023).

3. Colorado Encyclopedia (accessed online April 21, 2023).

4. Colorado River Basin Tribes Address a Historic Drought—and Their Water Rights—Head-On, Tim Vanderpool, November 14, 2022. https://www.nrdc.org/stories/colorado-river-basin-tribes-address-historic-drought-and-their-water-rights-head (accessed online April 21, 2023).

5. Colorado River Basin Tribes Address a Historic Drought—and Their Water Rights—Head-On, Tim Vanderpool, November 14, 2022. https://www.nrdc.org/stories/colorado-river-basin-tribes-address- historic-drought-and-their-water-rights-head (accessed online April 21, 2023). Id.; https://www.reviewjournal.com/news/politics-and-government/

officials-celebrate-colorado-river-drought-deal-at-hoover-dam-1668958/ (accessed online April 21, 2023).

6. https://tentribespartnership.org/wp-content/uploads/2019/12/WaterStudy.pdf (accessed online April 21, 2023).

7. ARTICLE: COMMUNITY IN THE COLORADO RIVER BASIN, 57 Idaho L. Rev. 1 (2021).

8. https://f.hubspotusercontent10.net/hubfs/6000718/Water%20Hub/Letter%20to%20Sec%20Haaland%2011.15.21.pdf (accessed online April 21, 2023).

Additional Articles:

Colorado River Basin Tribes Address a Historic Drought—and Their Water Rights—Head-On, Tim Vanderpool, November 14, 2022. https://www.nrdc.org/stories/colorado-river-basin-tribes-address- historic-drought-and-their-water-rights-head (accessed online April 21, 2023).

Historically excluded from Colorado River policy, tribes want a say in how the dwindling resource is used. Access to clean water is a start. Michael Elizabeth Sakas, December 7, 2021. https://www.cpr.org/2021/12/07/tribes-historically-excluded-colorado-river-policy-use-want-say-clean-water-access/ (accessed online April 21, 2023).

What part do Native American tribes play in fixing the Colorado River shortage? "How come we just get a drop in the bucket?" The Denver Post, Conrad Swanson, January 4, 2023. https://www.denverpost.com/2023/01/04/colorado-river-water-rights-native-american-tribes/ (accessed online April 21, 2023).

https://www.durangoherald.com/articles/tribes-assert-water-rights-on-colorado-river-basin/ (accessed online April 21, 2023).

9. https://www.sudrum.com/top-stories/2024/05/03/upper-basin-tribes-and-states-sign-historic-memorandum-of-understanding/ (accessed online June 23, 2024).

10. Tribes have rights to a quarter of Colorado River's water but have been excluded from decision-making. Will that change? Elise Schmelzer, July 3, 2024. https://www.denverpost.com/2024/07/03/colorado-river-compact-tribes-inclusion-water-negotiations/?clearUserState=true (accessed online July 3, 2024).

25

PRESERVING AMERICAN INDIANS' RELIGIONS, CULTURES AND LANGUAGES

At the turn of the century the federal government suppressed the practice of Indian religions and criminalized cultural traditions. Christianity was to be used to assimilate Indian people and to replace the "heathen" practices of the natives. Today, the SUIT and UMUT guard the religious and cultural heritage of their communities.

1800's BIA Prohibition on American Indian Religious and Cultural Practices

The Bureau of Indian Affairs promulgated "Rules Governing the Court of Indian Offenses" on April 10, 1883, which criminalized traditional Indian dances, traditional marriage and divorce, community and social gatherings, traditional probate, traditional burials and mourning practices, and religious practices of medicine men, etc.

NCAI Policy Issues

At present, a principal objective of the NCAI is the protection of the spiritual and cultural traditions of Indian people and communities.

> As Native people, we often witness threats to our traditions, languages, religions, histories, and more from mainstream society. NCAI works with partners across Indian Country to educate non-Native people and turn back these attacks on our cultures and lifeways. Protection of Native cultural resources is critical to the vitality of traditional religions, customs, languages, and status as sovereigns.[1]

Key issues for the survival of these traditions include access to and control of sacred sites, preservation of Native American languages, return of sacred artifacts, and maintenance of the integrity of religious knowledge and values.[2]

2019: United Nations Declares International Decade of Indigenous Languages

In 2019, the United Nations acknowledged the importance of Indigenous languages by declaring the decade ahead to be the International Decade of Indigenous Languages, recognizing the right to languages as an inherent right of Indigenous Peoples.[3]

Their declaration confirmed the following:

> *The loss of global language diversity has been greatly accelerated by colonization and globalization. Other significant factors in the erosion of Indigenous languages are the dispossession of lands, territories and resources; repression and assimilation; genocide and shrinking ageing communities in which language is not passed to next generations.* Indigenous languages are not merely a tool for communication. Indigenous languages are central to Indigenous Peoples' identity, the preservation of their cultures, worldviews and visions and something critical to them: an expression of their self-determination. (Emphasis added).[4]

Education and American Indian Boarding Schools Legacy

In his 1901 Annual Report, Commissioner of Indian Affairs W. A. Jones reported his view of Indian education to the Secretary of the Department of the Interior:

> There are in operation at the present time 113 boarding schools, with an average attendance of something over 16,000 pupils, ranging from 5 to 21 years old. These pupils are gathered from the cabin, the wickiup, and the tepee. Partly by cajolery and partly by threats; partly by bribery and partly by fraud; partly by persuasion and partly by force, they are induced to leave their homes and their kindred to enter these schools and take upon themselves the outward semblance

of civilized life. They are chosen not on account of any particular merit of their own, not by reason of mental fitness, but solely because they have Indian blood in their veins. Without regard to their worldly condition; without any previous training; without any preparation whatever, they are transported to the schools-sometimes thousands of miles away-without the slightest expense or trouble to themselves or their people.

The Indian youth finds himself at once, as if by magic, translated from a state of poverty to one of affluence. He is well fed and clothed and lodged. Books and all the accessories of learning are given him and teachers provided to instruct him. He is educated in the industrial arts on the one hand, and not only in the rudiments but in the liberal arts on the other. Beyond "the three r's" he is instructed in geography, grammar, and history; he is taught drawing, algebra and geometry, music, and astronomy, and receives lessons in physiology, botany, and entomology. Matrons wait on him while he is well and physicians and nurses attend him when he is sick. A steam laundry does his washing and the latest modern appliances do his cooking. A library affords him relaxation for his leisure hours, athletic sports and the gymnasium furnish him exercise and recreation, while music entertains him in the evening. He has hot and cold baths, and steam heat and electric light, and all the modern conveniences. All of the necessities of life are given him and many of the luxuries. All of this without money and without price, or the contribution of a single effort of his own or of his people. His wants are all supplied almost for the wish. The child of the wigwam becomes a modern Aladdin, who has only to rub the Government lamp to gratify his desires.

Here he remains until his education is finished, when he is returned to his home-which by contrast must seem squalid indeed-to the parents whom his education must make it difficult to honor, and left to make his way against the ignorance and bigotry of his tribe. Is it any wonder he fails? Is it surprising if he lapses into barbarism? Not having earned his education, it is not appreciated; having made no sacrifice to obtain it, it is not valued. It is looked upon as a right and not as a privilege; it is accepted as a favor to the Government and not to the recipient, and the almost inevitable tendency is to encourage dependence.[5]

In 2022, Secretary of the Interior Deb Haaland described the boarding school policy differently: The purpose of federal Indian boarding schools was to culturally assimilate American Indian, Alaska Native and Native Hawaiian children by forcibly removing them from their families, communities, languages, religions and cultural beliefs. While children attended federal boarding schools, many endured physical and emotional abuse and, in some cases, died.[6]

UMUT's Chairman Heart confirmed the "atrocity" of government boarding schools that sought to stamp out tribal heritage and language. "It had a devastating impact on three to four generations of tribal families in a very negative way, right up to today."[7]

In 1928, the Meriam Report—The Problem of Indian Administration—was completed. The study contained data on health, education, economic development, social life, and government programs. Historian Kathleen Chamberlain, writes: "The Meriam Report captured the attention of government officials with graphic descriptions of poverty, disease, inadequate diet, and substandard housing."

The report is particularly critical of the boarding schools: "The survey staff finds itself obligated to say frankly and unequivocally that the provisions for the care of the Indian children in boarding schools are grossly inadequate."[8]

June 2024: U.S. Catholic Bishops Formally Apologize for 'Trauma' Inflicted on Native American Communities

> "In these schools, Indigenous children were forced to abandon their traditional languages, dress, and customs," the bishops said in the document. "Boarding schools were seen as one expedient means to achieve this cultural assimilation because they separated Indigenous children from their families and Tribes and "Americanized" them while they were still malleable," the document adds.
>
> The guidelines issued Friday call on Catholic bishops to promote and expand healing and reconciliation with Native American communities, set up listening sessions and provide training for "clergy, religious, and lay leaders to better minister to the pastoral needs of Indigenous Peoples," according to the document.[9]

Notes:

1. https://www.ncai.org/section/policy/portfolios/cultural-protection (accessed online January 13, 2024).

2. American religions. https://www.britannica.com/topic/Native-American-religion (accessed online January 13, 2024).

3. https://theconversation.com/listen-why-preserving-indigenous-languages-is-so-critical-to-culture-204348 (accessed online January 13, 2024).

4. https://theconversation.com/listen-why-preserving-indigenous-languages-is-so-critical-to-culture-204348 (accessed online January 13, 2024).

5. Report of the Commissioner of Indian Affairs to the Secretary of the Interior, United States. Office of Indian Affairs, U.S. Government Printing Office, 1902.

6. https://www.doi.gov/priorities/strengthening-indian-country/federal-indian-boarding-school-initiative#:~:text=%E2%80%94%20Secretary%20Deb%20Haaland&text=The%20purpose%20of%20federal%20Indian,languages%2C%20religions%20and%20cultural%20beliefs (accessed online February 28, 2024).

7. https://ictnews.org/news/tribal-leaders-stress-education-water-issues-in-colorado (accessed online January 13, 2024).

8. Lewis Meriam, The Problems of Indian Administration (Baltimore: The Johns Hopkins Press), 1928.

9. Nicole Chavez, CNN, June 14, 2024.

26

WILLFUL VIOLATION OF STATE LAW REQUIRING COLORADO PUBLIC HIGH SCHOOLS TO TEACH CIVICS, INCLUDING SOCIAL CONTRIBUTIONS OF MINORITY GROUPS

In 1973, the Colorado state legislature enacted §123-21-4, C.R.S, requiring public schools to teach about the history and culture of Spanish-Americans and American Negroes.

While legislation was introduced in 1992 in an attempt to make it optional, it failed to pass (SB 108).

In 1998, it was amended to include American Indians at the urging of Comanche State Representative Suzanne Williams (HB 98-1186, enacted 4/17/1998)..

Fast-forward twenty-three years and the American Indian community has yet to see former Representative and Senator Williams' state legislative lobbying effort to get HB 98-1186 passed being fulfilled.

In 2003, the legislature mandated that students must satisfactorily complete a course on the civil government of the United States and the state of Colorado, as a condition of high school graduation, which expressly included the history and culture of certain minorities, effective with the graduating class of 2007 (SB 36, enacted 4/22/2003). The minorities included African-Americans, American Indians and Latinos.

In May 2019, teaching regarding Asian Americans and the lesbian, gay, bisexual and transgender individuals within these minority groups and the contributions and persecution of religious minorities were added to the statute (HB 19-1192, enacted 5/28/2019).

On April 29, 2021, it was further amended by SB 21-067 to address specific topics under federal and state constitutions and governments.

Colorado House Bill 19-1192: Codified as § 22-1-104, C.R.S.

On May 28, 2019, Colorado House Bill 19-1192 ("HB 19-1192") (codified as § 22-1-104, C.R.S.) was passed. It specifically became effective immediately. It provides as follows:

22-1-104. Teaching of history, culture, and civil government.

> The history and civil government of the United States and of the state of Colorado, which includes the history, culture, and social contributions of minorities, including, but not limited to, American Indians, Latinos, African Americans, and Asian Americans, the lesbian, gay, bisexual, and transgender individuals within these minority groups, and the intersectionality of significant social and cultural features within these communities, and the contributions and persecution of religious minorities, must be taught in all the public schools of the state.

> HB 19-1192 was introduced by Rep. Gonzales-Gutierrez, a granddaughter of Denver activist Rudolfo "Corky" Gonzales, a leader in the Crusade for Justice group. While a senior at Denver's West High School in 1969, Rep. Gonzales-Gutierrez's mother participated in protests on March 20-21, 1969. One grievance was the lack of Chicano curriculum. Students from Manuel, Thomas Jefferson, Lincoln and South High Schools, all came out and supported the students at West High School. The protests came to be known as the "blowouts." Numerous arrests occurred in what the demonstrators had hoped would be a non-violent presentation of their grievances to school administrators.

As reported by CPR News,

The West blowouts helped kick-start what became known as El Movimiento, the Chicano Movement. Just a few weeks later, the Crusade for Justice held the first ever Youth Liberation Conference. Nearly 1,500 young Chicanos from across the country were drawn to Denver.[1]

In a symbolic ceremony, Governor Jared Polis signed HB 19-1192 at Denver's Rudolfo "Corky" Gonzales Branch Library. Rep. Gonzales-Gutierrez stated: "Our diversity is what makes our country and our state strong, but for too long, individuals and communities that have moved or immigrated here and those that have been here for many centuries ... have been excluded from our teaching of history." Three generations later, one Latinx family seeking an inclusive curriculum has yet to see the fruition of its activism.[2]

Judicial Review of § 22-1-104

Colorado Attorney General Opinion on § 22-1-104

The Colorado Attorney General has upheld § 22-1-104 as follows:

> Generally the legislature has authorized local school district boards of education "to determine the educational programs to be carried on in the schools of the district" C.R.S. 1973, 22-32-109(1)(t). However, the legislature presently mandates certain minimum requirements as to what must be taught, including the history and civil government of the state and of the United States, C.R.S. 1973, 22-1-104, honor and use of the United States flag, C.R.S. 1973, 22-1-06, United States Constitution, C.R.S. 1973, 22-1-108, and the effects of the use of alcohol, C.R.S. 1973, 22-1-110 (Supp. 1982)."
>
> *"I conclude that a state has authority to impose academic and nonacademic requirements as a condition of promotion at various levels of K-12 education and/or as a condition of receiving a high school diploma, as long as constitutional rights of due process and equal protection are observed."* (Emphasis added).[3]

Colorado Appellate Court Decision on § 22-1-104

More importantly, a Colorado appellate court also upheld § 22-1-104 as follows:

> The board of education has been given statutory authority to "determine the educational programs to be carried on in the schools of the district." Section 22-32-109(1)(t), C.R.S. (1988 Repl. Vol. 9). However, the board's discretion is not unlimited, and the General Assembly has specified certain subjects that must be taught. These subjects are: the history, culture, and civil government of Colorado and the United States, including the history, culture, and contributions of minorities, see § 22-1-104, C.R.S. (1988 Repl. Vol. 9); honor and use of the flag, see § 22-1-106, C.R.S. (1988 Repl. Vol. 9); the federal constitution, see § 22-1-108, C.R.S. (1988 Repl. Vol. 9); and the effect of alcohol and controlled substances. See § 22-1-110, C.R.S. (1988 Repl. Vol. 9). See *Skipworth v. Board of Educ.*, 874 P. Ed. 487 (1994).

Colorado Federal District Court, *Lane v. Owens*, 2003, Cited § 22-1-104 in Dicta as Valid Example of Curriculum Requirement

A federal district court cited § 22-1-104 in dicta as an example of a valid curriculum requirement versus the rote recitation of the Pledge of Allegiance. See *Lane v. Owens*, U.S. District Court of Colorado, Civil Docket Case No 1:03-cv-01544- LTB, Judge Lewis T. Babcock, August 15, 2003, Ruling (pp. 6-7). Plaintiffs were successful in their Preliminary Injunction petition. Defendants included the CCSD, Adams-Arapahoe (Aurora), Denver County 1, and Jefferson County R-1 (Jeffco) Public School Districts.

Colorado Supreme Court Decision regarding Use of Term "Must" by General Assembly (aka State Legislature)

Also, according to the Colorado Supreme Court, the Colorado General Assembly's use of the term "must" "connotes a mandatory requirement." See *Waddell v. People*, 462 P.3d 1100, 1106 (Colo. 2020), citing *Ryan Ranch Cmty. Ass'n v. Kelley*, 380 P.3d 137, 146 (Colo. 2016).

Native American Holocaust in Colorado's Public High Schools

We survived or we died
> In Colorado's public high schools.
> Unable to get the school system to add one course,
> Only including, not wholly about, our history, culture and social contributions.
> Education paramount for the privileged Anglos.
> We failed to achieve, we failed to graduate
> We dropped out, we drugged ourselves into a stupor to escape
> We hated ourselves for being Indian or we assimilated into the Majority
> Unable to endure the ignominy of being different, of being less than.

We survived or we died
> Harshly, disproportionately disciplined. Captive this time in public schools. Alone, with no one to help.

We survived or we died
> Colorado's public high schools flaunting the law in our face.
> Enduring its continuing, unabated, injustices,
> Its quiet massacres.

Donna Chrisjohn, Sicangu Lakota/Diné, American Indian Educator

Donna Chrisjohn, a member of the Sicangu Lakota Nation and a descendant of the Diné Nation, teaches classes to teachers and administrators on Indigenous history and culture for a perspective they don't necessarily know or understand. In a 2021 interview with Jenny Brindin, Colorado Public Radio, Donna said the following:

'Our Invisibility and Our Erasure in This Country Is on Purpose'

> Chrisjohn said some individual teachers in Colorado make real efforts to include Indigenous content, often in a history or English class. But advocates say the content of most government courses, such as civics classes, far from satisfies what Colorado law specifies students be taught. Instead, Chrisjohn said, curriculum is often rife with generalizations, romanticization and stereotypes. Modern day

Indigenous issues are almost never discussed. Also often ignored is the fact that Indigenous people existed in America up to 20,000 years prior to 1492.

"There's actually no context to the fact we existed here prior to settler colonialism," Chrisjohn said. "Our invisibility and our erasure in this country is on purpose. It is built in through federal policies and it is institutionalized in our school systems."

She said a civics class could include Indigenous ways of governing, handling conflict, Indigenous values systems, the theory that U.S. democracy was influenced by the 6 Nations of the Iroquois Confederacy, federal policy and jurisdictional issues, and sovereignty rights.

"It's a totally different perspective. So how harmful is that for our Indigenous students to know that my culture, everything about myself can never come into this classroom because it will never be accepted?"

In a recent national report, the U.S. Commission on Civil Rights found that the lack of Indigenous representation in school curriculum harms students. It said without historically accurate representation or discussion of Native American people in curriculum, the education experience can be isolating and limiting. Donna Chrisjohn agrees.

"We know that right away, as soon as we start '1492 and sailing the ocean blue,' we know that that is not the truth of who we are and where we come from. And we are immediately erased," she said. "And then we're triggered that I'm just not included in this classroom perspective or this narrative."

Donna Chrisjohn's ancestors have been here for 20,000 years. They say they're not going anywhere—and they're not giving up.[4]

Notes:

1. https://www.cpr.org/2019/03/18/chicano-progress-today-owes-much-to-the-denver-west-high-blowouts-of-50-years-ago/ (accessed online March 1, 2021).

2. www.coloradopolitics.com/news/colorado-schools-to-teach-a-far-more-inclusive-version-of-history/article_07619028-8195-11e9-9f1a-63bd85281cbd.html (accessed online March 5, 2021).

3. See 1983 Colorado Attorney General Opinion State Legislature Has Authority to Impose Academic Graduation Requirements, including § 22-1-104, 983 Colo. AG LEXIS 33 (December 2, 1983). But see Comment: The Colorado Charter Schools Act and the Potential for Unconstitutional Applications Under Article IX, Section 15 of the State Constitution, 67 U. Colo. L. Rev. 171, Winter, 1996, FN 47.

4. https://www.cpr.org/2021/09/30/colorado-students-arent-supposed-to-graduate-without-learning-about-indigenous-history-and-culture-are-they/ (accessed online June 16, 2024).

27

UNITED NATIONS PERMANENT FORUM ON INDIGENOUS ISSUES

The U.N. Forum is to strengthen international cooperation for solution of problems faced by indigenous people in such areas as human rights, the environment, education and health.

United Nations Declaration on the Rights of Indigenous Peoples ("UNDRIP")

Adopted in 2007, the UNDRIP establishes a universal framework of minimum standards for the survival, dignity and well-being of indigenous peoples and elaborates on existing human rights standards and fundamental freedoms as they apply to the specific situation of indigenous peoples. The UNDRIP is not legally binding on States and does not impose legal obligations on governments, but like all human rights instruments, it carries moral force.[1]

Canada, the U.S., New Zealand and Australia initially voted against UNDRIP. They later endorsed it as 'aspirational' and non-binding. Canada, USA, New Zealand and Australia have similar colonial histories. They argued that autonomy recognized for indigenous peoples was problematic and would undermine sovereignty of their own states, particularly in the context of land disputes and natural resource extraction.

United Nations Summary of Damages to Indigenous Peoples

As identified by the United Nations,

> ...multiple threats and obstacles continue to hinder Indian social,

economic, political and legal development, including discrimination and marginalization; lack of rights to land and natural and productive resources; denial and lack of access to justice; violations of cultural rights; denial of the rights to legal recognition, political representation and participation; lack of access to basic social services; denial of the right to existence and self-development; violence against indigenous individuals and communities, including rape and death of indigenous women; and multiple-impact land conflicts arising from development and conservation projects that fail to take into account the rights and interests of indigenous peoples.

Extractive industries, infrastructure projects, large-scale agriculture or hydroelectric dams and the promotion of new technologies such as improved seeds, chemical fertilizers and pesticides, the introduction of cash-crop cultivation and large plantation schemes all impact indigenous ecosystems.[2]

Notes:

1. https://www.usaid.gov/indigenous-peoples-0#:~:text=Adopted%20in%202007%2C%20the%20UNDRIP,specific%20situation%20of%20indigenous%20peoples (accessed online November 22, 2020).
2. www.un.org/development/desa/indigenouspeoples/mandated-areas1/environment.html (accessed online November 22, 2020).

Appendix 1: U.S. Colorado American Indian Treaties

U.S. Colorado American Indian Treaties [This list is not meant to be inclusive. This list does not infer any legality or validity of any of the Treaties listed.]			
Year	Treaty	Purpose	Outcome
1849	Abiquiu	Pacify the Territory of NM and San Luis Valley acquired as result of Mexican-American War (1846-48).	Capote and Muache Ute bands agree to U.S. jurisdiction over them, safe passage for settlers, presence of military forts and trading posts.
1851	Fort Laramie	Ensure protected right-of-way for emigrants crossing Indian lands.	White travelers permitted free and unmolested travel across Great Plains and Army could build and man forts.
1861	Fort Wise	Allow for continued settlement and mining for gold in Colorado without fear of Indian violence.	Cheyenne and Arapaho cordoned onto small triangular reservation, cede lands granted them under 1851 Fort Laramie Treaty; 1/13 of their original land base retained.
1863	Conejos	Avoid hostilities that resulted when white immigrants occupied Ute lands during Colorado Gold Rush and after passage of the Homestead Act in 1862.	Relinquished claims to all land in Colorado Rocky Mountains east of Continental Divide (Front Range of the Rockies), along with Middle Park basin in Rockies n north-central Colorado.
1865	Little Arkansas Treaty	Remove Cheyenne and Arapaho Tribes from Colorado to Indian Territory in Oklahoma.	
1867	Medicine Lodge	Establish security for person and property along the lines of railroad.	Cheyenne and Arapaho chiefs sign treaty creating a reservation in western Indian Territory.
1868	Ute	Open Central Rocky Mountains for mining.	Utes cede Central Rockies; Reservation for Utes on Colorado's Western Slope; reservation for Uintah Utes in Utah.
1874	Ute	Brunot Agreement [Not Treaty]	Utes Cede Mineral Rich San Juan Mountains

Appendix 2: Presidential Viewpoints of American Indians

General George Washington: Americans' Sole Lords and Proprietors, Revolutionary War Victory Foundation of Empire

Prior to becoming president at the end of the Revolutionary War, General George Washington referred to Americans as "the sole Lords and Proprietors of a vast Tract of Continent" and believed the success of the Revolutionary struggle was nothing less than the "foundation of our Empire[.]"[1]

1791: Thomas Jefferson: War to Bribery

Bribery through annuities and treaties without substance were cheaper than outright warfare with the Indians.

From Thomas Jefferson to James Monroe, April 17, 1791:

> I hope we shall ***drub the Indians well this summer and then change our plan from war to bribery***. We must do as the Spaniards and English do, keep them in peace by liberal and constant presents. They find it the cheapest plan, and so shall we. The expence of this summers expedition would have served for presents for half a century.
>
> ...Every rag of an Indian depredation will otherwise serve as a ground to raise troops... (Emphasis added)[2]

In a letter dated April 15, 1791, from Thomas Jefferson to Charles Carroll, he repeated his bribery policy:

> "***The most economical as well as most humane conduct towards them is to bribe them into peace, and to retain them in peace by eternal bribes***." (Emphasis added)[3]

1798: President John Adams: Indian Trust Responsibilities Are Subordinate to Obligations to U.S. Citizenry

President John Adams (1797–1801) captured the essence well of the executive responsibility to its "white children" in this 1798 letter to the Cherokee Nation objecting to the invasion of squatters: His "stronger obligations" were to "hear the complaints, and relieve, as far as in my power, the distresses of my white children, citizens of the United States."[4]

1803: President Thomas Jefferson (1801–1805)

Thomas Jefferson (1801–1805) would become the (1) architect of the U.S.' Indian removal policy, well before the Indian Removal Act of 1830; and (2) the "Manifest Destiny" of the U.S. to expropriate Indian lands:

From Thomas Jefferson to John Breckinridge (U.S. Attorney General), 12 August 1803, regarding the Louisiana Purchase:

> ...the best use we can make of the country for some time will be to give establishments in it to the Indians on the East side of the Mispi in exchange for their present country, and open land offices in the last, & thus make this acquisition the means of filling up the Eastern side instead of drawing off its population. *when we shall be full on this side, we may lay off a range of states on the Western bank from the head to the mouth, & so range after range, advancing compactly as we multiply*. (Emphasis added)[5]

Bribery through annuities and treaties without substance were cheaper than outright warfare with the Indians. From the time of President Jefferson, the plan was to drub them or bribe them.

1816: President James Madison, Policy Is Precursor to Allotment

Our fourth President, James Madison, planned to complete the work of transitioning the Indians from the "habits of the savage to the arts and comforts of social life" and divide up their land in a terrifying precursor to future allotment. By the political administration of Indians in reduced areas, land expropriation and exploitation would be easier.

> 1816: [T]he facility is increasing for *extending that divided and individual ownership, which exists now in movable property only, to the soil itself,* and of thus establishing in the culture and im-

provement of it the true foundation for a transit from the habits of the savage to the arts and comforts of social life. (Emphasis added.)[6]

1817: The hunter state can exist only in the vast uncultivated desert. It yields to the more dense and compact form and great force of civilized population; and of right it ought to yield, for the earth was given to mankind to support the greatest number of which it is capable, and no tribe of people have a right to withhold from the wants of others more than is necessary for their own support and comfort.[7]

In Monroe's 1818 State of the Union address, he spoke these words:

"Experience has clearly demonstrated that independent savage communities can not long exist within the limits of a civilized population. The progress of the latter has almost invariably terminated in the extinction of the former, especially of the tribes belonging to our portion of this hemisphere, among whom loftiness of sentiment and gallantry in action have been conspicuous. To civilize them, and even to prevent their extinction, it seems to be indispensable that their independence as communities should cease, and that the control of the United States over them should be complete and undisputed. The hunter state will then be more easily abandoned, and recourse will be had to the acquisition and culture of land and to other pursuits tending to dissolve the ties which connect them together as a savage community and to give a new character to every individual. I present this subject to the consideration of Congress on the presumption that it may be found expedient and practicable to adopt some benevolent provisions, having these objects in view, relative to the tribes within our settlements."[8]

The hunter state can exist only in the vast uncultivated desert. It yields to the more dense and compact form and great force of civilized population; and of right it ought to yield, for the earth was given to mankind to support the greatest number of which it is capable, and no tribe of people have a right to withhold from the wants of others more than is necessary for their own support and comfort.[9]

1819: Indian Civilization Act

Congress responded in 1819 by approving $10,000 annually for Indian education under the Indian Civilization Act, also known as the Civilization Fund Act. The act was passed on March 3, 1819 to encourage benevolent societies to provide education for the Indian tribes and provided the authorization to encourage the civilization programs. The act led to the formation of 52 schools over the next decade which were administered either by the federal government or by Christian missions.[10]

1821: James Monroe - Removal of Indians Paramount; Assimilation Policy Defunct

Our fifth President, James Monroe, in his Second Annual Message to Congress in 1821 (1) discredited the U.S. recognition of Indian tribes as Nations; (2) disclaimed their sovereignty over their territorial lands; (3) relegated to them the right for a 'reasonable equivalent" to the lands they ceded; and (4) secured to each individual the right to a "competent" portion of land. Neither what was a "reasonable equivalent" nor a "competent" parcel were defined. His policies would essentially destroy Indian Nations as sovereigns with the fundamental right to govern their peoples and exercise control of their lands.

> The care of the Indian tribes...has not been executed in a manner to accomplish all the objects intended by it. *We have treated them as independent nations, without their having any substantial pretensions to that rank*. The distinction has flattered their pride, retarded their improvement, and in many instances paved the way to their destruction. The progress of our settlements westward, supported as they are by a dense population, has constantly driven them back, with almost the *total sacrifice of the lands which they have been compelled to abandon. Their sovereignty over vast territories should cease, in lieu of which the right of soil should be secured to each individual and his posterity in competent portions*. They have claims on the magnanimity and, I may add, on the justice of this nation which we must all feel. We should become their real benefactors; we should perform the office of their Great Father, the endearing title which they emphatically give to the Chief Magistrate of our Union. Their sovereignty over vast territories should cease, in lieu of which the right of soil should be secured to each individual and his posterity in competent portions; and for the territory thus ceded by each tribe some reasonable equivalent should be granted, to be vested in permanent funds for the support of civil government over them and for the education of their children, for their instruction in the arts of husbandry, and to provide sustenance for them until they could provide it for themselves. My earnest hope is that Congress will digest some plan, founded on these principles, with such improvements as their wisdom may suggest, and carry it into effect as soon as it may be practicable. (Emphasis added)[11]

1829: President Jackson suggested "the propriety of setting apart an ample district west of the Mississippi, and without the limits of any State or Territory now formed, to be guaranteed to the Indian tribes, as long as they shall occupy it; each tribe having a distinct control over the portion designated for its use." "There," he observed, "they may be secured in the enjoyment of governments of their own choice, subject to no other control from the United States, than such as may be necessary to preserve peace on the frontier and between the several tribes..."[12]

1839: President John Quincy Adams: Indian Right of Possession Questionable

Our sixth President, John Quincy Adams, proudly delivered his position regarding westward expansion. The United States would dominate the Americas, Adams said, and assert its hemispheric hegemony without challenge. He wrote, "We have it; we constitute the whole of it."[13]

On Indian land title, in his oration at the Jubilee of the Constitution, delivered at New York, April 30, 1839, before the New York Historical Society, he said the following:

> *The Indian right of possession itself stands, with regard to the greatest part of the country, upon a questionable foundation.*
>
> Their cultivated fields, their constructed habitations, a space of ample sufficiency for their subsistence, and whatever they had annexed to themselves by personal labor, was undoubtedly by the laws of nature theirs.
>
> But what is the right of a huntsman to the forest of a thousand miles over which he has accidentally ranged in quest of prey? ...
>
> Shall the lordly savage not only disdain the virtues and enjoyments of civilization himself, but shall he control the civilization of a world? (Emphasis added)[14]

Henry Clay, Secretary of State under John Quincy Adams, claimed that "it was impossible to civilize Indians; that there never was a full-blooded Indian who took to civilization. It was not in their nature."

Adams recorded the moment:

> He [Clay] believed they were destined to extinction, and, although he would never use or countenance inhumanity towards them, he did not think them, as a race, worth preserving. He considered them as essentially inferior to the Anglo-Saxon race, which were now taking their place on this continent. They were not an improvable breed, and their disappearance from the human family will be no great loss to the world. In point of fact they were rapidly disappearing, and he did not believe that in fifty years from this time there would be any of them left.[15]

By portraying Indians as unimportant and destined to become extinct, Henry Clay is employing a perception transfer of Indians which makes it easier to justify dispossession of their lands and extermination of them as a people.

1812, 1829: President Andrew Jackson: Kill and Lay Captive Their Women and Children

Our seventh President's (Andrew Jackson) despotic policy toward indigenous peoples is unquestioned. While a General in our armed forces, he appealed to the Tennessee legislature and implored them to approve and fund a military invasion of the Creek territory. In correspondence with Governor Blount, Jackson made it clear that he intended to invade the Creek Nation even without the authorization of the legislature "and think myself Justifiable, in laying waste their villages, burning their houses, killing their warriors and leading into Captivity their wives and children..." (1812). He would carry this attitude into the presidential office.[16]

1829: President Jackson suggested "the propriety of setting apart an ample district west of the Mississippi, and without the limits of any State or Territory now formed, to be guaranteed to the Indian tribes, as long as they shall occupy it; each tribe having a distinct control over the portion designated for its use." "There," he observed, "they may be secured in the enjoyment of governments of their own choice, subject to no other control from the United States, than such as may be necessary to preserve peace on the frontier and between the several tribes..."[17]

1860: President Buchanan: Extinguishment of Indian Title

In 1860, President Buchanan transmitted eight memorials to Congress from residents of New Mexico, Utah, Kansas, and Nebraska seeking "the early extinguishment of the Indian title."[18]

1868: President Garfield: Treaties with Savages Mockery

1868: Thirteen years before he took office as president of the United States, James Garfield predicted the extinction of the American Indian.

> "The race of the red men will...before many generations be remembered only as a strange, weird, dreamlike specter, which once passed before the eyes of men, but had departed forever," he said in 1868 when, as a member of the U.S. House of Representatives, he proposed a bill that would transfer Indian Affairs from the Interior Department to the War Department. He called it a "mockery...for the representatives of the great Government of the United States to sit down in a wigwam and make treaties with a lot of painted and half naked savages, only to have those treaties trampled under foot... This whole practice of making treaties with our wards is ridiculous."[19]

In a letter of advice to President-elect James A. Garfield, Interior Secretary Schurz warned Garfield of the corruption of the Department of the Interior.

> The Interior Department is the most dangerous branch of the public service. ... It is a constant fight with the sharks that surround the Indian Bureau, the General Land Office, the Pension Office and the Patent Office, and a ceaseless struggle with perplexing questions and situations, especially in the Indian Service. Unless the head of the Interior Department well understands and performs his full duty, your Administration will be in constant danger of disgrace..."[20]

Garfield's Presidency was abruptly terminated six months after his taking office by his assassination.

1873: President Grant's Peace Policy

In his inaugural address on March 4, 1873, President Grant stated: "The proper treatment of the original inhabitants of this land—the Indians—is one deserving of careful study. I will favor any course towards them which tends to their civilization and ultimate citizenship."[21]

1878: President Hayes: Moral Duty

In his 1878 State of the Union address, President Hayes acknowledged the moral duty of the U.S. to the Indians. Unfortunately, he was in the minority. Those that followed would violate his trust.

> It may be impossible to raise them fully up to the level of the white population of the United States; but *we should not forget that they are the aborigines of the country, and called the soil their own on which our people have grown rich, powerful, and happy.* We owe it to them as a moral duty to help them in attaining at least that degree of civilization which they may be able to reach. It is not only our duty, it is also our interest to do so. (Emphasis added)[22]

1880: Indians to Be Assimilated to and Merged in Body of U.S. Citizens

The Congressional testimony of Sec. of Interior Schurz on the Agreement with the Ute Indians to sell their reservation in Colorado, House bill No. 5092 and Senate bill No. 1509, stated as follows:

> *It has seemed to me...that the system of large reservations as has hitherto prevailed, is not only no longer desirable either in the interest of the Indians or of the whites, but will, in the course of time become utterly untenable.* As our white settlements in the West multiply, as the development of the country advances, available lands become more and more scarce and valuable, and so it is not unnatural that the withholding of large tracts from settlement and development so as to maintain a savage aristocracy in the enjoyment of their chivalrous pastimes, should be looked upon by many as a system incompatible with the progress of civilization and injurious to the material interests of the country. As an inevitable consequence, we have witnessed many encroachments, lawless and wrongful in character, upon Indian lands and rights, and constant efforts to drive the red men from the reservation belonging to them. (Emphasis added)

> *...as long as the Indians hold very large tracts of land, in great part useless to themselves...their tenure will, under existing circumstances become practically more and more precarious.* It is

most desirable for the interests of the Indians themselves, therefore, that we should substitute for the system of large reservations another system that will protect the rights and interests of the Indians without standing in the way of the progress and development of the country. ***The ultimate end of this new system, in my opinion, must necessarily be that the Indians be gradually assimilated to and merged in the body of citizens.*** In the direction of this end, some things are necessary, which have been done as far as the Executive could do them under the laws of the country as they stand: First, to set the Indians to work; second, to educate them; and, third, to individualize the Indians by settling them in severalty, with the expectation of giving them fee-simple title by patent to their allotments, the same title by which white citizens hold their lands under the protection of law. (Emphasis added)[23]

1889: Indians to be Absorbed into National Life, Not as Indians but as American Citizens

In 1889, Commissioner T.J. Morgan, just beginning his term as Commissioner, stated his "strongly-cherished convictions:"

> ***First. The anomalous position heretofore occupied by the Indians in this country can not much longer be maintained. The reservation system belongs to a "vanishing state of things" and must soon cease to exist. Second. The logic of events demands the absorption of the Indians into our national life, not as Indians, but as American citizens. Third. As soon as a wise conservatism will warrant it, the relations of the Indians to the Government must, rest solely upon the full recognition of their individuality. Each Indian must be treated as a man, be allowed a man's rights...***(Emphasis added)[24]

> ***So long as Indians continue to maintain tribal relations and so long as they are confined to the limits of their reservations, the Indian question will continue to be a problem. They must become more intimate with our citizenship.*** They must be taught by actual experience and association the important lessons of social economy. In our efforts to humanize, Christianize, and educate the Indian we should endeavor to divorce him from his primitive habits and customs. He should be induced to emulate

the white man in all things that conduce to his happiness and comfort. The best way to instruct an Indian in agriculture is to locate his land or farm in juxtaposition with that of thrifty and energetic farmers. (Emphasis added)[25]

1881: President Arthur: No Sovereigns

In his first message to Congress, in December 1881, President Arthur pointed to historic errors in the conduct of Indian affairs. His opinions of Indians wouldn't be propitious. He (1) opposed recognizing tribes as sovereigns; (2) protested the treaty and reservation policy; (3) disputed any support for pursuing their cultural practices; and (4) assailed the failure of civilizing them.

> "It was natural, at a time when the national territory seemed almost illimitable and contained many millions of acres far outside the bounds of civilized settlements, that a policy should have been initiated which more than aught else has been the fruitful source of our Indian complications," he said. "I refer, of course, to the policy of dealing with the various Indian tribes as separate nationalities, of relegating them by treaty stipulations to the occupancy of immense reservations in the West, and of encouraging them to live a savage life, undisturbed by any earnest and well-directed efforts to bring them under the influences of civilization."[26]

1885-1889: President Cleveland: Allotment

During President Cleveland's first term in office, from 1885 to 1889, Congress enacted three measures with devastating effects on Indians. First, the Major Crimes Act (18 U.S.C.S. §1153) instituted federal jurisdiction over serious crimes committed by Indians on their own land. This deprived Indian Nations of this vital aspect of sovereignty, especially since the federal government lacked the manpower and the will to prevent criminal activities. Second, the General Allotment Act (24 Stat. 388) authorized the President to divide Indian tribal land into individual allotments, forcing Indians into private property ownership whether they desired it or not. Third, the Indian Appropriations Act of 1889 (25 Stat. 980) opened "unassigned" lands to white settlers. This would lead, for example, to the Oklahoma Land Run of 1889.

1889: President Harrison: Eradicating Tribal Relations

President Benjamin Harrison was the grandson of the ninth U.S. president

William Henry Harrison. In his first message to Congress, in December 1889, Harrison called Indians an "ignorant and helpless people." In his opinion, breaking up tribal relations should have occurred much earlier.

> "It is to be regretted that the policy of breaking up the tribal relation and of dealing with the Indian as an individual did not appear earlier in our legislation," Harrison told Congress. "Large reservations held in common and the maintenance of the authority of the chiefs and headmen have deprived the individual of every incentive to the exercise of thrift, and the annuity has contributed an affirmative impulse toward a state of confirmed pauperism."[27]

1889: Theodore Roosevelt: We Are Indebted to Fierce Settler who Drives Savage from Land

The bias against Indians was still prevalent in 1889 when Theodore Roosevelt wrote *The Winning of the West*, a decade before he would be elected President:

> The most ultimately righteous of all wars is a war with savages, though it is apt to be also the most terrible and inhuman. The rude, fierce settler who drives the savage from the land lays all civilized mankind under a debt to him. American and Indian, Boer and Zulu, Cossack and Tartar, New Zealander and Maori,—in each case the victor, horrible though many of his deeds are, has laid deep the foundations for the future greatness of a mighty people. ... It is of incalculable importance that America, Australia, and Siberia should pass out of the hands of their red, black, and yellow aboriginal owners, and become the heritage of the dominant world races.[28]

In his First Message to Congress, December 1901, President Roosevelt advocated for breaking up tribes, distributing tribal funds, ending the leasing of allotments and Indians treatment as individuals like the white man.

> In my judgment the time has arrived when we should definitely make up our minds to recognize the Indian as an individual and not as a member of a tribe. The General Allotment Act is a mighty pulverizing engine to break up the tribal mass. It acts directly upon the family and the individual. Under its provisions some sixty thousand Indians have already become citizens of the United States. We should now break up the tribal funds, doing for them what allotment does for the tribal lands; that is, they should be divided into individual holdings. There will be a

transition period during which the funds will in many cases have to be held in trust. This is the case also with the lands. A stop should be put upon the indiscriminate permission to Indians to lease their allotments. The effort should be steadily to make the Indian work like any other man on his own ground. The marriage laws of the Indians should be made the same as those of the whites.

In the schools the education should be elementary and largely industrial. The need of higher education among the Indians is very, very limited. On the reservations care should be taken to try to suit the teaching to the needs of the particular Indian. There is no use in attempting to induce agriculture in a country suited only for cattle raising, where the Indian should be made a stock grower. The ration system, which is merely the corral and the reservation system, is highly detrimental to the Indians. It promotes beggary, perpetuates pauperism, and stifles industry. It is an effectual barrier to progress. It must continue to a greater or less degree as long as tribes are herded on reservations and have everything in common. The Indian should be treated as an individual--like the white man. During the change of treatment inevitable hardships will occur; every effort should be made to minimize these hardships; but we should not because of them hesitate to make the change. There should be a continuous reduction in the number of agencies.[29]

1924: Indian Citizenship Act

The Indian Citizenship Act of 1924 was approved by Congress on June 2, 1924, and was signed into law by Calvin Coolidge (1872–1933), in a ceremony attended by representatives of a number of Indian nations.

1934: Indian Reorganization Act

The 1934 Indian Reorganization Act (IRA) ended the policy of allotment, banned the further sale of Indian land and decreed that any unallotted land not yet sold should be returned to tribal control. Land was restored to the SUIT and UMUT. It also granted Indian communities a measure of governmental and judicial autonomy by authorizing tribes to organize governments and obtain charters.

1932: Franklin D. Roosevelt, Indian New Deal

With the election of Franklin D. Roosevelt in 1932, Collier was appointed commissioner of Indian affairs, taking office on April 21, 1933. He immediately began the Indian New Deal by convincing Congress to approve of the Pueblo Relief Act (1933) to compensate the Pueblo tribes for land lost to squatters. This was followed by the Johnson–O'Malley Act (1934) to authorize federal contracts with state and local governments for educational, health, and social services for tribes, and the Indian Reorganization Act (1934) that ended land severalty and supported tribal self-government. The Indian Arts and Crafts Act (1935) protected and promoted authentic Indian arts and crafts. Collier administratively closed a number of off-reservation boarding schools and constructed scores of day schools that he used to promote his ideology of community life. He also hired Willard Beatty as director of education to implement a progressive education that supported and reinforced rural Indian life while providing training for teachers in cross-cultural education.[30]

1946: Indian Claims Commission – Pre-Cursor to Termination of Indian Tribes

The first step towards terminating the reservations came in 1946 when Congress, in part to reward Native Americans for their contribution to the war effort, set up the Indian Claims Commission to hear Indian claims for any lands stolen from them from 1776 forward. The Commission would provide only financial compensation and not return any land. *The federal government regarded the Commission as the first step to 'getting out of the Indian business.'*

President Truman stated:

> I hope that this bill will mark the beginning of a new era for our Indian citizens. They have valiantly served on every battle front. ... With the final settlement of all outstanding claims which this measure ensures, Indians can take their place without special handicaps or special advantages in the economic life of our nation and share fully in its progress.[31]

The original intention was for the Commission to sit for five years, but there were so many claims that it remained in existence until 1978.

Termination

> Senate approved House Concurrent Resolution 108 establishing the congressional goal of subjecting American Indians "to the same laws

and entitled to the same privileges and responsibilities" as other Americans.³²

New Era of Indian Self-Determination

1968: President Lyndon B. Johnson, Indian Self-Determination

1970: President Richard M. Nixon, Indian Self-Determination

President Nixon: July 8, 1970 It was time for a policy of self-determination "without the threat of eventual termination."

1975: Indian Self-Determination and Education Assistance Act

Successive Presidential Administrations Confirm Tribal Sovereignty

Notes:

1. "From George Washington to The States, 8 June 1783," *Founders Online,* National Archives. https://founders.archives.gov/documents/Washington/99-01-02-11404 (accessed online November 13, 2020).

2. From Thomas Jefferson to James Monroe, 17 April 1791," *Founders Online*, National Archives, https://founders.archives.gov/documents/Jefferson/01-20-02-0051. [Original source: *The Papers of Thomas Jefferson*, vol. 20, *1 April–4 August 1791*, ed. Julian P. Boyd. Princeton: Princeton University Press, 1982, pp. 234–236.] (accessed online November 13, 2020).

3. "From Thomas Jefferson to Charles Carroll, 15 April 1791," *Founders Online,* National Archives. https://founders.archives.gov/documents/Jefferson/01-20-02-0046. [Original source: *The Papers of Thomas Jefferson*, vol. 20, *1 April–4 August 1791*, ed. Julian P. Boyd. Princeton: Princeton University Press, 1982, pp. 214–215.] (accessed online November 19, 2020).

4. Genovese, Michael A., and Alysa Landry. US Presidents and the Destruction of the Native American Nations. Palgrave Macmillan, 2021, p. 43. "From John Adams to Cherokee Nation, 27 August 1798," Founders Online, National Archives, https://founders.archives.gov/documents/Adams/99-02-02-2892 (accessed online July 14, 2024).

5. "From Thomas Jefferson to John Breckinridge, 12 August 1803," Founders Online, National Archives, https://founders.archives.gov/documents/Jefferson/01-41-02-0139. [Original source: The Papers of Thomas Jefferson, vol. 41, 11 July–15 November 1803, ed. Barbara B. Oberg. Princeton: Princeton University Press, 2014, pp. 184–186.] (accessed online November 19, 2020).

6. https://www.infoplease.com/primary-sources/government/presidential-speeches/state-union-address-james-madison-december-3-1816 (accessed online July 14, 2024).

7. https://millercenter.org/the-presidency/presidential-speeches/december-2-1817-first-annual-message (accessed online March 27, 2023).

8. https://www.presidency.ucsb.edu/documents/second-annual-message-1 (accessed online March 27, 2023).

9. https://millercenter.org/the-presidency/presidential-speeches/december-2-1817-first-annual-message (accessed online March 27, 2023).

10. https://www.stateoftheunionhistory.com/2017/04/1818-james-monroe-indian-civilization.html#:~:text=The%20act%20led%20to%20the,-to%20become%20part%20of%20it. (accessed online July 10, 2024).

11. https://www.presidency.ucsb.edu/documents/inaugural-address-24 (accessed online July 10, 2024).

12. See "Annual Message to Congress with Documents, President Jackson, December 8, 1829," Senate Document 1, Twenty-First Cong., First Sess., Congressional Serial Set 192.

13. Adams, John Quincy. *Memoirs of John Quincy Adams: comprising portions of his diary from 1795 to 1848*. JB Lippincott & Company, 1874, 5:176.

14. Orations, John Quincy Adams, "The Jubilee of the Constitution, delivered at New York, April 30, 1839, before the New York Historical Society." https://www.gutenberg.org/files/896/.

15. Adams, John Quincy. *Memoirs of John Quincy Adams: comprising portions of his diary from 1795 to 1848*. JB Lippincott & Company, 1874, 7:89.

16. Rogin, Michael P. *Fathers and Children: Andrew Jackson and the Subjugation of the American Indian*, 1975:147. Love, Christopher A. "Andrew Jackson and His Indian Wars." Air Force Law Review, spring 2002, pp. 221+. Gale Academic OneFile, link.gale.com/apps/doc/A103223914/AONE?u=anon~cd130ebe&sid=googleScholar&xid=58683e63. (accessed online July 14, 2024).

17. See "Annual Message to Congress with Documents, President Jackson, December 8, 1829,"
Senate Document 1, Twenty-First Cong., First Sess., *Congressional Serial Set 192*.

18. https://www.presidency.ucsb.edu/documents/special-message-2969 (accessed online October 4, 2022).

19. The works of James Abram Garfield. Volume 1, James A. Garfield, Best Books, 1882, p. 367.

20. Carl Schurz, Speeches. Correspondence and Political Papers. (New York, 1913).

21. https://www.presidency.ucsb.edu/documents/inaugural-address-37 (accessed online April 14, 2022).

22. http://www.let.rug.nl/usa/presidents/rutherford-birchard-hayes/state-of-the-union-1878.php (accessed online April 28, 2022).

23. H.R. Rep. No. 1401, 46th Cong., 2nd Sess. (1880), pp. 2-3. Congressional Record: Containing the Proceedings and Debates of the 46th Cong., 2nd Sess. Congress, Volume 10, U.S. Government Printing Office, 1880, p. 104.

24. Report of the Commissioner of Indian Affairs to the Secretary of the Interior. United States. Office of Indian Affairs. U.S. Government Printing Office, 1890, pp. XXXVIII-XXXIX.

25. Report of Superintendent of Indian Schools to the Secretary of the Interior, 1896, p. 17.

26. Indian Policy Reform Extract from President Chester Arthur's First Annual Message to Congress, https://www.presidency.ucsb.edu/documents/first- annual-message-13 (accessed online February 21, 2022).

27. http://www.let.rug.nl/usa/presidents/benjamin-harrison/state-of-the-union-1889.php (accessed online July 11, 2022).

28. Roosevelt, Theodore. *Winning of the west,* Vol. 4., Putnam, 1889: 56.

29. https://www.presidency.ucsb.edu/documents/first-annual-message-16 (accessed online December 12, 2020).

30. Dejong, David H. Paternalism to Partnership: The Administration of Indian Affairs, 1786– 2021. University of Nebraska Press, 2022.

31. https://www.trumanlibrary.gov/library/public-papers/204/statement-president-upon-signing- bill-creating-indian-claims-commission

32. Indians, HCR 108, 67 Stat. B132 (August 1, 1953).

Appendix 3: BIA American Indian Citizenship Ceremony

Representative of department speaking:

The President of the United States has sent me to speak a solemn and serious word to you, a word that means more to some of you than any other that you have ever heard. He has been told that there are some among you who should no longer be controlled by the Bureau of Indian Affairs, but should be given their patents in fee and thus become free American citizens. It is his decision that this shall be done, and that those so honored by the people of the United States shall have the meaning of this new and great privilege pointed out by symbol and by word, so that no man or woman shall not know its meaning. The President has sent me papers naming those men and women and I shall call out their names one by one, and they will come before me.

For Men:
(Read Name.)
_____ (white name). What was your Indian name? (Gives name.)
_____ (Indian name). I hand you a bow and an arrow. Take this bow and shoot the arrow. (He shoots.)
_____ (Indian name). You have shot your last arrow. That means that you are no longer to live the life of an Indian. You are from this day forward to live the life of the white man. But you may keep that arrow, it will be to you a symbol of your noble race and of the pride you feel that you come from the first of all Americans.
_____ (white name). Take in your hand this plow. (He takes the handles of the plow.) This act means that you have chosen to live the life of the white man—and the white man lives by work. From the earth we all must get our living and the earth will not yield unless man pours upon it the sweat of his brow. Only by work do we gain a right to the land or to the enjoyment of life.
_____ (white name). I give you a purse. This purse will always say to you that the money you gain from your labor must be wisely kept. The wise man saves his money so that when the sun does not smile and the grass does not grow, he will not starve.
I give into your hands the flag of your country. This is the only flag you have ever had or ever will have. It is the flag of freedom; the flag of free men, the flag of a hundred million free men and women of whom you are now one.

That flag has a request to make of you, _____ (white name), that you take it into your hands and repeat these words:

"For as much as the President has said that I am worthy to be a citizen of the United States, I now promise to this flag that I will give my hands, my head, and my heart to the doing of all that will make me a true American citizen." And now beneath this flag I place upon your breast the emblem of your citizenship. Wear this badge of honor always; and may the eagle that is on it never see you do aught of which the flag will not be proud.
(The audience rises and shouts: "_____(white name) is an American citizen.")

For Women:
_____ (white name). Take in your hand this work bag and purse. (She takes the work bag and purse.)
This means that you have chosen the life of the white woman—and the white woman loves her home. The family and the home are the foundation of our civilization. Upon the character and industry of the mother and homemaker largely depends the future of our Nation. The purse will always say to you that the money you gain from your labor must be wisely kept. The wise woman saves her money, so that when the sun does not smile and the grass does not grow, she and her children will not starve.
I give into your hands the flag of your country. This is the only flag you have ever had or ever will have. It is the flag of freedom, the flag of free men, a hundred million free men and women of whom you are now one. That flag has a request to make of you, _____ (white name), that you take it into your hands and repeat these words:
"For as much as the President has said that I am worthy to be a citizen of the United States, I now promise to this flag that I will give my hands, my head, and my heart to the doing of all that will make me a true American citizen." And now beneath this flag I place upon your breast the emblem of your citizenship. Wear this badge of honor always, and may the eagle that is on it never see you do aught of which the flag will not be proud.
(The audience rises and shouts: "_____(white name) is an American citizen.")

https://www.ndstudies.gov/curriculum/high-school/standing-rock-oyate/documents-standing-rock (accessed online April 9, 2023).

Appendix 4: Indian Child Welfare Act Case Study

Part 1: Haaland v. Brackeen, 599 U.S. 255, 268-270 (2023).
Part 2: Significant Parties Supporting ICWA.
Part 3: Significant Opposing Briefs in Haaland v. Brackeen.
Part 4: Colorado - Pioneering State for Adoption Intervention Cases: 2,500 Cases Filed by 2022 – Primary Attorney's Firm Used Discredited Child Adoption Expert.
Part 5: Federal and Colorado Adoption Legislation, Restricting Intervention.
Part 6: American Indian/Alaska Native (AI/AN) Families Attachment and Bonding Research.

Part 1: Haaland v. Brackeen, 599 U.S. 255, 268-270 (2023)

This case arises from three separate child custody proceedings governed by ICWA. 25 U.S.C. §§ 1901-63.

The Brackeens and their attorneys challenged ICWA on multiple grounds, claiming that it constitutes racial discrimination and, thus, a violation of the equal protection clause. They also argued that because ICWA is a federal law that states are being forced to implement, the legislation goes against the principle of anti-commandeering as articulated in the 10th Amendment.[1]

> Holding: In child custody proceedings governed by the Indian Child Welfare Act, ICWA is consistent with Congress's Article I authority, petitioners' anticommandeering challenges under the Tenth Amendment are rejected, and the parties lack standing to litigate their other challenges to ICWA's placement preferences.[2]

Brackeens

A. L. M. was placed in foster care with Chad and Jennifer Brackeen when he was 10 months old. Because his biological mother is a member of the Navajo Nation and his biological father is a member of the Cherokee Nation, he falls within ICWA's definition of an "Indian child." Both the Brackeens and A. L. M.'s biological parents live in Texas. After A. L. M. had lived with the Brackeens for more than a year, they sought to adopt him. A. L. M.'s biological mother, father, and grandmother all supported the adoption. The Navajo and Cherokee Nations did not. Pursuant to an agreement between the Tribes, the Navajo Nation designated A.

L. M. as a member and informed the state court that it had located a potential alternative placement with nonrelative tribal members living in New Mexico. ICWA's placement preferences ranked the proposed Navajo family ahead of non- Indian families like the Brackeens. See §1915(a). The Brackeens tried to convince the state court that there was "good cause" to deviate from ICWA's preferences.
They presented favorable testimony from A. L. M.'s court-appointed guardian and from a psychological expert who described the strong emotional bond between A.

L. M. and his foster parents. A. L. M.'s biological parents and grandmother also testified, urging the court to allow A. L. M. to remain with the Brackeens, "'the only parents [A. L. M.] knows.'" App. 96. The court denied the adoption petition, and the Texas Department of Family and Protective Services announced its intention to move A. L. M. from the Brackeens' home to New Mexico. In response, the Brackeens obtained an emergency stay of the transfer and filed this lawsuit. The Navajo family then withdrew from consideration, and the Brackeens finalized their adoption of A. L. M. The Brackeens now seek to adopt A. L. M.'s biological sister, Y. R. J., again over the opposition of the Navajo Nation. And while the Brackeens hope to foster and adopt other Indian children in the future, their fraught experience with A. L. M.'s adoption makes them hesitant to do so.

Librettis

Altagracia Hernandez chose Nick and Heather Libretti as adoptive parents for her newborn daughter, Baby O. The Librettis took Baby O. home from the hospital when she was three days old, and Hernandez, who lived nearby, visited Baby O. frequently. Baby O.'s biological father visited only once but supported the adoption. Hernandez is not an Indian. But Baby O.'s biological father is descended from members of the Ysleta del Sur Pueblo Tribe, and the Tribe enrolled Baby O. as a member. As a result, the adoption proceeding was governed by ICWA. The Tribe exercised its right to intervene and argued, over Hernandez's objection, that Baby O. should be moved from the Librettis' home in Nevada to the Tribe's reservation in El Paso, Texas. It presented a number of potential placements on the reservation for Baby O., and state officials began to investigate them. After Hernandez and the Librettis joined this lawsuit, however, the Tribe withdrew its challenge to the adoption, and the **Librettis finalized their adoption of Baby O**. The Librettis stayed in the litigation because they planned to foster and possibly adopt Indian children in the future.

Cliffords

Jason and Danielle Clifford, who live in Minnesota, fostered Child P., whose maternal grandmother belongs to the White Earth Band of Ojibwe Tribe. When Child P. entered state custody around the age of three, her mother informed the court that ICWA did not apply because Child P. was not eligible for tribal membership. The Tribe wrote a letter to the court confirming the same. After two years in the foster care system, Child P. was placed with the Cliffords, who eventually sought to adopt her. The Tribe intervened in the proceedings and, with no explanation for its change in position, informed the court that Child P. was in fact eligible for tribal membership. Later, the Tribe announced that it had enrolled Child P. as a member. **To comply with ICWA, Minnesota placed Child P. with her maternal grandmother**, who had lost her foster license due to a criminal conviction. The Cliffords continued to pursue the adoption, but, citing ICWA, the court denied their motion. Like the other families, the Cliffords intend to foster or adopt Indian children in the future.

The Brackeens, the Librettis, Hernandez, and the Cliffords filed suit in federal court... They were joined by the States of Texas, Indiana, and Louisiana. Several Indian Tribes intervened to defend the law alongside the federal parties. 599 U.S. 255, 268-270 (2023).[3]

Brackeen's Standing to Bring Federal Lawsuit

Federal courts only have constitutional authority to resolve actual disputes. Since the Brackeens had been able to adopt the Navajo child they were seeking to adopt, their controversy was over. The Navajo mother relinquished custody to the Brackeens.

GDC filed its federal suit on behalf of the Brackeens just two days before they overcame the final barriers to their adoption. As Journalist Rebecca Nagle summarized, "The Brackeens didn't file a federal lawsuit when they were losing custody. They filed the lawsuit when they were winning."[5] This raised questions about their case.[4]

Also, they sued the wrong party – the federal government. They did not cause the injury, nor could they redress it. State officials enforce ICWA, and any redress would be by them.
As stated by Stanford Law Professor Greg Ablavsky, whose amicus brief was cited by justices on both sides of the case, Justices Gorsuch in his concurring opinion and Justice Thomas in dissent:

> The Court fully rejected the Article I and anti-commandeering arguments. But on the equal protection and non-delegation questions, the Court found that the **plaintiffs lacked standing**—that they basically sued the wrong people. They brought the case against federal officials, but the federal officials are not the ones who enforce the statute. It's state officials who enforce the statute. And so, **the argument is that if they want to argue that they've been harmed, they have to sue state, not federal officials**.[5]

Those issues, the justices said, would be best resolved by state courts. As Mark Fiddler—perhaps the nation's foremost ICWA expert—put it, this means ICWA "lives to die another day."[6]

Basically, the constitutional requisites for the existence of standing were not met. The plaintiff must personally have: 1) suffered some actual or threatened injury; 2) that injury can fairly be traced to the challenged action of the defendant; and 3) that the injury is likely to be redressed by a favorable decision. The federal suit on behalf of the Brackeens was filed just two days before they overcame the final barriers to their adoption. They had no actual or threatened injury nor could a federal court redress their injury.

SCOTUS Decision Upholds ICWA as Constitutional

> In a 7–2 ruling, the Supreme Court affirmed the Fifth Circuit's determination that the ICWA is consistent with congressional powers. The appellant claims of state commandeering were rejected, reversing the Fifth Circuit's decision. No determinations were made as to appellant Fourteenth Amendment claims for lack of standing.

BARRETT, J., delivered the opinion of the Court, in which ROBERTS, C. J., and SOTOMAYOR, KAGAN, GORSUCH, KAVANAUGH, and JACKSON, JJ., joined. GORSUCH, J., filed a concurring opinion, in which SOTOMAYOR and JACKSON, JJ., joined as to Parts I and III. KAVANAUGH, J., filed a concurring opinion. THOMAS, J., and ALITO, J., filed dissenting opinions.

The U.S. government and the tribes argued Native identity is inherently political, and not racial, because Native nations are sovereign entities. SCOTUS' decision in Morton v. Mancari in 1974 established that federally recognized Indian tribes and their tribal members represent a "political classification," not a racial class. As such, Congress may enact legislation, and executive branch agencies may implement policy, that is unique to Indian peoples without violating the requirement of equal protection of the law, when such legislation or policies are reasonable and rationally designed to further tribal self-government.

> Literally every piece of legislation dealing with Indian tribes and reservations, and certainly all legislation dealing with the BIA, single out for special treatment a constituency of tribal Indians living on or near reservations. If these laws, derived from historical relationships and explicitly designed to help only Indians, were deemed invidious racial discrimination, an entire Title of the United States Code (25 U.S.C.) would be effectively erased

and the solemn commitment of the Government toward the Indians would be jeopardized. ... As long as the special treatment can be tied rationally to the fulfillment of Congress' unique obligation toward the Indians, such legislative judgments will not be disturbed. Here, where the preference is reasonable and rationally designed to further Indian self- government, we cannot say that Congress' classification violates due process.[7]

Notes: Part 1: Haaland v. Brackeen, 599 U.S. 255, 268-270 (2023).

1. https://www.deseret.com/2023/5/16/23680786/indian-child-welfare-act-future/ (accessed
online July 1, 2024).

2. https://www.deseret.com/2023/5/16/23680786/indian-child-welfare-act-future/ (accessed
online July 1, 2024).

3. https://www.supremecourt.gov/opinions/22pdf/21-376_7l48.pdf (accessed online June 1, 2014).

4. This Land. Rebecca Nagle. Podcast (19 Episodes). https://crooked.com/podcast-series/this-land/ (accessed online July 1, 2024).

5. Stanford's Greg Ablavsky on the Brackeen Indian Child Welfare Act Decision, June 30, 2023. https://law.stanford.edu/2023/06/30/stanfords-greg-ablavsky-on-the-brackeen-indian-child-welfare-act-decision/ (accessed online July 10, 2024).

6. What Does the ICWA Ruling Mean for Native American Kids, Timothy Sandefur, June 15, 2023. https://www.goldwaterinstitute.org/what-does-the-icwa-ruling-mean-for-native-american-kids/ (accessed online July 10, 2024).

7. Morton v. Mancari, 417 U.S. at 555 (1974).

Part 2: Significant Parties Supporting ICWA

87 Members of Congress
Many States with Significant American Indian Populations
180 INDIAN TRIBES AND 35 TRIBAL ORGANIZATIONS
American Academy of Pediatrics and American Medical Association
American Psychological Association
American Bar Association
American Civil Liberties Union

Senator James Abourezk

Robyn Bradshaw
Casey Family Programs, et al.
National Association of Counsel for Children
Former Foster Children
Family Defense Providers
Aubrey Nelson and Sam Evans-Brown

Administrative Law and Constitutional Law Professors
Professor Gregory Ablavsky
Indian Law Professors
American Historical Association and Organization of American Historians
Constitutional Accountability Center
County of Los Angeles
National Indigenous Women's Resource Center[1]

87 Members of Congress

INTEREST OF AMICI CURIAE

This brief is filed by 33 Senators and 54 Members of the House of Representatives, each of whom has taken an active role in legislation concerning Indian affairs during his or her tenure as a Member of Congress.

INTRODUCTION

ICWA is a valid and constitutionally sound exercise of the "[p]lenary authority" over Indian affairs that Congress has exercised "from the beginning" of the Republic. Lone Wolf v. Hitchcock, 187 U.S. 553, 565 (1903). BRIEF FOR 87 MEMBERS OF CONGRESS AS AMICI CURIAE IN SUPPORT OF FEDERAL AND TRIBAL DEFENDANTS.[2]

Many States with Significant American Indian Populations Support ICWA

Many states support ICWA including those that submitted an Amicus Brief in Support of the federal and tribal parties: BRIEF FOR THE STATES OF CALIFORNIA, ARIZONA, COLORADO, CONNECTICUT, IDAHO, ILLINOIS, IOWA, MAINE, MASSACHUSETTS, MICHIGAN, MINNESOTA, NEVADA, NEW JERSEY, NEW MEXICO, NEW YORK, NORTH CAROLINA, OREGON, PENNSYLVANIA, RHODE ISLAND, SOUTH DAKOTA, UTAH, WASHINGTON, AND WISCONSIN, AND THE DISTRICT OF COLUMBIA, AS AMICI CURIAE IN SUPPORT OF THE FEDERAL AND TRIBAL PARTIES.[3]

Tribes

NARF's Tribal Government and Organizations Brief. BRIEF OF 180 INDIAN TRIBES AND 35 TRIBAL ORGANIZATIONS AS AMICI CURIAE IN SUPPORT OF CHEROKEE NATION, ET AL.[4]

Medical Organizations

American Academy of Pediatrics and American Medical Association

> Tribes are, in a real way, extended families. AI/AN children have supportive connections not only with parents, and not only with their near relatives, but with a broader community that provides care and affirmative connections for nourishing growth. These connections are invaluable for the development of AI/AN chil-

dren. BRIEF OF AMERICAN ACADEMY OF PEDIATRICS AND AMERICAN MEDICAL ASSOCIATION AS AMICI CURIAE IN SUPPORT OF RESPONDENTS.[5]

The American Academy of Pediatrics affirms the continuing importance of ICWA as a gold standard child-welfare policy. The Academy urges the Court to leave this vital statute undisturbed to promote the optimal health and wellbeing of AI/AN children. ... A metaanalysis of studies covering over 600,000 children found that children in kinship care "experience better outcomes in regard to behaviour problems, adaptive behaviours, psychiatric disorders, well-being, placement stability (placement settings, number of placements, and placement disruption), guardianship, and institutional abuse than do children in foster care."[6]

American Psychological Association (specifically including the associations of Texas, Louisiana, and Indiana) and the Society of Indian Psychologists

... psychological research has confirmed Congress's determination that Indian children generally do best when they are placed with Indian families. Researchers have found that the formation of an Indian identity through enculturation—i.e., the process of learning about and adopting features of one's cultural heritage—provides Indian children with substantial mental health benefits, including increased self-esteem and resilience. BRIEF OF THE AMERICAN PSYCHOLOGICAL ASSOCIATION, SOCIETY OF INDIAN PSYCHOLOGISTS, INDIANA PSYCHOLOGICAL ASSOCIATION, LOUISIANA PSYCHOLOGICAL ASSOCIATION, AND TEXAS PSYCHOLOGICAL ASSOCIATION AS AMICI CURIAE IN SUPPORT OF THE FEDERAL AND TRIBAL PETITIONERS.[7]

American Bar Association ("ABA")

The ABA filed an amicus brief in support of ICWA stating: the ABA has been a consistent advocate for ICWA in part because it effectively implements broader legal principles that the ABA recognizes as foundational in the child welfare field. See, e.g., ABA Resolution 11819A (2019) (recognizing, inter alia, that children and parents have legally protected rights to family integrity and family unity). BRIEF OF THE AMERICAN BAR ASSOCIATION AS AMICUS CURIAE IN SUPPORT OF PETITIONERS IN 21-376 AND 21-377, AND IN SUPPORT OF RESPONDENTS IN 21-378 AND 21-380.[8]

In an ABA article, Kinship Care is Better for Children and Families, Am. Bar Ass'n (July 1, 2017), Heidi Redlich Epstein wrote that "kinship care is more likely to improve children's wellbeing, minimize trauma, increase permanency for children's home placement, improve behavioral and mental health outcomes, and preserve children's cultural identifies than foster care placement with non- relatives)."[9]

American Civil Liberties Union

In furtherance of their mission, the ACLU and its affiliates have supported federal laws designed to preserve Indian families and respect the cultural heritage of Indian Tribes. The ACLU and its affiliates have also advocated in favor of children's rights and a child's interest in family integrity. BRIEF OF THE AMERICAN CIVIL LIBERTIES UNION AND FOURTEEN AFFILIATES AS AMICI CURIAE IN SUPPORT OF FEDERAL AND TRIBAL DEFENDANTS.[10]

U.S. Department of Health & Human Services ("USDH&HS"), Admin. for Children and Families, Children's Bureau

The USDH&HS announced that "[k]inship care has become a preferred option in most U.S. child welfare systems."[11]

Other Amici Curiae briefs filed in support of the federal and tribal defendants:

Senator James Abourezk
Robyn Bradshaw

Casey Family Programs, et al. Former Foster Children Family Defense Providers
Aubrey Nelson and Sam Evans-Brown

Administrative Law and Constitutional Law Professors Professor Gregory Ablavsky
Indian Law Professors

American Historical Association and Organization of American Historians Constitutional Accountability Center
County of Los Angeles

National Association of Counsel for Children National Indigenous Women's Resource Center

Notes: Part 2: Significant Parties Supporting ICWA.

1. https://www.supremecourt.gov/docket/docketfiles/html/public/21-376.html (accessed online July 10, 2024).

2. https://www.supremecourt.gov/DocketPDF/21/21-376/234020/20220819125927143_21-376%20bsac%2087%20Members%20of%20Congress%20supporting%20Federal-Tribal%20Defendants.pdf (accessed online July 10, 2024).

3. https://www.supremecourt.gov/DocketPDF/21/21-376/234021/20220819125918797_21-376%20Brief%20for%20California%20et%20al.pdf (accessed online July 10, 2024).

4. https://www.supremecourt.gov/DocketPDF/21/21-376/195984/20211008165606962_41401%20pdf%20Jacket%20br.pdf (accessed online July 10, 2024).

5. https://www.supremecourt.gov/DocketPDF/21/21-376/234042/20220819140750948_21-376.amics.brief.FINAL.pdf (accessed online July 10, 2024).

6. Marc Winokur et al., "Kinship Care for the Safety, Permanency, and Wellbeing of Children Removed from the Home for Maltreatment: A Systematic Review," Campbell Systematic Reviews (Mar. 3, 2014), https://doi.org/10.4073/csr.2014.2. See also https://www.newyorker.com/magazine/2023/10/23/foster-family-biological-parents-adoption-intervenors (accessed online July 10, 2024).

7. https://www.supremecourt.gov/DocketPDF/21/21-376/234093/20220819161628388_APA%20Amicus%20Brief.pdf (accessed online July 10, 2024).

8. https://www.supremecourt.gov/DocketPDF/21/21-376/233915/20220818145927333_21- 376%2021-377%20 21-378%2021-380acTheAmericanBarAssociation.pdf (accessed online July 10, 2024).

9. https://www.americanbar.org/groups/public_interest/child_law/resources/child_la w_practiceonline/child_law_practice/vol-36/july-aug-2017/kinship-care-is-better-forchildren- and-families [https://perma.cc/8L6QJL6H] https://turtletalk.blog/wp- content/uploads/2023/07/article-5_fort.pdf, p. 1659 (accessed online July 10, 2024).

10.. https://www.supremecourt.gov/DocketPDF/21/21-376/233896/20220818142023980_21-376%2021-377%2021-378%2021-380%20American%20Civil%20 Liberties%20Union%20and%20Fourteen%20Affiliates.pdfA.pdf (accessed online July 10, 2024).

11. "Impact of Kinship Care on Permanency Outcomes," U.S. ADMIN. FOR CHILDREN & FAMILIES, CHILDREN'S BUREAU, https://www.childwelfare.gov/ topics/permanency/relatives/impact/ (last visited July 20, 2022). The AFCARS Report, "U.S. DEP'T OF HEALTH & HUMAN SERVS., ADMIN. FOR CHILDREN & FAMILIES" (Oct. 4, 2021) (estimating fiscal year 2020 data) (accessed online July 10, 2024).

Part 3: Significant Opposing Briefs in Haaland v. Brackeen

    Goldwater Institute, Texas Public Policy Foundation, and Cato Institute
    Pacific Legal Foundation
    Christian Alliance for Indian Child Welfare
    Citizens Equal Rights Foundation
    New Civil Liberties Alliance
    Project on Fair Representation
    State of Ohio

BRIEF AMICI CURIAE OF GOLDWATER INSTITUTE, TEXAS PUBLIC POLICY FOUNDATION, AND CATO INSTITUTE IN SUPPORT OF STATE OF TEXAS AND BRACKEEN, ET AL

The Goldwater Institute (GI) is a nonpartisan public policy foundation devoted to advancing the principles of limited government and individual freedom. ... GI's Equal Protection for Indian Children project is devoted to defending Native American children and families against the unconstitutional provisions of the Indian Child Welfare Act (ICWA). Through that project, GI has litigated or participated as amicus in ICWA cases nationwide, including in Arizona, California. Ohio, and Washington.

The Cato Institute is a nonpartisan public-policy research foundation established in 1977 and dedicated to advancing the principles of individual liberty, free markets, and limited government.

The Texas Public Policy Foundation (TPPF) is a non-profit, nonpartisan research organization founded in 1989 and dedicated to promoting liberty, personal responsibility, and free enterprise through academically-sound research and outreach. ... Through its Center for Families and Children, TPPF pursues policies that will preserve families, improve foster care, and protect parents and children from unjustified, often counterproductive, government interference. GI, Cato, and TPPF have participated as amici at every stage of this case.[1]

Funded by thousands of individuals, foundations, and corporations, the Foundation does not accept government funds or contributions to influence the outcomes of its research.[2]

Its position on ICWA is as follows:

"The federal Indian Child Welfare Act creates a separate and unjust set of rules for Native American children," said Brandon Logan, director of the Center for Families & Children at the Texas Public Policy Foundation. "Rather than looking to the best interests of the child in making decisions on foster care placement and adoption, federal law imposes an inferior, race-based standard on state courts. The standard set by this law can lead to racial segregation and injustice and deny Native American children the best opportunity to flourish."[3]

AMICUS CURIAE BRIEF OF FOSTER PARENTS AND PACIFIC LEGAL FOUNDATION IN SUPPORT OF CHAD EVERETT BRACKEEN, ET AL.

Founded in 1973, Pacific Legal Foundation is a nonprofit, tax-exempt corporation organized under the laws of the State of California for the purpose of engaging in litigation in matters affecting the public interest. PLF provides a voice in the courts for mainstream Americans who believe in the primacy of individual rights over collective interests. ... PLF has extensive litigation experience in the areas of racial discrimination, racial preferences, and civil rights. It has served as lead counsel in lawsuits challenging race-based laws ... and participated as amicus curiae in nearly every major United States Supreme Court case involving racial classifications in the past four decades. Amicus Curiae Brief of Foster Parents & Pacific Legal Foundation in Support of Chad Everett Brackeen, et al., Haaland v. Brackeen, Nos. 21-376, 21-377, 21-378 & 21-380 (U.S. June 1, 2022).[4]

GILA RIVER INDIAN COMMUNITY STATEMENT ON PACIFIC LEGAL FOUNDATION'S AMICUS BRIEF IN BRACKEEN V. HAALAND

Last week, the Pacific Legal Foundation—an organization recognized for its aggressive advocacy against Indian tribes over the past several years—filed an amicus brief in Brackeen v. Haaland, a case pending before the Supreme Court of the United States which challenges the sovereign status of tribes under the Indian Child Welfare Act. Anti-ICWA groups like PLF and the Goldwater Institute are challenging the sovereign status of tribes by attacking the constitutionality of ICWA, alleging that tribes have no sovereign interest in the health and welfare of tribal children. PLF's brief focuses on a single dependency case—Matter of C.J., Jr.—involving the Gila River Indian Community and which took place in Ohio. To create a legal argument that would somehow fit within the legal considerations of the Brackeen case, PLF distorts what actually happened in the case to "fit" a universally rejected view of ICWA (that ICWA is race-based), which the Ohio court of appeals itself rejected when it considered the case on appeal and remanded it to the Franklin County Juvenile Court in 2018 with the express direction that ICWA be applied to the case.[5]

BRIEF OF CHRISTIAN ALLIANCE FOR INDIAN CHILD WELFARE AND ICWA CHILDREN AND FAMILIES AS AMICI CURIAE SUPPORTING THE BRACKEEN AND STATE PETITIONERS

Christian Alliance for Indian Child Welfare ("Alliance") is a North Dakota nonprofit corporation with members in thirty-five states, including Texas. Alliance was formed, in part, to (1) promote human rights for all United States citizens and residents; (2) educate the public about Indian rights and issues; and (3) encourage government accountability to families with Indian ancestry.

Tania Blackburn, Andrew Bui, Leslie Cook, Sage DesRochers, Cari Esparza, Desirae French, Nina Martin De La Cruz, Rebecca McDonald, Christopher Moore, Elizabeth Morris, James Nguyen, Sierra Whitefeather, and Rachael Jean Wilbur are former ICWA Children ... who have been harmed by ICWA.

Amicus curiae Christian Alliance for Indian Child Welfare ("Alliance") is a Montana nonprofit corporation with approximately 400 members in 35 states, including South Carolina. Alliance seeks to help and protect the human, civil, and constitutional rights of all Americans, especially those of Native American ancestry, through education, outreach, and legal defense. One area of constitutional concern is the Indian Child Welfare Act of 1978, 25 U.S.C. §§ 1901–1963 ("ICWA").[6]

BRIEF FOR CITIZENS EQUAL RIGHTS FOUNDATION AS AMICUS CURIAE SUPPORTING NO PARTY. HAALAND V. BRACKEEN, NOS. 21-376. 21-377, 21-378 & 21-380 (U.S. JUNE 2, 2022)

Citizens Equal Rights Foundation (CERF/CERA) believes and defends the constitutional rights of Indians and non-Indians. Our mission is to change federal Indian policies that threaten or restrict the individual rights of all citizens living on or near Indian reservations. We do not tolerate racial prejudice of any kind. We do not knowingly associate with anyone who discriminates based on race.[7]

BRIEF AMICUS CURIAE OF THE NEW CIVIL LIBERTIES ALLIANCE IN SUPPORT OF PETITIONER IN NO. 21-378

The New Civil Liberties Alliance (NCLA) is a nonpartisan, nonprofit civil-rights organization devoted to defending constitutional freedoms from violations by the administrative state. Amicus curiae addresses the following question only: Whether the Indian Child Welfare Act, 25 U.S.C. §§ 1901-63, and its implementing regulations violate the nondelegation doctrine by allowing individual tribes to alter the child-placement preferences enacted by Congress.[8]

BRIEF FOR THE PROJECT ON FAIR REPRESENTATION AS AMICUS CURIAE IN SUPPORT OF PETITIONERS

The Project on Fair Representation is a public interest organization dedicated to equal opportunity and racial harmony. The Project works to advance race-neutral principles in education, government action, and voting. ... The Project has a direct interest in this important case. The Project opposes government imposed racial preferences, including racial preferences in state-administered adoption proceedings. Racial preferences, like those mandated by the Indian Child Welfare Act, contradict the Project's principles and the American ideal of individual equality.[9]

BRIEF OF AMICUS CURIAE STATE OF OHIO SUPPORTING PETITIONERS

Because Ohio has seen firsthand the harm that ICWA does to children, see In re C.J., 108 N.E.3d 677 (Ohio Ct. App. 2018), and because the Act unconstitutionally intrudes on a matter reserved to the States, Ohio urges this Court to grant certiorari and hold that Congress exceeded its constitutional authority when it enacted ICWA.[10]

Notes: Part 3: Significant Opposing Briefs in Haaland v. Brackeen

1. https://www.supremecourt.gov/DocketPDF/21/21-380/195908/20211008131937570_Brackeen%20Amicus%20Brief.pdf (accessed online July 15, 2024).

2. https://www.texaspolicy.com/about/ (accessed online July 15, 2024).

3. https://www.texaspolicy.com/press/tppf-applauds-texas-ags-challenge-to-discriminatory-federal-child-placement-law (accessed online July 15, 2024).

4. https://www.supremecourt.gov/DocketPDF/21/21-376/226812/20220601155110941_PLF%20Amicus%20Brief%20-%20BRACKEEN%20-%202022.06.01%20-%20FINAL.pdf (accessed online July 15, 2024).

5. https://turtletalk.blog/wp-content/uploads/2022/06/gric-statement-on-plf-brief-06-07-223.pdf (accessed online July 15, 2024).

6. https://sct.narf.org/documents/adoptivecouplevbabygirl/merits/christian_alliance_amicus. pdf (accessed online July 15, 2024).

7. https://www.supremecourt.gov/DocketPDF/21/21-376/227047/20220617165804413_lana_final.pdf (accessed online July 15, 2024).

8. https://www.supremecourt.gov/DocketPDF/21/21-376/227008/20220602161037969_21-378%20Amicus%20NCLA%20Supp.%20Pet..pdf (accessed online July 15, 2024).

9. https://www.supremecourt.gov/DocketPDF/21/21-376/226835/20220601163800814_21-376%20-377%20-378%20-380%20ICWA%20Amicus%20Brief.pdf (accessed online July 15, 2024).

10. https://www.supremecourt.gov/DocketPDF/21/21-380/194412/20211004114531726_Brackeen%20Amicus.PDF (accessed online July 15, 2024).

Part 4: Colorado - Pioneering State for Adoption Intervention Cases: 2,500 Cases Filed by 2022 – Primary Attorney's Firm Used Discredited Child Adoption Expert

> National Trend Is for Foster Parents Wanting to Adopt Child to Intervene in Court Cases Arguing Attachment "Theory"
>
> Diane Baird, Expert in Foster Care Cases across Colorado Admits Her Evaluations Are Unscientific
>
> According to Baird, Babies "Never Possessed" a Cultural Identity and Are "Not Losing Anything," by Being Adopted
>
> Colorado Expert Baird in Favor of Foster Parent Adoption

Diane Baird Online

Online Curriculum Vitae

CO County Service Provider

Colorado Supreme Court

Montana Case

Montana Training

Wyoming Training

WY Children's Justice Project, Wyoming Supreme Court Washington

Online Presentations

Media Expert

Indian Child Welfare Act Cases Require Review

National Trend Is for Foster Parents Wanting to Adopt Child to Intervene in Court Cases Arguing Attachment "Theory"

[A] ProPublica investigation co-published with The New Yorker in October revealed that there is a growing national trend of foster parents undermining the foster system's premise by "intervening" in family court cases as a way to adopt children. As intervenors, they can file motions and call witnesses to argue that they've become too attached to a child for the child to be reunited with their birth family, even if officials have identified a biological family member who is suitable for a safe placement.[1]

Colorado has been a pioneering state for intervention thanks mostly to [Timothy J.] Eirich, the lawyer whose firm represented Carter's foster parents. In 2013, he argued and won a state Supreme Court case that ended almost all limitations on the practice, and in the following five years there was a threefold increase in intervenor cases statewide, according to data from the Colorado Office of Administrative Courts. **By 2022, at least twenty-five hundred cases had been filed. A tenth of the state's child-welfare cases now have an intervenor. And with an intervenor, court data indicate, the chance that the birth parents' rights will be terminated surges from seventeen per cent to forty-three per cent.** (Emphasis added).[2]

Eirich's firm represents nine private-adoption agencies across Colorado, and he leads intervenor-training sessions for judges and foster parents. He told me that the idea that he helps adopters-to-be thwart the goal of birth-family reunifications is "absolute bullshit." Most of his clients intervene, he said, primarily in order to help the judge make an informed placement decision: one that considers the child as an individual, instead of prioritizing generalized arguments about biological ties or race. "Colorado empowers people who care about maltreated children to be part of the process," he says. (Emphasis added).[3]

He routinely relies on Diane Baird, whom his clients sometimes hire directly, or on an attachment expert whom she has trained. Baird told me that she decided to work so closely with Eirich because "he knew how to use me most effectively." They both often argue that birth-family visits are causing a child damaging emotional swings due to attachment issues. "A healthy attachment trumps biology in the first three years of life, period," Baird told me. (Emphasis added). Later, she e-mailed me something that one of her colleagues likes to say about biological families: "Blood is thicker than water but it's also a better carrier of disease," to which Baird added, "LOL."[4]

Last year, the Kempe Center's director asked Baird in an e-mail to stop using the Kempe name to describe her protocol and to make clear on her C.V. that she no longer works there.

[W]hen attorneys for poor birth families wrote to Kempe in late 2022 saying that Baird and experts she has trained "are doing real damage to families, and they are doing damage in the name of the Kempe Center," a CU lawyer responded by declining the

> advocates' request that the center "publicly disavow this protocol and correct the record." The reason, the lawyer said, was that the judge or jury on a particular case "is in the best position to evaluate arguments raised by involved parties" as to the scientific efficacy of the method. The lawyer added that the center has "worked with hundreds of individuals in its 50-year history in the child welfare arena and we have little ability to control testimony of each individual."[5]

It deliberately failed to take action to protect the trademark of the Kempe Center at CU and allowed an occult procedure using its name to be used publicly.

> **As Colorado grapples with how prevalent foster-parent intervention has become, other states are taking the intervenor concept further.** At least fifteen states, from New York to Tennessee to Arizona, now allow foster parents to directly file to terminate a biological parent's rights, as if they were prosecutors. (Emphasis added).[6]

Diane Baird, Expert in Foster Care Cases across Colorado Admits Her Evaluations Are Unscientific

> [Diane] Baird, a social worker and professional expert witness, has **routinely advocated in juvenile court cases across Colorado** that foster children be adopted by or remain in the custody of their foster parents rather than being reunified with their typically lower-income birth parents or other family members. (Emphasis added).[7]

Colorado Expert Baird Admits Her Evaluations Are Unscientific, Unpublished and Unstandardized

ProPublica found the following about Baird's Methodology, the "Kempe Protocol for Interactional Evaluation" after the Kempe Center for the Prevention and Treatment of Child Abuse and Neglect at the University of Colorado's Anschutz Medical Campus, the nation's leading academic institute focused on child welfare:

In a deposition, Baird responded as follows:

> Was Baird's method for evaluating these foster and birth families empirically tested? No, Baird answered: **Her method is unpublished and unstandardized, and has remained "pretty much unchanged" since the 1980s. It doesn't have those "standard validity and reliability things," she admitted. "It's not a scientific instrument."** (Emphasis added).[8]

According to Baird, Babies "Never Possessed" a Cultural Identity and Are "Not Losing Anything," by Being Adopted

> Had she considered or was she even aware of the cultural background of the birth family and child whom she was recommending permanently separating? (The case involved a baby girl of multiracial heritage.) **Baird answered that babies have "never possessed" a cultural identity, and therefore are "not losing anything," at their age, by being adopted.** Although when such children grow up, she acknowledged, they might say to their now-adoptive parents, "Oh, I didn't know we were related to the, you know, Pima tribe in northern California, or whatever the circumstances are." (Emphasis added).
>
> The Pima tribe is located in the Phoenix metropolitan area.[9]

Colorado Expert Baird in Favor of Foster Parent Adoption

> In interviews and emails with ProPublica, Baird said that she is simply opposed, in almost all cases, to rupturing the current healthy attachment of any child under 3 with that child's foster parents, even if a birth family member is available and family and cultural heritage stand to be lost forever. She said that this is the age when kids are developing their capacity to form healthy relationships, and that they may experience being removed from their foster parents as a rejection, causing a loss of trust going forward. She also said that kids who have a history of caregiver changes and trauma, which is true of many little ones in foster care, need a sense of "permanency," often meaning adoption.[10]

Diane Baird Online

The following information was located in a very cursory online query. It is not complete, but it is intended to give an example of the authoritative presence of Ms. Baird.

Online Curriculum Vitae

> Diane Baird (B.S.Ed., Oklahoma University; M.S.W., Tulane University Graduate School of Social Work) is a licensed clinical social worker and an instructor in the Department of Pediatrics at the University of Colorado School of Medicine, at the Kempe Center for the Prevention and Treatment of Child Abuse and Neglect. She holds a bachelor's degree in education and earned her master of social work from Tulane University Graduate School of Social Work. Her clinical work involves parent-child interactional evaluations and treatment, infant mental health, child and family therapy, therapeutic visitation, and post adoptive intervention. She is particularly interested in rehabilitation of parent-child relationships following abuse or neglect. Ms. Baird's interest in attachment and early childhood development is central to her clinical work; she has served as an expert in this area for the State of Colorado Department of Human Services (DHS) for more than 15 years. Ms. Baird was a child welfare caseworker and supervisor before beginning her employment with the Kempe Center in 1986. Her position is currently in the Training, Education, and Consultation Program at the Kempe Center. There, Ms. Baird codirects the State and Regional Team (START), a multidisciplinary consultation group that has reviewed complex cases of child maltreatment, from a civil and/or criminal perspective, for more than 20 years; cases may be referred from Colorado, Nebraska, Montana, Wyoming, Alaska, and other states in the region. Ms. Baird writes curricula, provides training for Colorado DHS and the State Judicial Office, and collaborates with other states in the region to develop and offer training to child welfare staff.[11]

CO County Service Provider

Ms. Baird has been used as a contract services provider in several CO Counties, including what would appear:

Clear Creek[12]
Douglas County[13]
Grand County[14]
Moffat County[15]
Montrose County[16]
Washington County[17] and
Yuma County.[18]

Colorado Supreme Court

She has given training and produced a Manual for the Colorado Supreme Court: Child development a multi-disciplinary curriculum for improvement of the child welfare system, Colorado Supreme Court. Court Improvement Program, 2010, Denver, Colo.[19]

Montana Case

She is serving as an expert in a pending foster care intervenor case in Montana: IN THE SUPREME COURT OF THE STATE OF MONTANA No. DA 23-0550 IN THE MATTER OF R.N., Youth in Need of Care, Montana Eighth Judicial District Court, Cascade County

APPELLANT'S OPENING BRIEF, filed Feb. 21, 2024, states as follows:

> Bringing R.N.'s best interest to the forefront of this case was the purpose of the Wagners' Motion for a Placement Hearing. In support of that motion, they provided the expert opinion of Diane Baird, LCSW who clearly set forth the risks associated with moving a child at R.N.'s tender age. **In further support of her opinion, Ms. Baird referenced that "the American Academy**

of Pediatrics has opinioned that changes of caregivers for children between the ages of six months and three to three and a half years are so psychologically dangerous that this should be undertaken only in matters of extreme urgency, e.g., for physical safety." (Emphasis added).[20]

American Psychological Association (specifically including the associations of Texas, Louisiana, and Indiana) and the Society of Indian Psychologists

Montana Training

Kempe Center's Diane Baird trains majority of Montana child welfare workers, The Kempe Foundation Staff

Throughout the summer, The Kempe Center's Diane Baird, LCSW visited 12 sites throughout Montana over a six week period and met with nearly all child welfare workers in the state. She presented her day-and-half presentation, "If You're Not Building Health, You're Reinforcing Pathology," traveling to five geographic regions in Montana. "Child welfare happens at the caseworker level," said Baird. "The focus of the training was on healthy, non-abusive parent child relationships." The training involved therapeutic visitation to change relationships, evaluate relationships and move toward a relationship focus. This means that professionals do not just treat the parent, then treat the child; instead, they work on the relationship between the two. Baird has visited Montana each year since 2005. Many of the workers she trained have been in their positions for 20 years or more and they value the relationship with The Kempe Center. "The Kempe Center has a great reputation among professionals throughout the region," said Baird. As a Kempe Center staff member, Baird has the ability to present current research and new ideas to many areas within the state of Montana including geographically isolated ones. Internet access and distance learning makes more of these trainings possible, but Baird enjoys visiting the locations and meeting one-on-one with people.[21]

Wyoming Training

WY Children's Justice Project, Wyoming Supreme Court

Regional Trainings were held in Gillette and Riverton on September 25-26, 2013. 50 attendees in Riverton, 37 in Gillette. Diane Baird and Gerald Glynn talked about case studies and factual stories to highlight why following the law is important (not just what the mandates and laws are). Dan emphasized how important the why part of this training is. Feedback was positive.[22]

Washington

While it is uncertain what Ms. Baird has done in Washington, the Washington State Office of Civil Legal Aid reproduced the ProPublica article discrediting her methods in its newsletter.[23]

Online Presentations

It would appear that she has given several presentations of varying topics which may be accessed online:

Child Abuse Services Team "CAST"[24]

Reactive Attachment Disorder[25]

Also, in CHILDREN SPEAK FOR THEMSELVES, "Kempe Interactional Assessment for Parent- Child Sexual Abuse," by Clare Haynes-Seman, Ph.D. and David Baumgarten, J.D., the "clinical work of Diane Baird, M.S.W., L.C.S.W." is acknowledged.

Media Expert

It would appear that she may be a media-go-to on child abuses issues: Experts Recommend When to Step Away from Crying Baby.[26]

Indian Child Welfare Act Cases Require Review

Baird notes that cases may be referred from Colorado, Nebraska, Montana, Wyoming, Alaska, and other states in the region. THESE ARE ALL STATES WITH AMERICAN INDIAN POPULATIONS. Training was given in Riverton, WY, near where the Wind River Indian Reservation is located.

> **Dr. Kathryn Wells, the Kempe Center's executive director, told ProPublica ... "that the use of attachment theory and parent-child interactional assessments, the procedure that Baird conducts with birth families, "in isolation" and "particularly in non-therapeutic settings and without attention to bias," is "not consistent with current best practices and can be abused by experts." Wells added that Kempe does not itself currently provide such evaluations for court proceedings or endorse the methodology for that purpose. (Emphasis added).**[27]

Indian Child Welfare Act cases should be reviewed to determine if Baird was an expert in the cases. Many times, it is simply wearing down family or kin in foster care/adoption proceedings, or if the cost is prohibitive, of if they are scared away by the credentials of the opposing party, or are fearful of drug claims, that is enough to cause a case to be abandoned. There may be no cases but again this is an incredible insight into how a person with no expert training is believed, merely because of their credentials and naming their product after a major entity.

Notes: Part 4: Colorado - Pioneering State for Adoption Intervention Cases: 2,500 Cases Filed by 2022 – Primary Attorney's Firm Used Discredited Child Adoption Expert

1. An expert who has testified in foster care cases across Colorado admits her evaluations are unscientific, Eli, Hager, ProPublica, March 18, 2024. https://www.denverpost.com/2024/03/18/diane-baird-kempe-protocol-colorado-foster- care/?clearUserState=true (accessed online July 2, 2024).

2. When Foster Parents Don't Want to Give Back the Baby. The New Yorker. https://www.newyorker.com›magazine›2023/10/23 (accessed online July 1, 2024).

3. When Foster Parents Don't Want to Give Back the Baby. The New Yorker. https://www.newyorker.com›magazine›2023/10/23 (accessed online July 1, 2024).

4. When Foster Parents Don't Want to Give Back the Baby. The New Yorker. https://www.newyorker.com›magazine›2023/10/23 (accessed online July 1, 2024).

5. An expert who has testified in foster care cases across Colorado admits her evaluations are unscientific, Eli Hager, ProPublica, March 18, 2024.
https://www.denverpost.com/2024/03/18/diane-baird-kempe-protocol-colorado-foster- care/?clearUserState=true (accessed online July 2, 2024).

6. When Foster Parents Don't Want to Give Back the Baby. The New Yorker. https://www.newyorker.com›magazine›2023/10/23 (accessed online July 1, 2024).

7. An expert who has testified in foster care cases across Colorado admits her evaluations are unscientific, Eli Hager, ProPublica, March 18, 2024.
https://www.denverpost.com/2024/03/18/diane-baird-kempe-protocol-colorado-foster- care/?clearUserState=true (accessed online July 2, 2024).

8. An expert who has testified in foster care cases across Colorado admits her evaluations are unscientific, Eli Hager, ProPublica, March 18, 2024.
https://www.denverpost.com/2024/03/18/diane-baird-kempe-protocol-colorado-foster- care/?clearUserState=true (accessed online July 2, 2024).

9. An expert who has testified in foster care cases across Colorado admits her evaluations are unscientific, Eli Hager, ProPublica, March 18, 2024. https://www.denverpost.com/2024/03/18/diane-baird-kempe-protocol-colorado-foster- care/?clearUserState=true (accessed online July 2, 2024)

10. An expert who has testified in foster care cases across Colorado admits her evaluations are unscientific, Eli Hager, ProPublica, March 18, 2024. https://www.denverpost.com/2024/03/18/diane-baird-kempe-protocol-colorado-foster- care/?clearUserState=true (accessed online July 2, 2024).

11. https://www.americanbar.org/content/dam/aba-cms-dotorg/products/inv/book/214953/5310429_author_abs.pdf (accessed online July 7, 2024).

12 https://co.clear-creek.co.us/AgendaCenter/ViewFile/Item/3902?fileID=1985 (accessed online July 7, 2024).

13. https://www.douglas.co.us/documents/2022-2nd-quarter-contract-log.pdf/ (accessed online July 7, 2024).

14. https://www.co.grand.co.us/AgendaCenter/ViewFile/Agenda/_05242022-2494 (accessed online July 7, 2024).

15. https://moffatcounty.colorado.gov/sites/moffatcounty/files/2017_05_09.pdf (accessed online July 7, 2024).

16. https://montrosecounty.granicus.com/MetaViewer.php?view_id=2&clip_id=1173&meta_id=646 01 (accessed online July 7, 2024).

17. https://www.9news.com/article/news/investigations/judge-orders-washington-county-human- services-internal-investigation-child-welfare-cases/73-62c35f96-eb32-4978-bc77-32c252699624 (accessed online July 7, 2024).

18. https://yumacounty.net/wp-content/uploads/2018/12/2018.08.31Minutes.pdf. (accessed online July 7, 2024).

19. https://www.cde.state.co.us/studentsupport/fostercare_resources (accessed online July 7, 2024).

20. https://juddocumentservice.mt.gov/getDocByCTrackId?DocId=463144 (accessed online July 7, 2024).

21. https://www.kempe.org/wp-content/uploads/2015/01/KempeChroniclesFall2011-web.pdf (accessed online July 7, 2024).

22. https://www.courts.state.wy.us/wp-content/uploads/2017/05/Oct2013CJPMinutes102513.pdf (accessed online July 7, 2024).

23. https://ocla.wa.gov/wp-content/uploads/2024/03/March-2024-Newsletter.pdf (accessed online July 7, 2024).

24. https://www.slideserve.com/maitland/child-abuse-services-team-c-a-s-t (accessed online July 7, 2024).

25. https://www.casappr.org/event/reactive-attachment-disorder/ (accessed online July 7, 2024).

26. https://www.casappr.org/event/reactive-attachment-disorder/ (accessed online July 7, 2024).

27. An expert who has testified in foster care cases across Colorado admits her evaluations are unscientific, Eli Hager, ProPublica, March 18, 2024. https://www.denverpost.com/2024/03/18/diane-baird-kempe-protocol-colorado-foster- care/?clearUserState=true (accessed online July 2, 2024).

Part 5: Federal and Colorado Adoption Legislation, Restricting Intervention
 Federal Law: Goal for Foster Care Is for It to Be Temporary and to Reunify Children with Family or Kin
 CO Law: Preference to Family Adult Relatives and Restricting Intervention
 Colorado House Bill 23-1024: Giving Preference to Relatives in Adoption Cases; Restricting Foster Family Interventions
 Proponent of Foster Care Adoption Argues 'Attachment Injury' Should Prevail Over Family Preferences
 Colorado's New Kinship Law Tested in Lawsuit: Attachment Injury Prevails over Family Preference

Federal Law: Goal for Foster Care Is for It to Be Temporary and to Reunify Children with Family or Kin

A fundamental goal of foster care, under federal law, is for it to be temporary: to reunify children with their birth parents if it is safe to do so or, second best, to place them with other kin. Extensive social science research has found that kids who grow up with their own families experience less long-term separation trauma, fewer mental health and behavioral problems as adolescents and more of an ultimate sense of belonging to their culture of origin.[1]

CO Law: Preference to Family Adult Relatives and Restricting Intervention

The National Coalition for Child Protection Reform cited data that Colorado used kinship care at a rate 30% below the national average.[2]

Foster parent intervention increased in Colorado in the past decade. In 2020, 10% of Dependency and Neglect cases had Intervenors. When foster parents intervene, the chance of reunification decreases from 62% to 22% for the birth parents. Once the foster parents intervened in case 19JV13, the court started hearing concerns about bonding and attachment.[3]

Colorado, though, enacted legislation in 2023 to align with federal law that "states should consider giving preference to adult relatives and kin." New legislation curbs (though does not end) one of the most pernicious practices - foster parents as "intervenors." The legislative declaration specifically addresses this strategy by providing: **"The number of months spent in foster care, or even a child's or youth's new attachment to foster parents, should [not] drive permanency decisions."** Even more significant, it bolsters the preference for placing children in kinship foster care, giving Colorado a chance to catch up to the nation.

In Feb. 2024, the Colorado Department of Human Services reported:

From February 2023 through January 2024, 50% of children and youth placed in foster care had their initial placement with kinship caregivers. This is the first time Colorado's child welfare system has hit this milestone, marking an important emphasis in practice, providing assurances that children and youth will remain in family-like settings whenever possible.[4]

Colorado House Bill 23-1024: Giving Preference to Relatives in Adoption Cases; Restricting Foster Family Interventions

DENVER (June 8, 2023) – Colorado House Bill 23-1024 (HB 23-1024), passed UNANIMOUSLY out of both the House and Senate, and was signed by Governor Polis on June 8, 2023. The key provisions are:

Requiring that **courts give preference to a relative** unless placement with that relative would negatively affect the child's or youth's mental, physical, or emotional needs, or hinder reunification with the child's or youth's family;

Creating a **rebuttable presumption that placement with a relative is in the child's or youth's best interest.** The presumption may be rebutted by a preponderance of the evidence, giving primary consideration to the child's or youth's mental, physical, and emotional needs, including the child's or youth's preference regarding placement.

Foster parents who have the child or youth in their care for twelve months or more may intervene, as a matter of right, with or without counsel, following adjudication. The **purpose of intervention is to provide knowledge or information** concerning the care and protection of the child or youth, including the child's or youth's mental, physical, and emotional needs. (Emphasis added).[5]

Be it enacted by the General Assembly of the State of Colorado: SECTION 1. Legislative declaration.

The general assembly finds and declares that:

Children and youth placed with relatives or kin experience greater placement stability, reduced separation trauma, lower rates of trauma from institutional abuse, better behavioral and mental health outcomes, preservation of identities, and higher rates of reunification with parents than children and youth placed in foster homes; **Federal law requires that children and youth be placed in the least restrictive, most family-like environment and that states should consider giving preference to adult relatives and kin;**
(i) The most critical factors for consideration in permanency planning should be the safety of the family home and a child's or youth's key attachments and family connections. **These factors, rather than the number of months spent in foster care, or even a child's or youth's new attachment to foster parents, should drive permanency decisions.** (Emphasis added)[6]

Proponent of Foster Care Adoption Argues 'Attachment Injury' Should Prevail Over Family Preferences

Lee Freeman, the founder of Foster Alight, stated: "This bill stands to put family placements, kinship placements, above other alternatives, and it does so at the cost of attachment."[7]

Colorado's New Kinship Law Tested in Lawsuit: Attachment Injury Prevails over Family Preference

The foster family retained Timothy Eirich as the attorney to represent them based on his extensive experience with foster families' cases. The judge determined that the child should remain with her foster parents, citing "attachment injuries."[8]

His website lists his experience as including "Intervention by a Native American tribe seeking to have an Indian child placed with a Native American family..."[9]

Notes: Part 5: Federal and Colorado Adoption Legislation, Restricting Intervention.

1. An expert who has testified in foster care cases across Colorado admits her evaluations are unscientific, Eli Hager, ProPublica, March 18, 2024.

2. https://coloradoreport.blogspot.com/p/executive-summary-full-report-and-all.html (accessed online July 1, 2024).

3. Family fights 3 years for custody of their own child - 9News. https://www.9news.com/article/news/investigations/washington-county-child-custody-fight/73- dd78d12c-01ea-4e40-a989-3d21e38f9050#:~:text=According%20to%20data%20provided%20by,22%25%20for%20the%20 birth%20parents (accessed online July 1, 2024).

4. Kinship care reaches a new statewide milestone. https://cdhs.colorado.gov/press- release/kinship-care-reaches-a-new-statewide-milestone (accessed online July 16, 2024).

5. https://leg.colorado.gov/bills/hb23-1024 (accessed online July 1, 2024).

6. https://leg.colorado.gov/sites/default/files/documents/2023A/bills/2023a_1024_01.pdf (accessed online July 1, 2024).

7. Colorado foster families concerned proposed legislation takes away their voice. https://krdo.com/news/top-stories/2023/03/22/colorado-foster-families-concerned-proposed- legislation-takes-away-their-voice/ (accessed online July 1, 2024).

8. https://www.9news.com/article/news/investigations/colorado-kinship-law-tested-court-decision/73-ca2f3a7c-ac02-45be-9515-04ac2674c472 (accessed online July 1, 2024).

9. https://www.grobeirich.com/adoption/contested-adoption/ (accessed online July 1, 2024).

Part 6: American Indian/Alaska Native (AI/AN) Families Attachment and Bonding Research

Contemporary attachment and bonding research related to American Indian/Alaska Native (AI/AN) families found that attachment theory focused on the dyad of parent and child is not congruent with AI/AN families culture. Their research supports the placement preferences with family/kin and keeping children connected to their AI/AN communities. Unfortunately, the National Indian Child Welfare Association found "[t]his research is infrequently cited in court cases involving the Indian Child Welfare Act (ICWA) and the placement of AI/AN children." Their research found:

> Historically, attachment theory focused on the dyad of parent and child, looking at the quality of relationship between the two as a predictor of well-being.[1]
>
> However, this model was based on Western cultural assumptions and did not account for cultural variation in family structures.[2]
>
> Extended family structures, traditional for many AI/AN communities in particular, were not accounted for in traditional attachment theory.[3]

Beyond Attachment Theory: Indigenous Perspectives on Child–Caregiver Bond from a Northwest Tribal Community

This study also found indigenous child development is supported by *"connection to extended kin, community, and place (e.g., land, water)."*

> Fundamentally, attachment theory is about connection, arguing that the secure emotional bond between a primary caregiver and

child is critical for early survival and foundational for healthy development. The current study centered the voices of Indigenous parenting adults to inform an expanded conceptualization of attachment. *An attachment theory that holds as integral to child development the formation of emotional bonds or connection to extended kin, community, and place (e.g., land, water) will support the well-being of Indigenous children.*[4]

As diverse as Indigenous cultures are, there are also some cultural commonalities. The interrelatedness or connectedness of all things, including humans and the ecosystem, is foundational to many Indigenous worldviews. This means that many Indigenous cultures ground identity, adaptation, and well-being in relationships beyond immediate family members and include community members, ancestors, land, waters, and the more-than-human relatives of the animal world.[5]

Participants concurrently expressed how the interconnectedness between those in the community is fostered by culture, language, food, and sovereignty—all of which contribute to the well-being of the community and influence a child's worldview. ....

This perspective aligns with the work of Bang et al.[6] who describe families as "the heart of Indigenous nations and communities" (p. 2) and also recognize an inclusive understanding of family as a "complex web of interdependence between all things" (p. 2). In fact, Carriere and Richardson (2009) argue for use of the term connectedness instead of attachment when working with Indigenous families because the term speaks to children's relationality beyond a single attachment figure.[7]

Notes: Part 6: American Indian/Alaska Native (AI/AN) Families Attachment and Bonding Research.

1. Flaherty, S., & Sadler, L. (2011). A review of attachment theory in the context of adolescent parenting. Journal of Pediatric Health Care, 25(2), 114-121.

2. Neckoway, R., Brownlee, K., & Castellan, B. (2007). Is attachment theory consistent with Aboriginal parenting realities? First Peoples Child & Family Review, 3(2), 65–74.

3. https://www.nicwa.org/wp-content/uploads/2020/10/Contemporary-Attachment-and-Bonding-Research-Final.pdf (accessed online July 3, 2024).

4. Waters, S. F., Richardson, M., Mills, S. R., Marris, A., Harris, F., & Parker, M. (2024). Beyond attachment theory: Indigenous perspectives on the child–caregiver bond from a northwest tribal community. Child Development, 00, 1–16. https://doi.org/10.1111/cdev.14127 (accessed online July 3, 2024).

5. Johnson-Jennings, M., Billiot, S., & Walters, K. (2020). Returning to our roots: Tribal health and wellness through land-based healing. Genealogy, 4, 91. https://doi.org/10.3390/genealogy4030091.

6. Bang, M. M., Nolan, C., & McDaid-Morgan, N. (2018).

7. Carriere, J., & Richardson, C. (2009). From longing to belonging: Attachment theory, connectedness, and indigenous children in Canada. In S. McKay, D. Fuchs, & I. Brown (Eds.), Passion for action in child and family services: Voices from the prairies (pp. 49–67). Canadian Plains Research Center.

Appendix 5: American Indian Country Criminal Jurisdiction Chart

for crimes committed within Indian country as defined by 18 U.S.C. '1151(a), (b) & (c) - **formal** [recognized reservation boundaries] **& informal** [tribal trust lands] **reservations** (including rights-of-way/roads), **dependent Indian communities,** & (c) **Indian allotments held in trust or restricted status** (including rights-of-way/roads). *(applies where no U.S. Congressional grant of jurisdiction to the state/municipal government over the Indian country involved exists)*

INDIAN OFFENDER :

VICTIM CRIMES: FOR OFFENSES AGAINST A PERSON OR A PERSON'S PROPERTY
(not a tribal govt.)

WHO IS THE VICTIM?	WHAT WAS THE CRIME?	JURISDICTION
INDIAN (enrolled or recognized as an Indian by a federally recognized tribe or the federal government <u>and</u> possessing some degree of Indian blood)	**Major Crimes Act Crimes:** murder; manslaughter; kidnapping; maiming; sexual abuse/assault under Ch. 109-A; <u>incest</u>; assault with intent to commit murder or in violation of 18 U.S.C. ' 2241 or '2242; assault with intent to commit any felony; assault with a dangerous weapon with intent to do bodily harm; assault resulting in serious bodily injury as defined in 18 U.S.C.§ 1365; assault resulting in substantial bodily injury of a spouse, intimate partner or dating partner, or on a person under 16 years old; assault of a spouse, intimate partner or dating partner by strangulation; <u>felony child abuse or neglect</u>; arson; <u>burglary</u>; robbery; felony theft under 18 U.S.C. ' 661. (Authority: Major Crimes Act - 18 U.S.C. § 1153) (underlined: assimilated state offense- 18 U.S.C. § 13) **All remaining crimes contained in tribal code:** (Authority: tribal code or 25 CFR Pt. 11, if a CFR Court of Indian Offenses)	FEDERAL# TRIBAL*

NON-INDIAN	**Major Crimes Act Crimes:** murder; manslaughter; kidnapping; maiming; sexual abuse/assault under Ch. 109-A; incest; assault with intent to commit murder or in violation of 18 U.S.C. ' 2241 or '2242; assault with intent to commit any felony; assault with a dangerous weapon; assault resulting in serious bodily injury; assault resulting in substantial bodily injury of a spouse, intimate partner or dating partner, or on a person under 16 years old; assault of a spouse, intimate partner or dating partner by strangulation; felony child abuse or neglect; arson; burglary; robbery; felony theft under 18 U.S.C. ' 661. (Authority: Major Crimes Act - 18 U.S.C. ' 1153) (underlined: assimilated state offense - 18 U.S.C. § 13)	FEDERAL #
	Federal Territorial Crimes: (unless the tribe has punished the Indian defendant) (Authority: General Crimes Act/Indian Country Crimes Act - 18 U.S.C. § 1152) **including crimes contained in state code (where there is no federal statute for the category of offense) under the Assimilative Crimes Act:** (18 U.S.C. ' 13)	FEDERAL #
	All remaining crimes contained in tribal code: (Authority: tribal code or 25 CFR Pt. 11, if a CFR Court of Indian Offenses)	TRIBAL *

VICTIMLESS CRIMES: NO PERSON OR PERSON'S PROPERTY INVOLVED

(e.g., traffic violations w/ no injury/damage to a person or their property, disorderly conduct, prostitution, violation of court order, etc.)

a. Crimes in state code (where there is no federal statute for the category of offense) under the Assimilative Crimes Act. (Authority: 18 U.S.C. ' '1152 and 13)	FEDERAL #
b. Crimes in tribal code. (Authority: tribal code or 25 CFR Pt. 11, if CFR Court)	TRIBAL *

SPECIAL CRIMES APPLICABLE TO INDIAN COUNTRY (Indian or Non-Indian): FEDERAL # (Federal prosecution based on crime committed in Indian country) (e.g., Habitual Domestic Violence, 18 U.S.C. ' 117; Failure to Register as Sex Offender, 18 U.S.C. ' 2250; Unauthorized Hunting/Fishing, 18 U.S.C. ' 1165 [tribal trust land and allotments only]; and other statutes) FEDERAL CRIMES GENERALLY APPLICABLE TO ANY PERSON NATIONWIDE: FEDERAL # (Indian or Non-Indian) (Crime Affecting Interstate Commerce or a Federal Interest)

(Federal prosecution NOT based on territorial jurisdiction over location of crime) (e.g., drug offenses, Violence Against Women Act (VAWA) offenses, firearm possession by prohibited person, tribal embezzlement, assault on a federal officer, theft from tribal casino, child porn., etc.) (Authority: individual federal statute)

NON-INDIAN OFFENDER:

1. **VICTIM CRIMES: FOR OFFENSES AGAINST A PERSON OR PERSON'S PROPERTY (not a tribal govt.)**

WHO IS THE VICTIM?	*WHAT WAS THE CRIME?*	*JURISDICTION*
INDIAN (enrolled or recognized as an Indian by a federally recognized tribe or the federal government and possessing some degree of Indian blood)	**Federal Territorial Crimes:** (Authority: General Crimes Act/Indian Country Crimes Act - 18 U.S.C. § 1152) **including crimes contained in state code (where there is no federal statute for the category of offense) under the Assimilative Crimes Act: (18 U.S.C. §§13)** **Assaults of tribal justice personnel, child violence, dating violence, domestic violence, obstruction of justice, sexual violence, sex trafficking, stalking, and violation of a protection order** *(Special Tribal Criminal Jurisdiction - "STCJ")* (Authority: tribal code under 25 U.S.C. ' 1304 – VAWA 2022) eff. 10/1/22 **All crimes in state code.** (Authority: *Oklahoma v. Castro-Huerta, No. 21-429 (U.S. Supr. Ct., 2022)*)	FEDERAL % TRIBAL *▲ STATE
NON-INDIAN	**All crimes in state code.** (Authority: *U.S. v. McBratney, 104 U.S. 621 (1881)*) **Assaults of tribal justice personnel or obstruction of justice** *(Special Tribal Criminal Jurisdiction - "STCJ")* (Authority: tribal code under 25 U.S.C. '1304 – VAWA 2022) eff. 10/1/22	STATE TRIBAL *▲

2. VICTIMLESS CRIMES: NO PERSON OR PERSON'S PROPERTY INVOLVED: STATE (e.g., traffic violations w/ no injury/damage to a person or their property, disorderly conduct, prostitution, violation of court order, etc.)

3. SPECIAL CRIMES APPLICABLE TO INDIAN COUNTRY (Indian or Non-Indian): FEDERAL # (Federal prosecution based on crime committed in Indian country) (e.g., Habitual Domestic Violence, 18 U.S.C. ' 117; Failure to Register as Sex Offender, 18 U.S.C. ' 2250; Unauthorized Hunting/Fishing, 18 U.S.C. ' 1165 [tribal trust land and allotments only]; and other statutes)

4. FEDERAL CRIMES GENERALLY APPLICABLE TO ANY PERSON NATIONWIDE: FEDERAL # (Indian or Non-Indian) (Crime Affecting Interstate Commerce or a Federal Interest) (Federal prosecution NOT based on territorial jurisdiction over location of crime) (e.g., drug offenses, Violence Against Women Act (VAWA) offenses, firearm possession by prohibited person, tribal embezzlement, assault on a federal officer, theft from tribal casino, child porn., etc.) (Authority: individual federal statute)

* A tribal court may be: 1) a tribal court established under tribal law; 2) or a "CFR" Court of Indian Offenses established under Title 25, Part 11, Code of Federal Regulations for a tribe without a court system; or 3) An Alaska Native Village Court with jurisdiction over Alaska Village land as defined by Section 812 (7) of VAWA 2022. 25 U.S.C. '1305 ▲ Applicable in an Alaska village only if part of a designated U.S. Department of Justice "Pilot Project"

\# includes juveniles (under 18 YOA at time of the incident) prosecuted as delinquents under 18 U.S.C. § 5032, if the state lacks or refuses to assume jurisdiction or it is a felony crime of violence or specified offense listed in 18 U.S.C. § 5032 and there is a substantial Federal interest

% includes juveniles (under 18 YOA at time of the incident) prosecuted as delinquents under 18 U.S.C. § 5032, if the state refuses to assume jurisdiction or it is a felony crime of violence or specified offense listed in 18 U.S.C. § 5032 and there is a substantial Federal interest

created by Arvo Q. Mikkanen, Assistant U.S. Attorney & Tribal Liaison, U.S. Attorney=s Office, Western District of Oklahoma **October 2022 Version** (may be reproduced with attribution)

Appendix 6: Major Congressional American Indian Affairs Statutes

Date	Major Congressional American Indian Affairs Statutes
1790	Non-Intercourse Act of July 22, 1790 (1 Stat. 131; 18 U.S.C. 1511 et seq.) extended in 1793, 1796, 1802, and Act of June 30, 1834 (4 Stat. 729; 25 U.S.C. 177) gave the Federal Government authority over American Indian matters and provided a base for United States American Indian policy.
1830	Indian Removal Act of May 28, 1830 (4 Stat. 411; 25 U.S.C. 174) enabled the President to negotiate in exchange for lands to relocate tribes east of the Mississippi to lands west of the Mississippi River. *Ended in forced removal for many tribes and large cession of lands by tribes west of Mississippi to open up lands for tribes removed under the Act without regard to impact on tribes ceding lands.* Over 60 removal treaties were signed which resulted in forced westward migration of approximately 80,000 American Indians.
1834	Congress Created Indian Territory in Present Day Oklahoma for Removal of Indians in Southeast.
1834	Trade and Intercourse Act of June 30, 1834 (4 Stat. 729) was the single most important measure of Indian-related legislation during the Trade and Intercourse Acts period. It defined the contemporary scope of Indian Country; prohibited alienation of lands by tribes unless the same be made by treaty or convention entered into pursuant to the constitution; provided remedies for the theft or destruction of property; and made liquor or distilleries in Indian Country illegal; provided for the punishment of crimes committed in Indian Country but excluded from such application crimes committed by one Indian against the person or property of another Indian.
1871	Indian Appropriations Act of March 3, 1871 (ch. 120, 16 Stat. 566; 25 U.S.C. 71) had a rider attached that effectively *ended the President's and Senate's treaty making by providing that no Indian Nation or tribe shall be acknowledged as an independent nation, tribe, or power with whom the United States may contract by treaty.* The Federal Government continued to provide similar contractual relations with the Indian tribes after 1871 by agreements, statutes, and executive orders.
1885	Major Crimes Act of March 3, 1885 (23 Stat. 362; 18 U.S.C. 1153) created Federal jurisdiction over seven crimes committed by Indians in Indian Country. *It was the first systematic intrusion by the Federal Government into the internal affairs of the tribes.*
1887	Dawes Act of Feb. 8, 1887 (ch. 119, 24 Stat. 388; 25 U.S.C. 331) provided for the allotment of lands to Indians on various reservations and public domain and extended the protection of United States laws to Indians. Cessation of Indian tribal holdings and division of lands among them was an attempt at assimilation and a way to open extensive Indian lands to western expansion and white settlement. It was hoped that Indians would establish homes, develop lands, and become a part of American society. *One of the results was the loss of more than 80 million acres of Indian lands into private ownership.*
1924	The Indian Citizenship Act of June 2, 1924 (P.L. 175, 43 Stat. 253) *unilaterally imposed* U.S. citizenship on all non-citizen Indians born in the U.S., though not *"full"* citizenship, making them subject to U.S. laws. The imposition of American citizenship is still contested by some tribes.

1934	Indian Reorganization Act of 1934 (P.L. 383, 48 Stat. 984; 25 U.S.C. 461–62) allowed Indian nations to establish governments or business committees, with constitutions, charters and by-laws, and to take over reservation governance, subject to the ultimate authority of the federal government. It ended allotments in severalty; and gave the Secretary of the Interior the authority to acquire lands inside or outside of reservations for American Indians.
1946	Indian Claims Commission Act of Aug. 13, 1946 (P.L. 725, 60 Stat. 1049; 25 U.S.C. 70–70v) established the Indian Claims Commission to determine claims in law or equity arising under the Constitution, laws, treaties of the United States, and all other claims in law or equity, and claims based upon dishonorable dealings not recognized by any existing rule of law or equity. The most fundamental problem with the act, from the tribes' point of view, was that it provided for payment in money and not land. The Indian Claims Commission arbitrarily assigned a monetary value to those lands, paid it into a trust fund of their own making, and declared the matter closed. As stated by Roger Buffalohead, Ponca: "We have had enough experience with the Indian Claims Commission Act to know that it has not benefited most tribes. Approximately $800 million was awarded through the Indian Claims Commission. If you divide the number of acres of land that those particular cases involved, the United States government ended up paying Indian people fifty cents an acre. The title was quieted, but in many cases it is still unsettled."
1952	McCarran Amendment (43 U.S.C. §666) enacted in 1952 allows for the adjudication of water rights which the United States holds in trust for Indians and tribes in federal and state courts by joining the United States as a defendant in any suit "for the adjudication of rights to the use of water of a river system or other source."
1953	Public Law 280; Act of Aug. 15, 1953 (P.L. 90–280, 67 Stat. 588; 18 U.S.C. 1360) gave jurisdiction to California, Minnesota, Nebraska, Oregon, and Wisconsin, and some other states, with respect to criminal offenses and civil causes of action committed or arising on Indian reservations within such states and for other purposes. Section 4(a) PL 98-290 further provides that "such territorial jurisdiction as the Southern Ute Indian Tribe has over persons other than Indians and the property of such persons shall be limited to Indian trust lands within the reservation."
1966	National Historic Preservation Act of 1966 ("NHPA") (54 U.S.C. 300101)
1968	Indian Civil Rights Act: The United States Constitution, Bill of Rights, does not apply to the activities of the tribal governments. However, Congress passed the Indian Civil Rights Act in 1968 which applies to all tribes in the United States. The Indian Civil Rights Act is very similar to the U.S. Bill of Rights. The Act requires tribes to provide due process for anyone who falls under their jurisdiction and tribes may not impose cruel or unusual punishment. One difference from the Bill of Rights is that the Indian Civil Rights Act does not require tribes to separate church and state. Another difference is that the Indian Civil Rights Act limits sentencing options for all tribes.
1974	The Indian Financing Act of 1974 stimulates and increases Indian entrepreneurship and employment through the establishment, acquisition or expansion of Indian-owned economic enterprises. Programs include loan guarantees and loan and bond insurance. (25 U.S.C. §§ 1498, 1511)
1974	Indians are entitled to social security and state welfare benefits on the same basis as all other state citizens. No limitation may be placed on social security benefits because of an Indian claimant's residence on a reservation. *Morton v. Ruiz*, 415 U.S. 199 (1974).
1975	Indians are entitled to state health care services on the same basis as all other state citizens. In *Penn v. San Juan Hospital, Inc.*, 528 F.2d 1181 (10th Cir. 1975), class-action plaintiffs obtained a consent decree enjoining a state hospital practice of denying Indians health care and forcing them to use an Indian Health Service facility.
1969	National Environmental Policy Act of 1969 ("NEPA") (42 U.S.C. 4321)

1975	Indian Self-Determination and Education Assistance Act of Jan. 4, 1975 (P.L. 93–638, 88 Stat. 2203; 25 U.S.C. 450 et seq.) allowed tribes, through grants and contracts, to assume program responsibility for Federally funded programs designed for their benefit and previously administered by employees of the Bureau of Indian Affairs and the United States Indian Health Service. These contracts are commonly called "638 contracts" for the public law number of the statute that authorized them. Hundreds of such contracts and funding agreements are signed each year, amounting to billions of dollars in value annually. Today, more than half of all federal programs are carried out by tribes instead of the federal government, with tribes contracting multiple federal programs on Indian reservations ranging from schools, hospitals, medical clinics, fire and police departments, and courts to natural resources, road construction, real estate management, and myriad other routine governmental functions serving tribal communities. Not all tribes participate in contracting.
1976	Colorado Commission of Indian Affairs ("CCIA") CRS §§24-44-101 through 108. CCIA serves as official liaison between State of Colorado, Southern Ute and Ute Mountain Ute Indian Tribes. Our ongoing goal is to positively impact the lives of Colorado's American Indians and communities statewide.
1978	American Indian Religious Freedom Act of Aug. 11, 1978 (P.L. 95–341, 92 Stat. 469, 42 U.S.C. 1996) ("AIRFA"), explicitly recognized the importance of traditional Indian spiritual practices and directed all Federal agencies to ensure that their policies will not abridge the free exercise of Indian religions.
1978	Indian Child Welfare Act of Nov. 8, 1978 ("ICWA") (P.L. 95–608, 92 Stat. 3969–3084; 25 U.S.C. 1901–1961) addressed the transfer of large numbers of Indian children to non-Indian parents in state adoption and guardianship proceedings. Enacted to protect American Indian families and nations, it promulgated procedures for termination of parental rights, adoptions, and foster care placement involving American Indian children, establishing preferences for Indian guardians and prior notification to tribes so they may protect their children. It requires many adoptions and guardianship cases to be held in tribal court. *Upheld by SCOTUS in 2023.*
1982	Federal Oil and Gas Royalty Management Act ("FOGRMA") of 1982 (30 USC § 1701 et seq.) grants the Secretary of the Interior authority for managing and collecting oil and gas royalties from leases on federal and Indian lands.
1988	Indian Gaming Regulatory Act ("IGRA"), 25 U.S.C. §§2701-2721, permits certain federally recognized tribes to engage in Class III gaming (casino-style games, slot machines and lotteries), subject to a tribal-state compact which must be approved by the Secretary of the Interior. IGRA requires that gaming revenues go toward tribal government operations, promotion of the welfare of the tribe and its citizens, economic development, support of charitable organizations, and compensation to local non-Native governments for support of services provided by those governments. It also waives tribal immunity from suit by a state to sue for violation of any tribal-state compact in effect. The Tribe has the sole proprietary interest in and responsibility for the conduct of any gaming operation on tribal lands. The regulation of gaming is vested in the Tribal Gaming Commission. The National Indian Gaming Commission ("NIGC"), established by IGRA, is an independent federal regulatory agency to oversee both Class II and III gaming.
1990	Native American Graves Protection and Repatriation Act of Nov. 16, 1990 ("NAGPRA"), (P.L. 101–601, 104 Stat. 3048; 25 U.S.C. 3001, 3001–3013), addressed the rights of lineal descendants and members of Indian tribes, Alaskan Natives and native Hawaiian organizations to certain human remains and to certain precisely defined cultural items with which they are related. These items include human remains from graves associated with a particular tribal group or individual offerings or artifacts associated with burials, and important religious items of cultural and spiritual importance to a tribal group. *Significantly amended in 2023 due to delays by organizations in compliance and totally insignificant financial penalties for non-compliance.*

2013	Colorado Protocol to Repatriate and Rebury Culturally Unidentifiable Native American Remains and Associated Funerary Objects In inaugurating Colorado's compliance with NAGPRA, Karen Wilde, Executive Secretary of the Colorado Commission of Indian Affairs collaborated with the Colorado Historical Society in procuring a precedent setting grant to implement a model NAGPRA program in the state.
1990	National Indian Forest Management Act
1993	American Indian Agricultural Resource Management Act
1996	Indian Employment, Training, and Related Services Demonstration Act of 1992, or P.L. 102-477, as amended by the Omnibus Indian Advancement Act of 2000, authorizes the programmatic integration of employment, training, and related services provided by tribal governments to demonstrate how tribes can improve the effectiveness of services, reduce joblessness in Indian communities and serve tribally determined goals. (25 U.S.C. § 3401 et seq.)
1996	Native American Housing Assistance and Self-Determination Act (NAHASDA) of 1996 addresses the need for affordable homes in safe and healthy environments on Indian reservations, in Indian communities and in Alaska Native villages. The Act assists Indian tribes and tribally designated housing entities with providing affordable housing to low-income families residing on reservations and in other tribal areas. (25 U.S.C. § 4101 et seq.)
2002	Federal Water Pollution Control Act ("Clean Water Act") Section 518 (e) authorizes Tribal programs (November 27, 2002). Treatment as a state is found in this section. The SUIT has completed the Clean Water Act Treatment as a State process. Environmental Protection Agency ("EPA") approved the Ute Mountain Ute Indian Tribe's water quality standards in 2011, and the Southern Ute Indian Tribe's in 2022. All water on reservation lands in Colorado will be protected by the Tribes. https://www.epa.gov/newsreleases/epa-approves-southern-ute-indian-tribes-water-quality-standards (accessed online April 20, 2023).
1998	Clean Air Act amendments of 1990 ("CAA") authorized the U.S. Environmental Protection Agency (EPA) to "treat tribes as states" for purposes of developing, administering, and enforcing air quality regulations within reservation boundaries, irrespective of land ownership. *EPA promulgated the Tribal Authority Rule (TAR) in 1998 to implement the CAA's "treatment as a state" provisions.* On March 6, 2012, the EPA approved the Southern Ute Indian Tribe's air permitting program.
2004	American Indian Probate Reform Act ("AIPRA") enacted on October 27, 2004, creates a uniform probate code for all reservations∗ across the United States. The Act applies to all individually owned trust lands, unless a tribe has its own probate code. AIPRA changes the way trust estates are distributed to your heirs after your death. This increases the importance and benefits of writing a will or doing an estate plan. AIPRA also improves your ability to consolidate your interests in trust or restricted land.
2004	The BIA Office of Law Enforcement Services which enforces federal law in Indian country as well as tribal law if requested, may commission state and local law enforcement officers to carry out federal functions (Internal Law Enforcement Services Policies, 69 Fed. Reg. 6321 (2004)). The Ute Mountain Ute Indian Tribe uses BIA Office of Law Enforcement Services.
2005	Indian Mineral Development Act and the Indian Energy Policy Act of 2005 streamline the planning and authorization for development of energy and mineral resources held in trust for the benefit of Indian owners. (25 U.S.C. § 2101 et seq.)

Appendix 7: Federal Executive Agencies with Tribal Trust Responsibilities

Department of the Interior	Secretary Deb Haaland, Laguna Pueblo Secretary of the Interior is trustee for U.S., responsible for fulfilling DOI's trust responsibilities to American Indian and Alaska Native tribes and individuals, promoting tribal self-determination and economic well-being, and supporting government-to-government relationship between federally recognized tribes and U.S. The 574 federally-recognized sovereign Tribal nations are part of U.S. family of governments that have a nation-to-nation relationship with federal government as a part of trust relationship.	U.S. Department of the Interior ("DOI") protects and manages Nation's natural resources and cultural heritage; provides scientific and other information about those resources; and honors its trust responsibilities or special commitments to American Indians, Alaska Natives, Native Hawaiians, and affiliated Island Communities. DOI has a staff of 70,000 employees.
Assistant Secretary - Indian Affairs	Bryan Newland, citizen of Bay Mills Indian Community (Ojibwe) in Michigan. Discharges duties of Secretary with authority and direct responsibility to: Strengthen government-to-government/nation-to-nation relationship with American Indian and Alaska Native tribes; Advocate policies that support AI/AN self-determination and tribal sovereignty; Protect and preserve AI/AN trust assets held by Federal Government for their benefit; and Administer a wide array of laws, regulations, and functions relating to AI/AN tribes, individual AI/AN trust beneficiaries, tribal members, and Indian Affairs bureaus, offices, and programs that are vested in Secretary by President and Congress.	Assist Secretary of the Interior in fulfilling Department's trust responsibilities to American Indian and Alaska Native tribes and individuals, promoting tribal self-determination and economic well-being, and supporting government-to-government relationship between federally recognized tribes and United States.
Solicitor's Office	Robert Anderson, Solicitor for Department of the Interior
Deputy Solicitor, Energy and Mineral Resources
Deputy Solicitor, General Law
Deputy Solicitor, Indian Affairs
Deputy Solicitor, Land Resources
Deputy Solicitor, Parks and Wildlife
Deputy Solicitor, Water Resources	Performs legal work for United States Department of the Interior, and manages Departmental Ethics Office and Departmental FOIA Office. With more than five hundred total employees, more than four hundred of which are licensed attorneys, Office strives to provide sound legal services to fulfill Department's diverse and wide-ranging mission.

Office of Natural Resources Revenue	Howard Cantor	Office of Natural Resources Revenue ("ONRR") has a trust responsibility to American Indians and Alaskan Natives. It collects, accounts for, verifies, and disburses energy and mineral revenues on Indian lands.
Bureau of Indian Affairs ("BIA")	Darryl LaCounte, member of Turtle Mountain Band of Chippewa Indians, North Dakota	Maintain federal government-to-government relationship with federally recognized Indian tribes, and promote and support tribal self-determination. Bureau implements federal laws and policies and administers programs established for American Indians and Alaska Natives under trust responsibility and government-to-government relationship.
Bureau of Trust Funds Administration	Jerry Gidner, citizen of Sault Ste. Marie Chippewa Tribe	Manages financial assets of American Indians held in trust by DOI. Maintains official archive of American Indian Records.
Bureau of Indian Education ("BIE")	Tony Dearman, member of Cherokee Nation of Oklahoma	Provide quality education opportunities. Employs thousands of teachers, administrators and support personnel, while many more work in tribal school systems. There are 183 Bureau-funded elementary and secondary schools, located on 64 reservations in 23 states, serving approximately 42,000 Indian students. Of these, 55 are BIE –operated, and 128 are tribally operated.

Bureau of Land Management ("BLM") BLM has a broad range of responsibilities that impact tribes, including, but not limited to: • Ca-	Tracy Stone-Manning	Administer lands, cultural heritage, natural, and minerals resources programs in a manner consistent with Indian treaty rights, other applicable legal statutes, and BLM's responsibility to work in partnership with Indian tribes on a government-to-government basis. Land use planning and environmental review. Agreements pertinent to tribal relations include— 1. Memorandum of Understanding among the U.S. Department of Defense, U.S. Department of the Interior, U.S. Department of Agriculture, U.S. Department of Energy, and the Advisory Council on Historic Preservation Regarding Interagency Coordination and Collaboration for the Protection of Indian Sacred Sites (December 4, 2012); 2. Programmatic Agreement Among the Bureau of Land Management, the Advisory Council on Historic Preservation, and the National Conference of State Historic Preservation Officers regarding the Manner in which the BLM Will Meet its Responsibilities under the National Historic Preservation Act (February 9, 2012); and 3. Onshore Federal and Indian Energy and Mineral Lease Management Standard Operating Procedures (SOP) (signed by the DOI Assistant Secretary, PMB, on September 18, 2013, and amended on September 23, 2013).
Environmental Protection Agency ("EPA")	• Michael S. Regan, Administrator • Office of International and Tribal Affairs, Daniel Vaught • Number of EPA Tribal Program Managers	American Indian Environmental Office Mission ("AIEO") leads EPA's efforts to protect human health and environment in Indian country by supporting implementation of federal environmental law consistent with federal trust responsibility and government-to-government relationship.
Department of Energy Office of Indian Energy Policy and Programs	Office of Indian Energy Policy and Programs Wahleah Johns (Director)	Authorized to provide, direct, foster, coordinate, and implement energy planning, education, management, development and efficiency.

Department of Health and Human Services Office of Intergovernmental and External ("IEA") Tribal Affairs	HHS Secretary Kathleen Sebelius Secretary's Tribal Advisory Committee signals a new level of attention to Government-to-Government relationship between HHS and Indian Tribal Governments	Tribal Affairs component of Office of Intergovernmental and External serves as official first point of contact for Tribes, Tribal Governments, and Tribal Organizations wishing to access Department of Health and Human Services (HHS). U.S. Health and Human Services Administration for Native Americans ("ANA") Annual Grants of $43 Million
Department of Justice Federal Bureau of Investigation Office of the Solicitor General Office of Tribal Justice	Merrick B. Garland, Attorney General FBI Director Christopher Wray Solicitor General Elizabeth B. Prelogar Tracy Toulou, Director, Office of Tribal Justice: Office of Tribal Justice is primary point of contact for Department of Justice with federally recognized Native American tribes, and advises Department on legal and policy matters pertaining to Native Americans.	Mission of Department of Justice is to uphold rule of law, to keep our country safe, and to protect civil rights. OSG's mission is to represent interests of United States before Supreme Court and to oversee appellate and certain other litigation on behalf of United States in lower federal and state courts.
Indian Health Service (IHS)	Roselyn Tso, an enrolled member of Navajo Nation, is Director.	Ensures availability of comprehensive and culturally acceptable public health services to American Indian and Alaska Native people.
Office of Public and Indian Housing (PIH)	Office of Assistant Secretary for Public and Indian Housing	PIH Office works to guarantee safe, decent, and affordable housing.
Office of Indian Education	Julian Guerrero, Jr., Director	Helps American Indian and Alaska Native students achieve state performance standards.
National Indian Gaming Commission (NIGC)	E. Sequoyah Simermeyer, Chairman	Commission's primary mission: regulation of gaming activities conducted by tribes on Indian lands to fully realize IGRA's goals.
Internal Revenue Service IRS Office of Indian Tribal Governments		Tax Information for Indian Tribal Governments